Women's Lives, Women's
Rituals in the Hindu Tradition

Women's Lives, Women's Rituals in the Hindu Tradition

Edited by
TRACY PINTCHMAN

UNIVERSITY PRESS
2007

OXFORD
UNIVERSITY PRESS

Oxford University Press, Inc., publishes works that further
Oxford University's objective of excellence
in research, scholarship, and education.

Oxford   New York
Auckland   Cape Town   Dar es Salaam   Hong Kong   Karachi
Kuala Lumpur   Madrid   Melbourne   Mexico City   Nairobi
New Delhi   Shanghai   Taipei   Toronto

With offices in
Argentina   Austria   Brazil   Chile   Czech Republic   France   Greece
Guatemala   Hungary   Italy   Japan   Poland   Portugal   Singapore
South Korea   Switzerland   Thailand   Turkey   Ukraine   Vietnam

Copyright © 2007 by Oxford University Press, Inc.

Published by Oxford University Press, Inc.
198 Madison Avenue, New York, New York 10016

www.oup.com

Oxford is a registered trademark of Oxford University Press

Library of Congress Cataloging-in-Publication Data
Women's lives, women's rituals in the Hindu tradition /
edited by Tracy Pintchman.
   p. cm.
Includes bibliography and index.
ISBN 978-0-19-517706-0; 978-0-19-517707-7 (pbk.)
1. Hindu women—Religious life.   2. Hinduism—Rituals.
3. Hindu women—Social life and customs.   I. Pintchman, Tracy.
BL1237.46.W67 2007
294.5'38082—dc22   2006021014

9 8 7 6 5 4 3 2 1

Printed in the United States of America
on acid-free paper

For my son,

Noah Lawrence French,

born August 4, 2002

Acknowledgments and Note on Transliteration

I would like to thank all of the contributors for their hard work and their patience during the years this volume was in process. Thank you, thank you, thank you! I would like to express my gratitude as well to the editorial staff at Oxford University Press, especially Theo Calderara, who cheered us on and never seemed to doubt that some day we would actually finish this book and get it to press. Many thanks, too, to Corinne Dempsey for her very helpful comments on the manuscript.

We have chosen to eliminate all diacritical marks from the book and to minimize the use of terms from Indian languages in order to make the chapters more accessible to a nonspecialist audience.

Contents

List of Illustrations

Contributors

Elaine Craddock is an associate professor and chair of the Department of Religion and Philosophy at Southwestern University. She teaches courses in Hinduism, Buddhism, and feminist studies. Her research interests include Hindu goddesses, tantra in South India, Tamil *bhakti* poetry, and religion and the body. Her publications include "Reconstructing the Split Goddess as Shakti in a Tamil Village," in *Seeking Mahadevi: Constructing the Identities of the Hindu Great Goddess*, edited by Tracy Pintchman (2001).

Kathleen M. Erndl is an associate professor of religion at Florida State University, where she teaches undergraduate and graduate courses on Hinduism, South Asian religions, Sanskrit, gender and religion, and theory and method in the study of religion. She is the author of *Victory to the Mother: The Hindu Goddess of Northwest India in Myth, Ritual, and Symbol* (1993), and with Alf Hiltebeitel she co-edited the volume *Is the Goddess a Feminist? The Politics of South Asian Goddesses* (2000). She has also published numerous essays on goddess traditions and women in South Asian religions. She is currently writing a book entitled *Playing with the Mother: Women, Goddess Possession, and Power in Kangra Hinduism*. Her other research interests include gender and religious hybridity in India and the United States.

Joyce Burkhalter Flueckiger is a professor in the Department of Religion at Emory University. She specializes in performance studies, with a particular interest in religion and gender. She has carried out extensive fieldwork in India, working with both Hindu and Muslim popular traditions. Her most recent book, *In Amma's Healing Room: Gender and Vernacular Islam in South India* (2006), addresses questions of religious and gender identities and boundaries in the healing practice of a female Muslim folk healer in the city of Hyderabad. Her most recent fieldwork was conducted in Tirupati with the goddess tradition of Gangamma. She is also the author of *Gender and Genre in the Folklore of Middle India* (1996) and has published numerous articles on South Asian performative traditions.

Lindsey Harlan is a professor of religious studies at Connecticut College. She is the author of *The Goddesses' Henchmen: Gender in Indian Hero Worship* (2003) and *Religion and Rajput Women* (1992). With Paul Courtright, she edited the volume *From the Margins of Hindu Marriage* (1995). Her most recent work has focused on cultic heroic traditions in India and traditions of hero memorialization in the United States. She also writes on Hinduism in Trinidad.

June McDaniel is a professor of religious studies at the College of Charleston, where she teaches classes on world religions, women and religion, the religions of India, the phenomenology of religion, mysticism and religious experience, and other topics. Her publications include a number of articles and book chapters and three books: *Offering Flowers, Feeding Skulls: Popular Goddess Worship in West Bengal* (2004); *Making Virtuous Daughters and Wives: An Introduction to the Brata Rituals of Bengal* (2003); and *The Madness of the Saints: Ecstatic Religion in Bengal* (1989). Her current research is on Hindu *bhakti*, Shakta tantra, world mysticism, and religious ecstasy.

Vijaya Rettakudi Nagarajan is an associate professor of South Asian religions in the Department of Religious Studies and Environmental Studies at the University of San Francisco, where she teaches courses on Hinduism, religion and ecology, religion and nonviolence, and other topics. Her publications include a number of articles and essays on the *kolam* and Hinduism and ecology, as well as a forthcoming book, *Drawing Down Desires: An Exploration of the Kolam: Women, Ritual and Ecology in Southern India*. Her current research focuses on tree temples, sacred groves, and the commons in Tamilnadu, India.

Vasudha Narayanan is a professor of religion at the University of Florida and a past president of the American Academy of Religion (2001–2002). Her fields of interest include the Sri Vaishnava tradition; Hindu traditions in India, Cambodia, and America; and gender issues. She is the author and editor of six books, including, most recently, *Hinduism* (2004) and a forthcoming work, *A Hundred Autumns to Live: An Introduction to Hindu Traditions*. She is currently researching Hindu temples and Vaishnava traditions in Cambodia.

Leslie C. Orr is an associate professor in the Department of Religion at Concordia University in Montreal, Canada. Her research is concentrated in two overlapping areas: first, the roles and activities of women in Hinduism, Buddhism, and Jainism; and, second, the organization of religious life in the history of South India up to the late medieval period, including the examination of institutional structures, religious authority and social hierarchy, ritual forms and ritual performers, and the physical space in which social and ritual dynamics transpired, with a particular focus on the interactions among religious communities. She is the author of a number of articles in these fields and the book *Donors, Devotees and Daughters of God: Temple Women in Medieval Tamilnadu* (2000). She has a book in progress on the sociology of the medieval South Indian temple.

Laurie L. Patton is Winship Distinguished Research Professor in the Humanities at Emory University. She has authored two books on early Vedic interpretation of mythology and ritual: *Myth as Argument* (1996) and *Bringing the Gods to Mind* (2005). She has also served as editor or co-editor of five volumes on myth theory, Vedic hermeneutics, the Indo-Aryan controversy, history of religions, and gender and early Hinduism. She is currently working on a book on women and Sanskrit as well as a book on scandal in the study of religion. She has recently completed a book of poetry, *Fire's Goal: Poems from the Hindu Year* (2003), and a translation of the *Bhagavad Gita*.

Tracy Pintchman is a professor of religious studies and Hindu studies at Loyola University Chicago, where she teaches courses on Hindu traditions and women and religion. Her previous publications include a number of articles and book chapters; two monographs, *The Rise of the Goddess in the Hindu Tradition* (1994) and *Guests at God's Wedding: Celebrating Kartik among the Women of Benares* (2005); and an edited volume, *Seeking Mahadevi: Constructing the Identities of the Hindu Great Goddess* (2001). She is currently researching narratives of meaning surrounding motherhood.

Women's Lives, Women's Rituals in the Hindu Tradition

Introduction

Tracy Pintchman

We give birth to a child, we put oil on the child's body, and we massage the child. Men can't do all this. So ritual worship [*puja*] is like this. Men cannot do as much as we do.

The woman who spoke these words, Bhagavanti, was reclining on the floor of her home in the city of Benares, North India, and watching her daughter-in-law sort rice as my research associate, Sunita Singh, and I sat before her, trying to interview her. It was November 1997, and I had come to Bhagavanti's home to ask about her participation in Kartik *puja*, a tradition of women's devotional practices specific to the month of Kartik (October–November). Bhagavanti sat before us, her elbow resting on a pillow as she responded patiently to the questions we put before her. She was quite elderly at the time of our interview and had lost a good deal of her hearing, so Sunita and I had to shout to make ourselves heard, drawing the attention of many neighborhood women and children, who came to peer through the windows to see what was going on. Bhagavanti's daughter-in-law kept getting up and milling about, but she also chimed in whenever she had a point she wanted to make. At this particular moment, I was asking Bhagavanti why men don't participate in the particular ritual tradition, called Kartik *puja*, about which I was asking her. Like many other women I interviewed, Bhagavanti attributed men's absence to differences between men's and women's natures and social roles in ways that seemed to favor women as the more virtuous and disciplined gender (cf. Pintchman 2005).

Bhagavanti's words quoted above bring to mind the common perception among many Indian Hindus that women have a special aptitude for ritual performance. During the years from 1995 to 1998, when I was conducting field research in Benares, on numerous occasions both women and men suggested to me that, in India, women are more religious than men and do the lion's share of the day-to-day religious work. Like other women I interviewed, Bhagavanti also drew a clear parallel between the work women do in the household and the work they do in this particular *puja* tradition, comparing ritual tasks specifically with maternal tasks and the responsibilities involved in birthing and caring for children. For Bhagavanti, the domain of ritual practice is not separated from day-to-day existence but instead involves the kinds of skills and commitments that appear regularly and without special notice in the mundane arena of ordinary life.

The chapters in this book explore the relationship between women's ritual practices and the lives and activities of Hindu women beyond the ritual sphere. Bhagavanti's words provide a helpful point of departure for our collective inquiry into the nature of this relationship. Like Bhagavanti, we presume that Hindu women are deeply engaged and invested in the performance of religious practice. Rituals that take place in Sanskritic, Brahminical Hindu environments continue to be instituted and directed largely by Brahmin males, but women largely control many types of ritual practice that occur outside of such contexts, including many household, calendrical, and local devotional practices. Even in environments where Sanskritic traditions maintain a strong presence, women often sustain active ritual agendas and function as engaged actors in many types of ritual work. Indeed, in some parts of India, women are taking leadership roles in Sanskritic ritual performance as well.

Like Bhagavanti, too, we maintain that Hindu women's religious practices are not isolated from social, cultural, domestic, or larger religious roles or frames of meaning but tend to engage realms that transcend individual ritual contexts. Contemporary scholarship pertaining to both ritual and women's religiosity provides support for such a premise. Recent work on ritual practice emphasizes its nature as a type of performance that is inherently constructive and strategic, producing specific types of meaning and values through particular strategies. Because it is constructive and strategic, ritual practice facilitates the ability of ritual agents to appropriate or reshape values and ideals that help to mold social identity (Bell 1997, 82, 73). Elizabeth Collins observes that thinking of ritual as performance also requires greater sophistication in thinking through issues of agency. Collins notes:

> The model of performance implies several different agents
> and different kinds of agency. There is the agency of the author of
> the text, but also the agency of the performers who choose to per-
> form a particular ritual or a particular variant of a ritual text and who

may even revise the text or tradition in their performance. There is [also] the agency of those who participate as audience. (Collins 1997, 183–184)

In different contexts, women may function as ritual authors, performers, audience, or any combination of these, and the chapters in this book collectively address women's ritual agency in all of these ways.

People who participate in ritual practices are also embedded in larger communities that maintain particular social norms and values. When individuals engage in ritual performances as agents, their engagement may function to help produce, reproduce, transform, resist, or even defy these larger norms. The constructive nature of ritual in this regard extends to ideologies and practices that concern gender. Judith Butler has argued that gender is primarily performative and that gender identity is constituted through a stylized repetition of acts (Butler 1990, 171–180). Religious practice, which certainly entails a stylized repetition of acts executed in a ritual arena, is, in this regard, clearly an engendering process. Lesley Northup notes that rituals are, at least in part, "constitutive of persons," helping to construct, enhance, and enable personhood (Northup 1997, 87). Ritual engenders through the performance of actions that help to produce identity, including gender identity, in relation to predominant social norms in ways that may be compliant, resistant, or both, complexly and simultaneously. In her work on Hindu women's domestic rituals in South India, for example, Mary Hancock explores ways that domestic ritual practice acts simultaneously as a site for both "reproduction of and resistance to hegemonic images of female subjectivity" in Sanskritic Hinduism (Hancock 1999, 32, 137).

Recent work on women's religiosity further corroborates an emphasis for women in particular, including Hindu women, on the continuity between religious and social domains, affirming that women appropriate religion in ways that tend to engage women's gender-specific social roles, experiences, and values. Meena Khandelwal, for example, notes that female renunciants in the Hindu tradition tend to identify themselves as mothers, emphasizing the moral and spiritual strengths particular to women in the mothering role and adapting the term Ma ("mother") as a form of address (Khandelwal 2004, 184–185). Susan Sered (1992, 1994) observes that women often personalize religion, emphasizing practices and symbols that give spiritual meaning to women's everyday lives. In speaking of the relationship between religion and other dimensions of women's lives, Marjorie Proctor-Smith distinguishes between what she calls the emancipatory function of religion (including ritual practices), where religion may help women to transcend existing social restraints and behave in ways contrary to social expectation, and a sacralizing function, where religion may serve to establish women's traditional roles and experiences as sacred (1993, 25–28). While the sacralizing function can serve to justify traditions that limit women's power and freedom in both public and private spheres, at its best it may serve to reveal "the dignity and holiness of women's work" (28) and to enhance women's self-esteem and feelings of self-worth.

In engaging Bhagavanti's words as our point of departure, it is important to acknowledge one important way in which the chapters in this book may depart from the assumptions that Bhagavanti seems to bring to the table: the chapters do not necessarily affirm a straightforward correlation between women's daily work in the domestic arena and women's religious practices. Instead, we interrogate the relationship of women's ritual activities to normative domesticity, exposing and exploring the nuances, complexities, and limits of this relationship. Here we understand domesticity in terms that are primarily spatial and relational. We take "the domestic" to refer to a place, a domicile or home, including the activities that occur therein and the kinship relations among particular individuals. In many cultural and historical contexts, including contemporary India, women's everyday lives tend to revolve heavily around domestic and interpersonal concerns, especially care for children, the home, husbands, and other relatives; hence, women's religiosity also tends to emphasize the domestic realm and the relationships most central to women. Within the study of Hinduism, work by Susan Wadley, Mary McGee, and Anne Pearson has elucidated the concern for familial relationships and domestic well-being that permeates some women's rituals, especially votive rituals (Wadley 1989; McGee 1987, 1991; Pearson 1996). But these scholars also remind us that such rituals involve other goals and concerns—spiritual liberation, for example. Furthermore, even the domestic religious activities that Hindu women perform may not merely replicate or affirm traditionally formulated domestic ideals; rather, these activities may function strategically to reconfigure, reinterpret, criticize, or even reject such ideals.

The contributions in this book form a collective commentary on the relationship of Hindu women's ritual practices to the domestic arena in particular. Women may challenge normative domesticity by reinterpreting, expanding, or rejecting prescribed spatial restrictions, domestic practices, ideologies of kinship, or familial expectations. Traditional domesticity intersects with women's lives ambiguously, providing freedoms as well as constraints, danger as well as protection, devalued as well as heightened status; women's challenges to normative domesticity may be similarly ambiguous.[1] We emphasize female innovation and agency in constituting and transforming both ritual and the domestic realm, and we call attention to the limitations of normative domesticity as a category relevant to at least some forms of Hindu women's religious practice.

Many chapters in this volume also consider the relationship between Hindu women's ritual practices and political, religious, or sociocultural concerns and values beyond the domestic. Some, for example, explore larger questions of power and women's empowerment, asking whether women's rituals empower women in Hindu society and, if so, how (e.g., Erndl, McDaniel). Several consider ways that women's ritual practices engage cultural notions of beauty and artistic ideals or, conversely, ascetic ideals that are often relegated to the male sphere (e.g., Nagarajan, Narayanan, Craddock, Orr). Other chapters explore ways that women's religious practices may engage ethical, devotional, or social values that diverge from or even challenge those more central to Brahmanical traditions and institutions (e.g., Harlan, Flueckiger, Pintchman). And one chapter (Patton) addresses how Sanskritic knowledge might be transformed by women from within. No matter what particular issues they address, however, all of the chapters sustain a focus on the fundamental theme of this volume: the relationship between specific forms of Hindu women's religious praxis and the lives of women outside of these ritual contexts. This is the essential axis around which every chapter in the book revolves.

Notes on the Scholarly and Historical Context for This Study

In her edited book *Roles and Rituals for Hindu Women*, Julia Leslie noted the challenge faced by contemporary scholars of Hinduism in "hearing the voices of women" in our research on Hindu traditions. Leslie argued that this challenge means "not only seeking out the voices of women but also hearing their own evaluations" of the traditions in which they participate (Leslie 1991, 3). In the early 1990s, this was something of a new challenge; the relatively small amount of Western scholarship that had been produced about Hindu women in earlier decades tended to focus more on what authoritative Hindu texts said about Hindu women than on what Hindu women themselves said and did within the context of their own religious values and convictions. In the last decade and a half, however, a number of works have been published that are perhaps more apt to meet the kind of challenge Leslie put before us in her pathbreaking book. These include works like Gloria Raheja and Ann Gold's *Listen to the Heron's Words* (1994), Meena Khandelwal's *Women in Ochre Robes* (2004), Anne Pearson's *"Because It Gives Me Peace of Mind"* (1996), and several of the essays in Laurie L. Patton's edited book, *Jewels of Authority* (2002).

Hearing the voices of women certainly seems to be a great deal easier for those of us interested in the present than it is for those whose scholarly interests focus on the historical past. Through ethnography, we can observe the practices of contemporary Hindu women, ask them to talk to us, and solicit their opinions and interpretations regarding ritual performance. The historical record gives us rather less to go by, since authoritative Hindu texts are predominantly male-authored. Yet even the male-authored texts clearly reveal that Hindu women have always been active, engaged ritual actors, and sophisticated readings of the historical record can tell us a great deal about their involvement in religious practice, even when we are unable to actually hear the voices of the women themselves in these texts. Here I might mention, as examples, Stephanie Jamison's *Sacrificed Wife/Sacrificer's Wife* (1996), which does a masterful job of reading and interpreting the role of the sacrificer's wife in the practice of ancient Vedic ritual, or Mary McGee's work on ancient *mimamsaka* debates concerning women's eligibility to perform Vedic sacrifices (McGee 2002). Furthermore, historically we do have a limited number of texts that were authored by women, and these serve as rich resources for those interested in the religious lives of Hindu women in past centuries, including their participation in ritual performance. Eleanor Zelliot (2000), for example, engages the recorded songs of female saints in medieval Maharashtra to explore tensions that emerge in these songs between the performance of household duties and the performance of meditation. Women's agency and active participation in various forms of Hindu ritual practice is clearly evident in a number of ways throughout the history of the Indian subcontinent.

The contributions in this book are indebted to the existing body of scholarship on the religious lives of Hindu women, past and present. We hope to move the conversation forward through our specific interrogation of the relationship between women's ritual practices and women's lives outside of ritual practice.

Organization of the Volume

This book is divided into two parts: "Engaging Domesticity" and "Beyond Domesticity." The first part consists of five chapters that engage domestic and interpersonal values in relation to women's ritual practices that tend to expand the boundaries of normative domesticity. Laurie L. Patton's "The Cat in the Courtyard: The Performance of Sanskrit and the Religious Experience of Women," for example, demonstrates how contemporary female Sanskritists in Maharashtra reconfigure Sanskrit, the "father language" of Brahminical Hinduism, as a "grandmother language" that women engage in new ways to imbue the practices and activities of everyday life with religious meaning. Female Sanskritists unite their *stridharma*, or ritual duties as women, with the use of Sanskrit in everyday life, importing Sanskrit into mundane events and practices like childbirth, daily food preparation, and the feeding of loved ones. In so doing, these women reconstitute Sanskrit as a domestic language of interpersonal care and personal transformation; they also reconfigure the "profane" moments of everyday life, imbuing them with religious meaning by sacralizing them with powerful religious mantras.

In the second chapter, "Wandering from 'Hills to Valleys' with the Goddess: Protection and Freedom in the *Matamma* Tradition of Andhra," Joyce Burkhalter Flueckiger explores the ways that South Indian Hindu women also expand the boundaries of domesticity, this time through a ritual alliance forged between women and the goddess Gangamma. In many Indian contexts, marriage is understood to be the quintessential domestic institution, serving most often to curtail significantly women's freedom and agency in the public sphere. Flueckiger explores a form of marriage that is socially liberating for Hindu women—a form of ritual marriage that women may enact with Gangamma. When illness strikes in villages around the pilgrimage town of Tirupati in Andhra Pradesh, particularly illnesses of poxes, rashes, and high fevers associated with the hot season and particular village goddesses, little girls may be offered to the goddess Gangamma (or one of her sisters) in exchange for the latter's protection and healing. When these girls reach puberty, they exchange *talis* (wedding necklaces) with the goddess and are considered married to her. The girls are called *matammas* in Telugu. Women who have been pledged in marital alliance to Gangamma serve the goddess first and hence are subject to male control only secondarily; since their primary marital allegiance is to a divine female, not a human male, these women are not bound by the same social rules as are other married women. Hence, they are able to move in and through public space and claim a place in the public sphere much more easily than are most married women. Their alliance with the goddess, formalized by the ritualized exchange of *talis*, affords these women protection, freedom of movement, and agency outside the domestic sphere.

Like Flueckiger's, my chapter, "Lovesick *Gopi* or Woman's Best Friend? The Mythic *Sakhi* and Ritual Friendships among Women in Benares," engages a form of religious practice that functions to establish an ongoing relationship, one that continues beyond the ritual performance itself. The ritually established relationships we both explore, furthermore, share common ground in that they mimic human marriage but function as lifelong bonds between two females. In the materials highlighted in my chapter, however, the bond is not between a woman and a goddess but between human women who establish ritual friendships. I focus on a tradition undertaken by women living in Benares, Uttar Pradesh (North India), in which the *gopis*, the famous cowherdesses of Krishna mythology, become the model for ritually based human female friendships. The *gopis* are also referred to as the *sakhis*, or "female friends," and in ordinary speech the term *sakhi* is used to refer commonly to a girl's or woman's female friend. The tradition I explore involves a ritual process of "becoming" or "tying" *sakhi*, which entails pledging lifelong friendship. For many Benarsi women, the *sakhi* relationship represents a female-female union that imitates the marital bond but may surpass blood or marital kinship bonds in terms of its professed meaningfulness in women's lives. The appropriation of the *sakhi* figure in this ritual tradition also demonstrates how women have adapted Krishna traditions in ways that engage their own interpersonal concerns and values.

The fourth chapter, Lindsey Harlan's "Words That Breach Walls: Women's Rituals in Rajasthan," explores women's ritual practices in Rajasthan, North India. Harlan echoes Flueckiger in emphasizing ways that ritual functions to facilitate women's movement across domestic boundaries and among various spaces beyond individual domiciles. The materials Harlan engages, however, move us in a different direction, emphasizing the permeability of domestic space, the flexibility of the category "domestic," and the continuity between domicile and extra-domestic spaces. Harlan explores Rajput women's performance of *ratijagas*, women's "wake" rituals, which women perform for weddings and other important occasions. *Ratijagas* are domestic ritual performances inasmuch as they occur in household spaces. But Harlan uses her exploration of *ratijagas* to interrogate and render problematic any simple distinction between public and private domains when it comes to women's ritual performance. As travelers to other households for *ratijaga* performances, for example, women may transform the environments from which they come and to which they travel; what goes on in one household may affect processes in other households. Harlan engages the popular film *Chocolat* as a comparison, demonstrating that the dynamics she highlights so beautifully in the materials she explores are not specifically Hindu or Indian but may be seen as broader insights about women's potential influence on religious praxis.

The fifth chapter, Vijaya Rettakudi Nagarajan's "Threshold Designs, Forehead Dots, and Menstruation Rituals: Exploring Time and Space in Tamil *Kolams*," brings us back to South India, this time to Tamilnadu. Like Harlan, Nagarajan explores the ways that women's religious practices cross boundaries and traverse thresholds, and she also emphasizes continuity and overlap between private and public domains. The focus of this chapter is the relationship between *kolams*, auspicious designs that women create daily at their domiciles' thresholds, and *pottus*, the auspicious red dots that adorn Tamil women's foreheads. Nagarajan argues that the *kolam* and the *pottu* are parallel ritual expressions that embody larger Hindu cultural values, especially auspiciousness and inauspiciousness, purity and pollution. Both *kolam* and *pottu* mark thresholds, those of the home and the body, and function to mark spatial and temporal transformations: from auspicious to inauspicious times or pure to impure ones, as in the erasure of the *pottu* and the absence of *kolam* production during menstruation and their reappearance following the period of menses. *Pottu* and *kolam* both embody the status of married women as auspicious householders, a status that is rooted in their domestic location, but both send that auspiciousness forth beyond the domestic threshold into the larger communities in which female Hindu householders are embedded.

Together, these first five chapters demonstrate ways that women exercise agency in religious performance as ritual authors, performers, and consumers. The practices these chapters explore expand notions of what constitutes domesticity in Hindu women's ritual traditions, and they dissolve conceptual boundaries that serve to divide the sacred from the profane and domestic spaces and performances from public ones, demonstrating the ways that women's ritual practices, and the women who engage in them, cross thresholds, traverse boundaries, reposition or reinterpret larger cultural formations and social norms, and provide room for relationships beyond the terms dictated by predominant patriarchal family norms.

The five chapters in part II, "Beyond Domesticity," similarly reveal the many ways that women's religious performances permeate diverse realms and breach borders. These chapters collectively take up a somewhat different challenge, however, exploring women's ritual practices outside the confines of strictly domestic contexts and contesting the impulse to link women's ritual performance primarily with domestic realms and concerns.

Leslie C. Orr's chapter, "Domesticity and Difference/Women and Men: Religious Life in Medieval Tamilnadu," questions any special emphasis on domestic values in evidence pertaining to women's ritual practices in medieval Tamilnadu. Orr compares the practices and goals of women and men in medieval South India, particularly with respect to gift giving and vow taking, as these are revealed in Tamil inscriptions engraved on the stone walls of Jain and Hindu temples of the ninth through thirteenth centuries. Women seem to have been especially involved in the sponsorship of images, notably images of goddesses, to be worshipped, and they used their gifts to forge links with family members. Somewhat different patterns are seen in the case of men's donations, but they also demonstrate familial involvement in, for example, men's gifts of thanksgiving for the births of sons or gifts for the merit of their fathers.

Orr observes, perhaps surprisingly, that "domestic" motives are not in evidence in the few records we have of women's vows and self-immolation, which do not indicate that these acts were performed for the sake of offspring or a husband. There seems to be nothing particularly feminine about such acts, which appear to be expressions of values of valor and loyalty shared with men and akin to vows of political allegiance, whose character as "religious" undertakings is questionable. Orr argues that men's and women's activities recorded on temple walls did indeed have distinctive colorings, but that the contexts, roles, and motives for these actions were overlapping and often congruent. Men expressed "domestic" concerns through their ritual activity, and women, through theirs, not only participated in the public religious space of the temple, but also shared in wider social and political worlds that transcended both the domestic and the religious. Orr concludes her chapter by questioning the conceptual boundaries that divide religion from political and economic realms, domestic ritual from "high" public ritual, and interpersonal religious aims from ultimate, transcendent ones in relation to the materials she explores.

Elaine Craddock also questions these kinds of conceptual boundaries in her chapter, "The Anatomy of Devotion: The Life and Poetry of Karaikkal Ammaiyar." Karaikkal Ammaiyar, a.k.a. Punitavati, was one of the Tamil *nayanmar*, or Shaivite saints. Before Punitavati became Karaikkal Ammaiyar, she was married to a merchant, but her ardent devotion to Shiva conflicted with her ritual duties as a wife. Her husband became frightened by Shiva's response to her devotions and released her from marriage; she immediately made a devotional pilgrimage to the Himalayas, where Shiva granted her wish to obtain a demon form and to be the eternal witness to his fierce dance in the cremation ground at Tiruvalankatu. There, she composed 143 verses, which represent the earliest Tamil poetry to Shiva. Some of these poems describe the cremation ground as a scene of ghoulish domesticity, relocating the center of existence in Shiva's presence: the site of death and burning flesh is repositioned as the domicile, and "home" is redefined as anyplace where one dwells in Shiva's presence. Karaikkal Ammaiyar's own life embodies a shift in emphasis from the performance of wifely domestic rituals, normally the primary ritual domain of married women, to the understanding of her entire life as a ritual offering to Shiva. This move from domestic practice to devotional practice as the central sphere of ritual concern pushes both women and men to see ordinary household rituals as meaningless and to transcend values like human beauty, promoting the view that only a life lived entirely as a ritual offering to Shiva has meaning. Like Orr, Craddock stresses the importance of religious values other than domesticity in women's ritual performance; in the materials Craddock explores, however, there is a self-conscious appropriation and repositioning of "the domestic" as a suitable site for women's religious performance.

The eighth chapter, Kathleen M. Erndl's "The Play of the Mother: Possession and Power in Hindu Women's Goddess Rituals," explores questions of Hindu women's power in connection with goddess possession rituals in the Kangra Valley area of Himachal Pradesh, North India. In Kangra, as in many other regions of India, it is not uncommon for women to become possessed by a goddess, to speak with her voice, and to act as healers and mediums in their communities. Divine possession as a form of religious expression is interconnected with such practices as pilgrimage to temples, *puja* (image worship), recitation of sacred texts, fasting, and meditation, practices that comprise the religious complex of Shaktism or goddess worship in the region. Erndl argues that possession practices can be a source of both religious and social empowerment for women, providing opportunities for women to improve their lives and to help other women. Like Harlan, Erndl stresses the mobility that religious practice, in this case possession performance, affords, granting householder women in particular opportunities to travel beyond their domiciles and to form with other women a female community, however temporary, which in turn may provide women access to advice, support, or even material assistance. She describes these ritual spaces as "cracks" in a patriarchal system that cannot be completely controlled by patriarchal norms and that provide sites for women's creativity and interconnection.

Erndl notes that goddess-possessed women, or *matajis*, may be married or single, householders or renunciants. The same is true of the women whom June McDaniel explores in her chapter, "Does Tantric Ritual Empower Women?

Renunciation and Domesticity among Female Bengali Tantrikas." McDaniel, however, emphasizes renunciation, not domesticity, as the preferred locus of women's religious expression in the materials she explores, namely, the ritual practices of women active in tantric traditions in West Bengal. These female tantrikas tend to reject the traditional domestic values associated with women's householder rituals, emphasizing instead ritual practices allied more closely with renunciation and its goals. In this context, renunciation is highly valued in women, as it is in men, while sexuality returns a woman to the sphere of traditional domesticity, where she takes on the role of supporter and helper of a man rather than the role of individual seeker. Hence, the world of female tantric ritual challenges the connection between domesticity and women's ritual practices predominant in other contexts. Like Orr and Craddock, McDaniel demonstrates that women's religious practices may engage ascetic goals and activities as fully as or even more fully than domestic ones, sometimes rejecting domesticity or subordinating the domestic realm of householder life to the goals associated with religious renunciation and celibacy.

The final chapter, by Vasudha Narayanan, "Performing Arts, Re-forming Rituals: Women and Social Change in South India," addresses the expression of Hindu women's religiosity through music and dance. Narayanan observes that in contemporary Hinduism the performing arts, which she argues are essentially forms of religious performance, may serve as vehicles not only for women's religious expression, but also for dynamic social commentary and reform. Narayanan points to dancers like Mallika Sarabhai and Chandralekha, who use dance to highlight women's issues and to express themes of anguish and strength, as examples. As authors, performers, and consumers of the performing arts, women may engage music and dance both to express their own subjectivities and to help effect social change.

Collins articulates two distinctive approaches to the study of ritual: one that emphasizes what ritual does to people and another that emphasizes what people do with ritual (Collins 1997, 17). The first approach elicits a hermeneutics of suspicion, seeking to elucidate ways that ritual practices affirm and reproduce larger relations of social power, often without the conscious assent of ritual actors. The second approach emphasizes instead the ways that people use ritual forms to pursue their own individual and collective interests, appropriating and sometimes modifying rituals when convenient (178). While the first approach stresses the nature of ritual actors as (often unwitting) recipients of larger ideological and hegemonic structures, the second stresses their nature as agents who may creatively deploy ritual for their own purposes. Both approaches certainly have a role to play in shedding light on the nature of ritual practice. But the chapters in this volume overwhelmingly stress the second approach, highlighting what Hindu women do with their rituals to shape their worlds as agents acting in pursuit of their own desired ends. The women

whose traditions and lives we explore in this book exercise initiative, inge-
nuity, and resolve in creating and sustaining female-centered traditions and
practices that are uniquely meaningful to women's experience in Hindu
culture. This volume as a whole suggests that those interested in Hindu wom-
en's ritual practices would do well to attend fully to women's ritual creativity
and to the religious concerns of women beyond the sphere of conventional
domesticity.

NOTE

    1. Many thanks to Corinne Dempsey, whose commentary on and description
of "domesticity" I am borrowing here from her helpful manuscript review.

REFERENCES

Bell, Catherine. 1997. *Ritual: Perspectives and Dimensions.* New York: Oxford Uni-
    versity Press.
Butler, Judith. 1990. *Gender Trouble: Feminism and the Subversion of Identity.* New
    York: Routledge.
Collins, Elizabeth Fuller. 1997. *Pierced by Murugan's Lance: Ritual, Power, and
    Moral Redemption among Malaysian Hindus.* DeKalb: Northern Illinois University
    Press.
Hancock, Mary Elizabeth. 1999. *Womanhood in the Making: Domestic Ritual and
    Public Culture in Urban South India.* Boulder, CO: Westview.
Jamison, Stephanie. 1996. *Sacrificed Wife/Sacrificer's Wife: Women, Ritual, and
    Hospitality in Ancient India.* New York: Oxford University Press.
Khandelwal, Meena. 2004. *Women in Ochre Robes: Gendering Hindu Renunciation.*
    Albany: State University of New York Press.
Leslie, Julia, ed. 1991. *Roles and Rituals for Hindu Women.* Rutherford, NJ: Fairleigh
    Dickinson University Press.
McGee, Mary. 1987. "Feasting and Fasting: The Vrata Tradition and Its Signifi-
    cance for Hindu Women." Th.D. diss., Harvard University Divinity School.
————. 1991. "Desired Fruits: Motive and Intention in the Votive Rites of Hindu
    Women." In *Roles and Rituals for Hindu Women,* ed. Julia Leslie, 71–88.
    London: Pinter.
————. 2002. "Ritual Rights: The Gender Implications of Adhikara." In *Jewels of
    Authority: Women and Textual Tradition in Hindu India,* ed. Laurie Patton, 32–50.
    New York: Oxford University Press.
Northup, Lesley A. 1997. *Ritualizing Women.* Cleveland, OH: Pilgrim.
Patton, Laurie. 2002. *Jewels of Authority: Women and Textual Tradition in Hindu India.*
    New York: Oxford University Press.
Pearson, Anne Mackenzie. 1996. *"Because It Gives Me Peace of Mind": Ritual
    Fasts in the Religious Lives of Hindu Women.* Albany: State University of New York
    Press.

Pintchman, Tracy. 2005. *Guests at God's Wedding: Celebrating Kartik among the Women of Benares*. Albany: State University of New York Press.

Proctor-Smith, Marjorie. 1993. "'In the Line of the Female': Shakerism and Feminism." In *Women's Leadership in Marginal Religions: Explorations Outside the Mainstream*, ed. Catherine Wessinger, 23–40. Chicago: University of Illinois Press.

Raheja, Gloria Goodwin, and Ann Grodzins Gold. 1994. *Listen to the Heron's Words: Reimagining Gender and Kinship in North India*. Berkeley: University of California Press.

Sered, Susan Starr. 1992. *Women as Ritual Experts*. New York: Oxford University Press.

———. 1994. *Priestess, Mother, Sacred Sister: Religions Dominated by Women*. New York: Oxford University Press.

Wadley, Susan. 1989. "Hindu Women's Family and Household Rites in a North Indian Village." In *Unspoken Worlds: Women's Religious Lives in Non-Western Cultures*, ed. Nancy A. Falk and Rita M. Gross, 94–109. San Francisco: Harper and Row.

Zelliot, Eleanor. 2000. "Women Saints in Medieval Maharashtra." In *Faces of the Feminine in Ancient, Medieval, and Modern India*, ed. Mandakranta Bose, 192–200. New York: Oxford University Press.

PART I

Engaging Domesticity

I

The Cat in the Courtyard: The Performance of Sanskrit and the Religious Experience of Women

Laurie L. Patton

Will the nature of Sanskrit and Hindu religious experience change as a result of its being increasingly in the hands of women? One young woman Sanskritist, Pradnya Deshpande, makes the following comparison:

> Sanskrit is difficult, but it is also like *prasadam*. When someone offers you *prasadam*, you have to eat it, even when there is a stone in it. Modern people reject the stone—they say, "There's a stone in this!" And throw it away. It is also like a cat: When the cat comes into the courtyard, the older women will call it *bhau-ji* [brother-in-law]. Even the cat is *bhau-ji*, like a brother-in-law, in that house. But the modern girl will say, "Go away, cat!" In this way, the modern researchers can accept some doubt about the tradition. They can be critical. Now these teachers still love Sanskrit, and they love anyone who is learning Sanskrit.

Background

This young woman's comments indicate a certain domestic welcoming of the opportunity to learn and study Sanskrit, even if it comes in the less pleasant form of a cat. Before I explore this idea in more detail, let me begin with some background. What is the situation of Sanskrit education in contemporary India? In his recent volume on the role of the *pandita*, Alex Michaels (2001) outlines the dual education system in contemporary India in which traditional teachers find themselves caught: the university system, based loosely on the English model of governments, schools, and universities, and the *pathshalas* and *samskrita-vidyapithas*, where Sanskrit is taught according to the traditional methods. There, the *guru-shishya sambandha*, or relationship between teacher and student, is the primary model, where the teacher stands for wisdom, memory, and personal and moral guidance. Michaels mentions the various ways in which, after the publication of the report of the government of India's Sanskrit Commission (1958), various agencies have been implementing its recommendations—especially the Rashtriya Sanskrit Sansthan, formed in 1970.

Despite dire predictions, Sanskrit has hung on. According to one report, almost all of the recommendations of the Sanskrit commission have been implemented; there are now 4,000 *pathshalas* funded by the Rashtriya Sanskrit Sansthan, as well as many other *vidyapithas* and Sanskrit colleges, which are funded independently or by local communities and temples. The study of Sanskrit in secondary schools has also been a major priority, with more limited success because of the other options for language study (English, regional languages, Hindi) recommended by state governments in India. The Bharatiya Janata Party (BJP) government's support for Sanskrit study in the 1990s was stronger than that of previous governments, but there was little improvement in the overall system of traditional education as India increasingly competed on the global stage in technology, science, and engineering. In the English university system, Sanskrit has become a "humanities" subject, with less qualified students, or students with a lesser need for high income, flocking to the registration desks.

While several other scholars[1] have recently commented on the dual education system and its effect on the study of Sanskrit in India, one crucial and overlooked element in this system is gender. Recent academic work is commendable indeed for keeping the study of Sanskrit alive in the scholarly imagination; however, this work has totally ignored the role of women in this sea change in the study of Sanskrit. In many parts of India, the dual education system is also clearly a dual gender system.

Let me be more specific. In postcolonial India, Sanskrit has become a marker of the Hindu religiosity of women as well as men. In certain places, if the trend continues, it will soon become entirely the prerogative of women. With the massive entry of men into the fields of science, technology, and engineering, this change has happened without the help of postcolonial theory or secular feminism, either Indian or Western. It will continue without that help. My larger book project, *Grandmother Language*, from which this chapter is derived, is a study of women Sanskritists through their personal narratives. Its chapters will comprise an examination of their lives, their religious commitments and practices, and their understandings of their roles as teachers and scholars. Such change is only possible with an unlikely amalgamation of factors: traditional Hindu ideologies of gender combine with a historical emphasis on women's educational reform in Maharashtra to create a unique environment for innovation. This combination makes it possible for women to take on new roles as caretakers of a classical language which has been prohibited to them for millennia.

Let me begin with some facts about Maharashtra, the area where I did my research. In Maharashtra, Sanskrit is still alive and well within the educational system: there are eight major independent research institutes in Pune and Bombay; six universities that offer degrees up to the master's and doctoral levels; thirty-three major Sanskrit manuscript collections; and nine Indological journals published in the state. The personnel needed to maintain this large educational tradition is extensive.

The bulk of that personnel is increasingly composed of women. With one retirement, the University of Pune's Department of Sanskrit will consist entirely of women. The ratio of male to female students registered for the M.A. degree in Sanskrit in 2004 was one to six. In the Deccan College Dictionary Project, Pune, there are seven women and two men on the regular research staff. Bhandarkar Oriental Research institute has 50 percent women researchers on its staff. The number of *stri-purohits*, or women ritual specialists, is growing rapidly, and, according to one report by V. L. Manjul, women ritual specialists now outnumber their male counterparts in certain neighborhoods in Pune. On a nationwide scale, the chairs of six of the major universities— Delhi, Madras, Nagpur, Pune, Calcutta, and Hyderabad—are women.[2]

I have completed eighty oral life narratives of women in the field of Sanskrit in Maharashtra, using as my starting point (and my starting point only) a questionnaire with ten questions about family life, educational experience, and vision for the future. The conversations were long and meandering, lasting about two to three hours each, and longer if necessary. They were conducted mostly in my native language of English, about eight in conversational Hindi, and some with occasional short exchanges in conversational Sanskrit. My collaborator in this project, Maitreyee Deshpande, also conducted several interviews in Marathi. She was able to clarify questions in Marathi during our conversations as well. All of the conversations except eleven were recorded.

Perhaps a story from my fieldwork best sums up the tensions that we might see in the coming years, as the dual education system unfolds. One young woman in my study, who requested not to be named, was part of a team that hired two young traditional *panditas* to teach at a major Indian university. The students wanted to get exposure to this method of learning, and the local *pathshala* was happy to help. One of the young *panditas* approached her, red-faced, and asked embarrassedly whether the young women he would be teaching could absent themselves during their menstrual periods so that he would be spared the problems of impurity that might result. She replied:

Sir, perhaps I might ask you to consider where our respective institutions might be in fifty years. I can as much as guarantee you that my university will be here and standing, and probably teaching Sanskrit then. However, neither I nor you can guarantee that your *pathshala* will survive that long. Given that this is the case, I suggest you comply with the university system, where no such concerns about monthly cycles apply.

Definitions

So much, then, for the basic background. While there are many other aspects of this change I will explore in my book, such as the role of caste, region, educational institution, and postcolonial status of Sanskrit, the purpose of this chapter is to explore only one small aspect of this rather large change: the more explicit inclusion of Sanskrit utterance in "domestic" moments of personal change and transformation. I want to formulate the issue in this way because I want to nudge the basic categories in which we tend to view Sanskrit—as either a dead language or an artificial language. In the case of Sanskrit as a dead language, we tend to hear this from non-Indological colleagues who may not be aware of the places it is still used, such as at academic conferences, in villages in Karnataka and Himachal Pradesh, and during revivals of sacrificial performances. The artificial language definition of Sanskrit is perhaps more accurate, describing as it does the fact that Sanskrit remains an elite, father language learned at one's male teacher's or father's feet—the opposite of the natural language learned at one's mother's knee. However, this definition implies that Sanskrit has nothing to do with the household, with the world of the domestic sphere, and with personal changes involving the heart as well as the head.

My preliminary research results show that even such a characterization of Sanskrit as an "artificial" language tends to be misleading. I would like to spend the time remaining to me arguing that, in the hands of Brahmin as well as some non-Brahmin women guardians, Sanskrit's cultural placement is shifting. Let me put my two basic points more accurately and specifically: first, Sanskrit's domestic usages, which have always been present in Hindu cultures, are now even more pronounced. Second, Sanskrit's relevance as a language which can be used in everyday moments and in moments of personal transition is increasing.

Let me begin by focusing on the contexts of Sanskrit and the ways in which we might view Sanskrit as we already do, as a partly formal language, but also as a partly proverbial language, one which depends upon informal contexts and particularly defined moments for its utterance. Notice that both of the characterizations of Sanskrit mentioned above, as either dead or artificial, are dependent upon performative context for their definitions. In the case of a dead language, there is assumed to be *no* performative context, hence the language's morbidity. In the case of an artificial language, the performative context is not "natural," but learned as a secondary and not a primary skill. But the emergence of performance studies would insist that we be even more specific and careful about such definitions, because language is performed in a much wider variety of contexts than these definitions tend to suggest. As Charles Briggs (1988: 372) puts it, "The emergence of contextual and performance-based studies is crucial, since they point to the status of contextual elements as central elements of the performance."[3]

Moreover, it is crucial to acknowledge, as linguists rarely do, the role of the local influence of Sanskrit in places such as Maharashtra. As Dandekar has noted in his excellent, but now somewhat dated, *Sanskrit and Maharashtra* (1972),[4] Sanskrit influenced and was influenced by local cultural movements throughout the history of the region. Most notably for our purposes, the political events of the late colonial and postcolonial periods provided ample opportunity for creative work in Sanskrit. Maharashtrian authors K. V. Chitale and V. Bagewadikar produced Sanskrit works on colonial figures such as Lokmanya Tilak, as well as Sanskrit biographies of Nehru, Gandhi, and the Freedom movement. Short story, poetry, and drama competitions have dotted the region, beginning from the 1930s and onward to this day. Translations of English works into Sanskrit by Marathi authors include Wordsworth (C. T. Kenghe), Longfellow (G. B. Palsule), Keats (N. P. Gune), the Sermon on the Mount (S. N. Tadpatrikar), and Goethe's *Faust* (L. V. Deshpande). In 1961, A. R. Ratnaparakhi composed the Samvadamala, which is a series of thirteen dialogues on daily subjects like breakfast, office, shopping, and so on, which might be the precursor of the Speak Sanskrit movement of Krishnashastri, called Samskriti Bharati today. While these examples may be well known to people within scholarly or literary circles, their existence does not seem to have affected the definition or treatment of Sanskrit in any demonstrable way until recently.

One exception to this is Jan Houben's edited volume, *Ideology and Status of Sanskrit* (1996).[5] There, Madhav Deshpande discusses the changing nature of priestly "recited" Sanskrit, from the early treatment of changes in mantra to the present-day usage of Sanskrit in American temples. Saroja Bhate writes of a "renaissance" in Sanskrit literature in the same period mentioned above, as well as its current role in public education and scientific research. Victor van Bijlert comments on the role of Sanskrit in the Bengal intellectual formation of nationalism. And Albrecht Wezler does a first pass through the "spoken Sanskrit" practices and their related grammars of the Middle Ages. All of these perspectives bode well for the treatment of Sanskrit as a living, breathing language with its own organic life, learned and used in a variety of contexts.

Formal Language within the Household: Women
and the Flexibility of Sanskrit

It is a truism and fairly uninteresting to state the obvious—that Sanskrit is
performed regularly in household *puja* rituals throughout India, at the time
of major festivals such as Ganeshotsav, Sarasvati Puja, Krishna Jayanti,
Diwali, and many others. What is more interesting is the ways in which wom-
en's increasing participation and leadership as guardians of mantric recita-
tions at these celebrations and their leadership in Sanskrit instruction within
the home are changing our understanding of why and how they are performed.

The stereotypes have been that Sanskrit *japa*, or low-toned recitation,
lends a certain inflexibility and even inaccessibility to even domestic ritual
performances. Kumud Pawde (1992), a Dalit Sanskritist at the University of
Nagpur, describes her Brahmin neighbors as "The Splendid People," whose
performance of Sanskrit in their home rendered them removed from their
Dalit neighbors—cleaner, more learned, and "shining" in a way that she could
never emulate.[6] This view is clear in a near-endless number of examples, from
the early sixth-century *bhakti* poets (see Ramanujan, 1973) to A. K. Murthy's
now-classic novel *Samskara* (1978).[7] The performance of *japa* is sometimes
even beyond the performer's comprehension and is invested with an aura of
elitism and oppression, combined with the formal exactitude of sound.

Yet there is another side to ritual performance—one in which, even in
highly formal situations, actors react to and improvise on their surroundings
in subtle ways. To put it theoretically, performance studies has suggested that
ritual worlds are created worlds governed by roles and instruments, and therefore there is a higher likelihood of ritual actors using pragmatic forms of communication and metonymically referring to and identifying with those roles
and instruments. Many performance theorists[8] (Tedlock, 1993; Tedlock and
Mannheim, 1995; Gill, 1987; Laderman, 1991; Driver, 1993; Mudimbe, 1997;
Spiziri, 1997; Grimes, 1990, 1995, 2000) have examined the linguistic aspects
of performance in ethnographic contexts similar to the highly structured world
of domestic *puja* ritual.

Further, as these authors have argued, in these structured ritual contexts,
while the verbal "text" may be fixed, the world constructed around that text, and
the actors' connection of that text to the world around them, does vary in fascinating ways. Briggs uses the example of the Easter liturgy in Mexicano verbal
art to demonstrate this: while the prayers and the hymns are the same, the
volume, the emphasis, the processions, and the placement of the ritual vary
according to the status, age, and disposition of the person performing the text,
as well as more external factors such as the weather, the current political
climate of the village, and the priest in charge (1988: 289–340). Moreover, as

THE CAT IN THE COURTYARD   25

Briggs also notes, these "fixed" texts are as much about the emotions and events they evoke as they are about the words contained in them.

Relatedly, in his article "Contextualizing the Eternal Language: Features of Priestly Sanskrit," Madhav Deshpande (1996)[9] also speaks about the ways in which ritual situations might change seemingly fixed ritual language. Some of the changes have to do with the influence of the vernacular language, leading to the term "vernacular Sanskrit." Others have to do with the actual ritual situation in which participants find themselves, such as priests wishing to make sure that the individual participants are acknowledged in American temples in a particular way.

Domestic Worlds

My research to date suggests a similar richness and variety in women's experiences of the domestic performance of Sanskrit in the home—whether it is through elaborate rituals or simple recitation. First, at a general level, it should be noted that, in sixty-two out of the eighty interviews, the women reported that it was the domestic use of Sanskrit in the childhood home that was in part responsible for their continuing with the study of Sanskrit as a profession.

One woman recounts her childhood experience of learning Sanskrit by having her mother teach her as she worked on the household chores: "Every household item we were cleaning or dusting, she would give me the Sanskrit name for it. In this way I learned simple Sanskrit words, and I began to associate in my mind the work my mother did for all of us in the family with the Sanskrit language. I still feel as [if] I am doing some of that today." A younger woman said that her connection with her grandfather and his kindness was integrally bound up with learning Sanskrit. "Since I was five we had to recite chapters from the *Gita*, and the *subhashitas*. It was a compulsion for us—not our wish—but we loved our grandfather because he never punished us. He died in 1986, and some spirit has carried on in my mind."

Second, and relatedly, for sixty-five out of the eighty women I interviewed, Sanskrit is associated with respect and honor for women as well as for men in the early family history. As one scholar, Mrs. Manik Thakar, told me, "Eminent scholars like S. D. Joshi, and so on, came to see us. They were all a keen group. I recited a few *shlokas* and felt very much a part of the group. I was respected as a child, and what is more, my mother was interested in educating girls." Mrs. Shailaja Bapat, currently the head of the Sanskrit Department in Pune, commented, "I learned it from *puja* only—in my childhood. In the morning, the priest used to come for worship; he used to tell us how to worship. Also, with *Ramaraksha* mantra—our father and grandmothers used to tell us how to recite everyday." Relatedly, Ranjana Date tells of her teacher:

He used to teach only for boys, but by special tuition he taught girls on Sundays. First girls' batch he taught. The amount wasn't much—seven or eight rupees per month. But that was an age-old matter of prestige, not of money for scholarship. He used to teach not only Sanskrit, but chemistry and French. Our headmistress said, "OK, we'll observe the rules of purity, so what harm is there in learning?" He had many different sides to him. [My teacher] Bhide taught us Panini [the Sanskrit grammarian]. We became familiar with that, and then we learned *Laghukaumudi*. We would memorize certain portions, and as we recited he would explain.

Third, and most important for our purposes, the women report their memories of domestic Sanskrit rituals as filled with color, light, fascination, and variation. More than half of those interviewed spoke of fascination for the ritual use of Sanskrit as part of their ongoing interest in the field, and forty-two mentioned morning *pujas* (both positively and negatively). One very prominent Sanskritist spoke of morning *pujas* as the thing that oriented her and grounded her as a child. Saroja Bhate commented, "Sanskrit, one can do at home, through morning *pujas*, as well as being a teacher in a college." One woman reminisced that she became fascinated with Sanskrit from her weekly and holiday trips to the temple. As she put it, her trips to the family temple continued back inside the household: "The chanting from the temple was so beautiful, and there was so much time we would spend together with my aunts and uncles and cousins—the whole family. We would continue the chanting from the temple back into our living room, and even some of the tunes I would hear from my father in the *puja* room the next morning too."

Several of the women spoke about negotiating with the priest in learning how to do the *pujas*; for each of them, understanding Hindu practices was a matter of trial and error, learning and perfecting. Mandakini Kinjavadekar had very powerful memories of such learning:

I remember my father's teacher, Pandit Khareshastri from Gokarna-Mahabaleshwar. Ganesh-shastri Khare was the guru of my father. While coming, he used to bring Konkan products—jackfruit chapati, mango chapati. He was for us as a loving grandpa bringing all these products. More than one year he lived with us, and he was observing "cleanliness." After a bath, nobody would touch him, not speak, etc. Also we had to obey all these things. When my father and his teacher were discussing all these things, we were not supposed to talk or go there. The teacher was observing no speaking, *maunavrata*. We felt that day very pure—that something pure is in our house.

None of these women actually performed the ritual in their childhoods, but it was clear that Sanskrit was a part of their negotiations in their narratives of childhood learning.

Most important, following Briggs's insight above about the emotional impact of a fixed text, the women reported that Sanskrit recitation was experienced in different ways in different climates. Forty-three of them mentioned that, while reciting had no meaning for them initially, they were moved by the beauty of Sanskrit to create a mood. As Saroja Bhate put it, "I remember the Hindu *vaidikas* of my childhood, where pronunciation was down to the minute details, in the exact and correct way. I was so impressed by the beauty of the language."

Yet many of these same women also reported that Sanskrit verses—sometimes even the same verses—created a mood of seriousness and respect when publicly recited outside of the home. Mrs. Asha Gurjar actually reported that her father did not allow her to recite the *Gita* because it seemed "too big" for her, but over time she began to experience it as "smaller" and eventually learned how to recite it publicly. Mrs. Menakshi Kodnikar also connected the work of the *stripurohits*, or women priests, with the work of women Sanskritists:

> There are a large number of women priests now—and they want to do service, to be of service like we do. And so whatever branch of knowledge they know, they perform this service for the family line. Many women, they don't take a degree. They teach more in the household, and they perform service for the householders—*Shrisukta* and things like that. And there are many ladies now doing this. Ladies also teach *puja-vidhi*—the rules about worship.

Sanskrit as the Scriptural Utterance of Transformation

In my research with these women, the second arena of Sanskritic performance had to do with its ability to transform a personal situation—a function I would identify closely with Charles Briggs's analyses of proverbial and scriptural utterances. As Briggs writes of both genres:

> The two genres [scriptural and proverbial] each revolve around the stylistic and ideological intrusion of a third party into the speech event; whereas the elders of bygone days enter the proverb[ial] performance, God or Christ emerges in the scriptural allusion, often through the mediation of a sacred text. In both cases, the quotation addresses the audience and elevates the social interaction. (1988: 158)

In the case of the scriptural quotation, however, the focus is moved back to the "earlier times" of the scripture itself and becomes a subject in its own right. As Briggs puts it, "Scriptural allusions are able to break out of the interactional setting that gave rise to them and become the *raison d'être* of the discourse" (1988: 169).

While I will discuss particular instances of Sanskrit quotation below, it is important to note here some overall ideologies about the effect that Sanskrit recitation has on social situations. Intriguingly, Briggs articulates in his own anthropological language an idea that the women themselves also articulated, albeit in a slightly different intellectual vernacular. From the basis of fifty-six out of the eighty responses, it was quite clear that the women have a general ideology behind Sanskrit quotation as a practice in its own right. As one senior woman put it, "Sanskrit has a purifying effect on the mind. It opens up a whole world once you recite it." And Asha Gurjar, also a senior, said, "If your mind is already accepting *samskaras*, then you will have better *samskaras* in Sanskrit." A younger woman said, "Whatever conversation is happening in your mind, you feel as if you have answered the voices if you recite at the beginning of the day." Menakshi Kodnikar also mentioned the effect that reciting a mantra has on cooking. When she recites mantras, the food has a special quality to it, and it affects everyone whom she feeds in an auspicious and peaceful way.

Again, at a general level, these women reported frequently that their Sanskrit ability, particularly the ability to recite, became in its own right a form of negotiation with their fathers and brothers. A rather striking fifty-two out of eighty women narrated some version of a story of their father's negative evaluation of them as women who could study and teach on their own right or as weaker compared to their brothers. One woman's father studied Sanskrit with her elder brother, but forbade her to come. Her insistence on continuing on the path was a means of gaining his respect, if not his approval. She felt she had done that when he didn't object to her accepting a scholarship to "offer" the subject of Sanskrit at a women's college. Another was encouraged to study Sanskrit because she didn't need a job that paid well, as her brother did. Others articulated the same interesting connection between a woman's status as a wife and her ability to take the lower-paying job of Sanskrit professor.[10]

However, for thirty-seven of these eighty women, their ability to recite Sanskrit somehow resolved the family situation and acted in part as a commentary on the relationship between the women and the men in their families, whether they be fathers or brothers. Even though I heard no specific story of Sanskrit recitation suddenly creating peace in the family, many women reported that they were able to prove themselves or, as one woman put it, "play a role in the family" after they had persevered and succeeded in learning Sanskrit. Lalita Marathe, a researcher in the Prakrit Dictionary Project, spoke of this in the following way:

When I was about five, six years old, I recited the twelfth chapter of *Bhagavad Gita*, and I got a prize. My parents taught me some *stotras*, like *shubham karoti kalyanam*. In this way, I was acquainted with Sanskrit in my home only, and my mother, father, uncles, *mama* [uncle], and *mausi* [aunt] all helped me in reciting Sanskrit. My younger brothers do *sandhya* [daily recitation]. I also recite with them.

On a general level, then, in Briggs's terms, the women's overall ability and competence in Sanskrit recitation and study "addressed the audience and elevated the social interaction."

However, specific instances of the kind of scriptural allusion that Briggs analyzes did arise in our conversations. One older woman spoke of recitation of the *Gita* as the "capstone" to her everyday experience. As she put it, "Only *Gita* can be an answer to our quest." Here, she did not mean simply the substance of the text of the *Gita*, but its actual recitation at certain moments. She mentioned that she recited the *shlokas* of the *Gita* that involve the word *kartavyam*—what is to be done—because they give her a sense of duty and direction when she is unsure. They also help her to meditate on the purpose and nature of duty toward family in her life.

> There is the idea of *pitridev* and *matridev* [mother and father honored as divine]. You shouldn't first cut the roots and then try to join them. And the *Gita* doesn't say *na kartavyam*, it says *kartavyam*. [Recites *Gita* 3.19]:
>
>> *tasmad asaktah satatam karyam karma samacara*
>> *asakto hy acarankarma param apnoti purushah*
>
> [My translation: So, without clinging, always perform action to be done. When one performs actions to be done without clinging, one attains the highest.]
>
> And I feel that only *Gita* can be an answer to the quest. My brother should have done Sanskrit. . . . I tried to carry on the tradition of my father, even if my brother didn't. I am not taking his place, but trying to help society today. Sanskrit is a kind of personality development program, as your mind becomes pure when you speak it and study it. I use it when I teach the *Shrisukta* and other things.

Here again, we see that in her own experience, reciting such *Gita* verses had both social and personal benefits and could act as a kind of commentary on a situation—both her own situation and those of her family and society. And the *Gita* itself, as Briggs also notices, becomes its own *raison d'être* for the conversation. God literally became part of the conversation, as Mrs. Gurjar recited Krishna's words. Another woman, one of the coordinators for the Samskriti Bharati movement in Mumbai, pushed this idea of speaking Sanskrit as the "divinization" of an ordinary situation even further. She told me: "I was literally cured of my illness after I began to speak Sanskrit. *Deva, guru, samskritam*—they are all the same for me. They are the same words."

Other Sanskrit scriptural allusions used by women tend to push us beyond Briggs's definitions and more into the realm of effecting difficult personal transitions. Dr. Kala Acharya, in the prime of her career as director of the Sanskrit Institute, spoke of helping her mother as she was dying. As she put it, "If some difficulties come in life, mantras will work. First when my mother was ill, I recited prayer[s] from the *Gita*. I alternated with other prayers I knew, and then went back to the *Gita*. At midnight she expired. I know it helped with the difficulty."

So too, a very senior woman who was involved in the Freedom movement in Pune spoke of her father's friend, who was a *shastri*, or learned person, teaching her an *ashirvad*, a prayer of hope and aspiration. She told me, "When I first began to study Sanskrit, before Pune University was even founded, this is how I got confidence every day, and got confidence in my heart. When my husband was ill I also recited it; it gave me psychological satisfaction, and I know I could face the future without him."

She then recited, *udvayam tamasaspari pashyanto jyotir uttamam; devam devatra suryam aganma jyotir uttamam* (Rig Veda 1.50.10; Atharva Veda 7.50.7; Shukla Yajur Veda 20.21, 27.10, 35.14, 38.24; Krishna Yajur Veda 4.17.4; "Beholding a higher light beyond this darkness, we have come to a highest light, Surya, god among gods"). She went on, "Even the use of the verb tense there expresses that something is about to happen in the immediate future—that we have almost reached a stage. And that should give us courage." She went on to explain to me that this mantra is one of the *Sandhya* mantras—defined usually as the meeting point between night and day, but also to be recited as part of the daily canon of mantras. She then concluded, "But this is truly a twilight mantra, in that it has helped me in the twilight of my life, to make it through the sunset period." This woman was able to understand the double meaning of *sandhya*—both as twilight language and as daily recitation practice—in a transformative way.

Perhaps the most common example of this transformative use of a mantra is the *Ramarakshastotram*—the mantra for protection. Most of the interviewees in the study learned this mantra as a child and would recite it for visitors and family. A short version of it (and it has many variations) goes as follows:

> *Om rama candraya vidmahe raghunandaya dhimahi*
> *tan no vishnuh pracodayat*

Almost all of the women in Maharashtra spoke of this *shloka* as a kind of talisman, to be used in many different circumstances—some of them very gendered indeed. The one above is modeled on the *Gayatri* mantra and has the same all-purpose function. As one young Sanskrit schoolteacher from Mumbai put it, that mantra got her through both labor and delivery. "I recited the *Ramarakshastotram* all the way to the hospital, and then in the delivery room too." She told me this as she spoke Sanskrit with her mother in the kitchen, both of them laughing as they tried various Sanskrit phrases for "The baby is crying. You go take care of her!" It may be perhaps unremarkable, but at another level quite remarkable, that Sanskrit would find itself happily in kitchens and hospital labor rooms. It would be hard to imagine more domestic situations in which the transformation of Sanskrit recitation might take place.

Concluding Thoughts

We return, then, to the cat in the courtyard. The story itself suggests a number of different aspects to the study of Sanskrit and its religious and ritual meanings—aspects which are borne out in this chapter. First, Sanskrit has underscored its presence in the home, and women are there to greet it in a new way. Second, there is a flexibility of response to Sanskrit—and women are part of that flexibility. The preliminary data from my interviews suggest that in their own experiences of recited Sanskrit, as well as in their use of it in their daily lives, women will give it yet another new place in postcolonial society. Contra the traditional definitions, Sanskrit is alive in a new way. Many of the women in this study were able to use *shlokas* to help them through moments of transition, crisis, or grief, whether it was to remove difficulty in childbirth in the Mumbai hospital, or to learn to face a new future as a widow. In a certain sense, based on these women's experiences, the cultural meaning of Sanskrit will have as much to do with the use of Sanskrit to negotiate domestic life and personal transformation as it does with the more public ritual life of the temple or the sacrifice. This change may be a gentler form of innovation, where the cat is welcomed, especially in the courtyard.

NOTES

1. See in particular Saroja Bhate (1996: 383–400); Victor van Bijlert (1996: 347–366); Crostiann Van Der Burg (1996: 367–382); Harry Falk (1993: 103–120); Pierre Sylvain Filliozat (2000); K. K. Mishra (1997); Ralph Marc Steinmann (1986).

2. Personal communication, V. L. Manjul and Devi Tai, Upasani Kanya Kunari Sthan, August 2004. Also see Manjul (2003: 64–68; 1996: 38–39); Damle (1997); and anonymous (2004; 2002).

3. Charles Briggs's analysis is very astute here; in a performative tradition with very strict rules like Sanskrit, there is a motivation to vary the performance according to subtle contextual cues shared by the audience. As the women described their participation in Sanskrit elocution and drama contests, the bulk of their stories was made up of some contextual variation (a different stage, a sudden noise) that varied the otherwise quite strict performative script.

4. R. N. Dandekar himself was always interested in cultural variations and local transmutations of Sanskrit practices. In a personal conversation (1997), he told me that he was sad that the "village" Sanskritists were fewer and fewer these days, because they provided the most interesting studies of "Sanskrit dialect."

5. On the "ideology" of Sanskrit, one of the larger points of my study will be that there is far more variation in ideology than is presumed by Western scholars. Partly because of a lack of enrollment in classes and partly because of a Brahminical exodus to technology and science, the study of Sanskrit in the major universities is now well populated with non-Brahmin students. In addition, there are several activist women Sanskritists on the Left of the political spectrum who are left out of the discussion altogether in the West—if Western scholars pay any attention to these women at all.

6. Kumud Pawde's influence is felt keenly among activist women on the Left in Maharashtra and in other parts of the feminist movement in India.

7. The scene which is most ironic on this score depicts the *acharya*, bursting with disease, leaving his temple and planning to cleanse and heal the town in all kinds of ways. The author goes on: "For quite some time he muttered to himself like a chant, 'The Idiots, The Idiots!'. . ."

8. I am grateful to my colleague Joyce Flueckiger for insight into this material as well as long conversations about my various case studies.

9. The question of "American Sanskrit" has just begun to be studied; a larger view of the Hindu education system in America is a desideratum at this point. Arthi Devarajan at Emory has just begun this important work, focusing on educational practices and aesthetics. The current generation of graduate students (both Hindu American and non-Hindu) have a wide field open to them.

10. I treat this subject at length in my book project.

REFERENCES

Anonymous. 2004. "Maidens Mastering Man's Mantra-Veda." *Sunday Herald Spectrum* 11.24, June 4.
———. 2002. "Starting Vedic Studies." *Hinduism Today* (October–December): 59.
Bhate, Saroja. 1996. "Position of Sanskrit in Public Education and Scientific Research in Modern India." In *Ideology and Status of Sanskrit*, ed. Jan Houben, 383–400. Leiden: Brill.
Briggs, Charles. 1988. *Competence in Performance: The Creativity of Tradition in Mexicano Verbal Art*. Philadelphia: University of Pennsylvania Press.
Damle, Manjiri. 1997. "Women Priests Win Hearts for Dedication." *Times of India*, November 29.
Dandekar, R. N. 1972. *Sanskrit and Maharashtra: A Symposium*. Pune, India: University of Pune.
Deshpande, Madhav. 1996. "Contextualizing the Eternal: Features of Priestly Sanskrit." In *Ideology and Status of Sanskrit: Contributions to the History of the Sanskrit Language*, ed. Jan E. M. Houben, 401–436. Leiden: Brill.
Driver, Tom Faw. 1993. *Life in Performance: Reflections on Ritual, Religion, and Social Value*. Washington, DC: Society for Values in Higher Education.

Falk, Harry. 1993. "Goodies for India: Literacy, Orality, and Vedic Culture." In
  Erscheinungsformen cultureller Prozesse, ed. Wolfgang Raible, 103–120. Tubingen:
  Gunter Narr.
Filliozat, Pierre Sylvain. 2000. *The Sanskrit Language: An Overview*. Varanasi, India:
  Indica.
Gill, Sam D. 1987. *Native American Religious Action: A Performance Approach to
  Religion*. Columbia: University of South Carolina Press.
Grimes, Ronald. 2000. *Deeply into the Bone: Reinventing Rites of Passage*. Berkeley:
  University of California Press.
———. 1995. *Beginnings in Ritual Studies*. Columbia: University of South Carolina
  Press.
———. 1990. *Ritual Criticism: Case Studies in Its Practice, Essays in Its Theories*.
  Columbia: University of South Carolina Press.
Hastings, Adi. 2003. "Simplifying Sanskrit." *Pragmatics* 13(3/4): 499–513.
———. "From Ritual to Grammar: Sacrifice, Homology, Metalanguage." *Language &
  Communication* 23(3/4): 275–285.
Houben, Jan, ed. 1996. *Ideology and Status of Sanskrit: Contributions to the History
  of the Sanskrit Language*. Leiden: Brill.
Laderman, Carol. 1991. *Taming the Wind of Desire: Psychology, Medicine, and
  Aesthetics in Malay Shamanistic Practice*. Berkeley: University of California
  Press.
Manjul, V. L. 2003. "Shirdi-Sakuri Don Upasana Kshetre." *Sri Sadguru Sairkrpa*,
  Oct.–Nov. Dassara-Diwali Issue, 64–68.
———. 1996. "A Hitherto Forbidden Realm." *Manushi* 97 (November–December):
  37–39.
Michaels, Alex. 2001. *The Pandit: Traditional Scholarship in India*. New Delhi: Manohar.
Mishra, K. K., ed. 1997. *Sanskrit Studies in India*. New Delhi: Rasthriya Sanskrit
  Sansthan.
Mudimbe, V. Y. 1997. *Tales of Faith: Religion as Political Performance in Central Africa*.
  London and Atlantic Highlands, NJ: Athlone.
Murthy, A. K. 1978. *Samskara*. Translated by A. K. Ramanujan. Delhi: Oxford
  University Press.
Patton, Laurie. 2002. *Jewels of Authority: Women and Textual Tradition in Hindu India*.
  New York: Oxford University Press.
———. 2001. "The Prostitute's Gold: Women and Sanskrit in One Corner of India."
  In *Postcolonialism, Feminism, and Religious Discourse*, ed. Kok Pui-Lan and
  Laura Donaldson, 123–141. New York and London: Routledge.
Pawde, Kumud. 1992. "The Story of My Sanskrit." In *Poisoned Bread: Translations
  from Modern Marathi Dalit Literature*, ed. Arjun Dangle, 96–107. Delhi: Orient
  Longman.
Ramanujan, A. K. 1973. *Speaking of Siva*. Harmondsworth, England: Penguin.
Ramirez, Olga. 1997. *La Fiesta de los Tastoanes: Critical Encounters in Mexican
  Festival Performance*. Albuquerque: University of New Mexico Press.
Spiziri, Frank S. 1997. *A Cobbler's Universe: Religion, Poetry, and Performance in the
  Life of a South Italian Immigrant*. Edited and translated by Catherine L. Albanese.
  New York: Continuum.

Steinman, Ralph Marc. 1986. *Guru Shishya Sambandha: Das Mesiter-Schuler-Verhaltnis im traditionallen und modernen Indien.* Wiesbaden, Germany: Steinder, 1986.

Tedlock, Dennis. 1993. *Breath on the Mirror: Mythic Voices and Visions of the Living Maya.* San Francisco: Harper.

———, and Mannheim, Bruce, eds. 1995. *The Dialogic Emergence of Culture.* Urbana: University of Illinois Press.

van Bijlert, Victor. 1996. "Sanskrit and Hindu National Identity in Nineteenth Century Bengal." In *Ideology and Status of Sanskrit,* ed. Jan Houben, 347–366. Leiden: Brill.

Van Der Burg, Crostiann. 1996. "The Place of Sanskrit in Neo-Hindu Ideologies: From Religious Reform to National Awakening." In *Ideology and Status of Sanskrit,* ed. Jan Houben, 367–382. Leiden: Brill.

Wezler, Albrecht. 1996. "'Do You Speak Sanskrit?' On a Class of Sanskrit Texts Composed in the Late Middle Ages." In *Ideology and Status of Sanskrit,* ed. Jan Houben, 327–346. Leiden: Brill.

2

Wandering from "Hills to Valleys" with the Goddess: Protection and Freedom in the *Matamma* Tradition of Andhra

Joyce Burkhalter Flueckiger

The goddess used to . . . take me from hill to valley [*konda-kona*], village to village. That's why I go wherever [the goddesses] like; I go and play and come back. This is my story.
                                                              —Govindamma, 2000

If I want to go to my native place and stay there for a few days, there's no one there for me. I have no one. Whenever I feel sad, I come here to the temple and stay. She [the goddess] is my mother and father, and my mother-in-law, too.
                                                              —Veshalamma, 1999

Govindamma and Veshalamma are women who have exchanged *tali*s (gold disk pendants most often associated with marriage) with one of the many forms of the South Indian village goddess.[1] The *tali* binds these women to the goddess but, just as important, signals her protection. Women who have formed such a *tali* relationship with the goddess are called *matamma*s; they are freed from the constraints of human marriage, but may form nonmarital sexual relationships with men and have children. Like the women who wear her *tali*s, the goddess herself wears a *tali*, has no husband, but may have children. This chapter explores the relationship between the goddess Gangamma and *matamma*s who are protected by her and thus given freedom to "wander." While the *tali* of human marriage has analytic connotations of binding a woman, restricting her movement, holding her in both physical and social "place," this chapter suggests that the *tali* of the goddess has given Veshalamma and Govindamma freedom to move across the traditional social and spatial boundaries observed by most Hindu women in similar stages of life.

Gangamma is one of the seven village goddess sisters who traditionally live on the boundaries of villages. (These seven sisters are not the same as the Sanskritic *saptamatrikas*, having different characters, images, and narratives altogether.) Depending on the context, the sisters may be conflated or individuated, although it is rare that all seven are named individually when someone is listing them—and the sets of names vary from village to village. The South Indian sisters are guardians of village welfare, protecting humans from disease (particularly poxes and fevers associated with the hot season) and ensuring fertility and the health of crops and animals. However, they may also cause disease if they are left unsatisfied/hungry/heated and if their *ugram* (potentially destructive power) overflows its boundaries; much of the worship of these village goddesses consists of calibrating the heat/desire/hunger of the goddess and feeding her. Gangamma and her sisters are characterized in both narrative and ritual as moving/fluid goddesses; they traditionally reside in open-air sites under trees or on boundaries between village settlements and paddy fields and often actively resist human suggestions for enclosed shrines. The seven sisters, although they may have children and are called "mother/Amma," are not householders. For their annual festivals (*jataras*), they are called to village centers, temporary structures are often built around them, and village boundaries are literally "bound" shut so that the goddesses will remain stable long enough through these ritual periods so that they may be served, fed, satiated.

In the countryside around the South Indian temple town of Tirupati, Andhra Pradesh, young girls or babies may be dedicated to Gangamma or one of her sisters when illness or drought strikes the village or the girl herself becomes ill with one of the diseases associated with the goddess. Upon reaching puberty, these girls ritually exchange *talis* with the goddess (sometimes this is called "marrying the goddess") and are thereafter called *matammas*. Traditionally, *matammas* do not enter human marriages with men. In some villages, *matammas* dance at the festivals of the goddess and otherwise serve her at her shrines; other *matammas* live more independently of temples or shrines and serve the goddess in less institutional contexts (including by becoming regularly possessed by the goddess in their homes and serving as her medium). The *matamma* tradition is shifting in the contemporary contexts of reform movements, middle-class sensibilities, and modernization; however, it is still practiced under the radar, so to speak.

Several middle-class Tirupati residents whom I initially asked about the term *matamma* explained, "You know, like *devadasis*," assuming I would know that more linguistically widespread word (for a tradition that is no longer practiced in the large South Indian temples with which it used to be associated).

While there are significant differences between the traditions of *matammas*, who form relationships with local village goddesses, and *devadasis*, who were temple dancers "married to the god" of more Sanskritic temples, both classes of women are or were under obligation to the deity and were freed from obligations of human marriage.[2] Further, they are ritual specialists whose ritual acts avert inauspiciousness and bring auspiciousness (Kersenboom 1987: 67, 192, 205). They themselves are never widowed since they are married to the deity and are, therefore, called *nityasumangali*, ever-auspicious women (Kersenboom 1987: xv). Nevertheless, today there is a societal ambivalence about these women who do not marry humans, even though the social institutions with which they are or were associated may have once been conceptually and ritually acceptable and even necessary. This ambivalence may be created, in part, by the perceived threat to the social order posed by a woman not "tied down," who moves across, and thereby challenges, traditional social, gendered boundaries. As Katherine Ewing suggests in writing about the threat of the wandering *sadhu/faqir* to the colonial order, their very movement itself "exposed contradictions and challenged the naturalness of the [colonial] order" (1997: 63).

Supported by legislation outlawing the practice of dedicating women to temples (particularly the Devadasi Act of 1947) and accompanying reform movements, several nongovernmental organizations (NGOs) based in Tirupati work with *matammas*. Specifically, their mission is to encourage *matammas* to marry the men with whom they may be living (the persuasion is actually most frequently directed at the men), to run schools for their children, and more generally to encourage an end to a tradition that is perceived, from a middle-class sensibility, to be exploitative of women. The assumptions of the NGOs seem to be that *matammas* are being taken advantage of sexually, either being forced into relationships against their wills or choosing to enter these relationships without being given the protections of the institution of marriage.

Because of these contemporary social and political contexts, the institution of *matammas* is rarely openly talked about to outsiders by those who participate in the village goddess traditions and festivals with which the institution is still associated. I attended three annual *jataras* and lived in Tirupati for nearly four months before I heard about the tradition; but, conducting my fieldwork primarily in women's ritual environments, once I did become aware of *matammas*, I heard and saw multiple signs of the tradition and ultimately met the two women whose personal narratives are the basis of this chapter.

Perhaps because of the contemporary ambivalence toward the tradition and the fact that Veshalamma and Govindamma had both married human males, neither woman self-identified as a *matamma*. But they both had exchanged *talis* with the goddess, and the temple flower sellers at one of Gangamma's Tirupati temples referred to them as *matammas*.[3] I think it is not a coincidence that the *matammas* whom I personally met *had* married humans. Govindamma and Veshalamma have a certain social "respectability" because of their married status, whatever else they may also be. This status may also have freed them to speak more openly to me than they would have had they remained unmarried. They are also unusual in the fact that they live in the town of Tirupati and are thus associated with the powerful Tirupati goddess rather than one of her (arguably) less-powerful village sisters. One flower seller told me that the more powerful the goddess, the more protection a *matamma* has—that if a woman has exchanged *tali*s with Tirupati Gangamma, no one will dare to harm her for fear of the wrath of this powerful goddess.

Govindamma is a sixty-five-year-old widow, and Veshalamma is a thirty- to thirty-five-year-old mother of three young children.[4] Upon first meetings, both women stood out as unique and unusually independent. Their life stories share themes of protection by the goddess and the resulting freedom to move and act in public spheres, although each narrative addresses some possible different aspects of a *tali* relationship with the goddess at different life stages of a woman.

I first met Veshalamma at Gangamma's largest Tirupati temple during the fall festival days of Navratri (Nine Nights of the Goddess) in 1999. For each evening of the nine nights, a different pan-Indian form of the goddess was installed in the courtyard in front of Gangamma,[5] and each evening Veshalamma swept the courtyard and drew a ritual rice-flour design in front of the goddesses before the nightly rituals began. Veshalamma was not accompanied to the temple by female relatives or friends (as are most women who come to the temple), although sometimes she brought along her young daughter and baby son. She told me she walked about a half hour to and from the temple every day and, even on nonfestival days, spent hours sitting in front of the goddess, sweeping the temple, or sleeping in the shade of the temple gate or courtyard trees. She was marked as unique by her freedom of movement, without accompaniment by family members, and her presence in public space with no particular agenda, except to be in the presence of the goddess.

I first met Govindamma in her home, so I did not notice her freedom of physical movement until I heard her extended personal narrative. However, she was visibly marked by the goddess in that she wore a large, pronounced red vermilion forehead marking (*bottu*) and had matted hair. When I registered surprise upon learning that she was a widow but still wore the *bottu* and *tali* associated with married women, she answered, "One hundred and one Gangammas gave me my *bottu*s; why should I take them off when my husband dies?" (One hundred and one is being used here as an auspicious number of power; literally, there are only seven sisters, although they may have different sets of names in different villages.) At another point in the conversational narrative, she similarly asserted, "Because 101 Gangammas gave me the *pasupu/kumkum* [auspicious vermilion-turmeric marking], I haven't taken it off [upon becoming a widow]."

We do not have historical evidence as to how the institution of *matammas* actually worked, whether or not these women were sexually exploited in premodern and contemporary India (as reform movements suggest), or whether the institution provided some women with agency that they may not have otherwise had. However, the personal narratives of Veshalamma and Govindamma provide traces of the protection, agency, and freedom of movement in public and "jungle" spaces[6] that the tradition may have offered *matammas* generally and these two women specifically, one a widow and the other an orphan and abused wife.

The freedom provided by the *tali* in this context raises questions about the significance of the *tali* in premodern South India, before it became so closely tied to marriage. Is the auspiciousness attributed to a married woman given by marriage itself (i.e., a husband), or is it inherent to a fertile woman? Here, I first examine several implications of the *tali* for both the goddess and non-*matamma* women, and then look at the implications of the *tali* for *matammas* as suggested through the oral narratives of two *matammas* (who are, albeit, atypical since they also married men).

Talis of Women

Talis in contemporary South India are most often associated with human marriage; a woman's *tali* is tied by her husband during the wedding ritual sequence. However, it may not have always been associated with marriage per se, but more specifically with a woman's inherent auspiciousness, her embodied creative power, and fertility potential. In a chapter about the goddess in Kerala, M. J. Gentes describes a pre-twentieth-century *tali* ceremony that used to be performed for pubescent girls (1992: 317). While the girl was joined with a male partner, it was not as "wife," but as "one who has the power to create and withhold life" (318). Gentes suggests that the *tali* ceremony

> may facilitate a young woman's claiming of her *shakti* (power)
> and role and her control of her own chastity (in the South Indian
> sense) without expressing it as dissolution of her life into that of a
> man.... As a necessary ceremony it marks and values the young
> females of the lineage and of society as a whole.... From the cere-
> mony onward, the girl was considered a reproducer of the matrilin-
> eage. (1992: 318)

The young woman was auspicious because she was a potentially fertile woman, marked by the *tali*, rather than because she was a potentially fertile *married* woman. Vasudha Narayanan describes a female puberty ritual among the Pillai community of Tamilnadu in which a young girl is given the authority to light the oil lamp on the family altar. On this occasion, she is given a gold necklace called a *nava tali* (lit. necklace of nine), strung with nine gold beads and corals. She wears this *tali* until she gets married, at which time it is replaced with that given by her husband (Narayanan forthcoming, 220). Other South Indian traditional puberty rituals similarly approximate some elements of marriage celebrations, the pubescent girl being dressed in silks and new jewelry (Reynolds 1991: 42).

Another trace of earlier associations of the *tali* may be found in the custom observed in some Telugu communities in which the bride is given a *tali* by her mother during pre-wedding rituals, before her husband ties one around her neck during the wedding itself. This "mother's *tali*" is called *puttininti tali* (lit. of the house of birth) and should be worn for at least forty days after the wedding.[7] It is sometimes then strung on the same chain/thread with the *tali* tied by the husband. I suggest that these rituals suggest the association of *tali* and a woman's auspiciousness/fertility independent of marriage, although for most women marriage is the context within which their fertility comes to fruition.

Later, in Kerala and elsewhere in South India, the *tali* began to be given by a woman's husband during the marriage ritual and has come to be strongly associated with marriage itself. (Leslie Orr, in her chapter in this volume, citing Jayadev, suggests this association began to be made in Tamilnadu as early as the eleventh century.) Holly Reynolds interprets the *tali* in contemporary South Indian contexts as follows:

> When a man ties a *tali* around the neck of a woman, he binds her to him with a symbol of all his culturally and socially derived identities, makes that woman a cumankali [*sumangali*], and entrusts to her the well-being of himself and his lineage, an act that paradoxically makes the wife the protector of the husband.... In owning the *tali*, the husband controls the auspiciousness of his wife: he confers cumankali [*sumangali*] status upon her at marriage and deprives her of it at his death. (1991: 45–46)

In marriage, the *tali* serves as a sign of the husband's protection, but also often restricts the movement of the bride/wife to staying within the confines of "women's space." Reynolds continues:

> The *tali* delimits boundaries, sets up barriers, confines [a] woman to a specified domain, that of her husband, a situation captured in one of the words for "wife," *taram*, limit, boundary. It declares that sexual relations are permissible only with the owner of the *tali*, for at issue here is control over and possession of female generative power. (1991: 46)

The *tali*'s earlier association with female auspiciousness/fertility, which has now been subsumed within the institution of marriage, suggests an alternative interpretation/ideology of the *tali* and marriage: marriage (the husband, the *tali*) does not *give* a woman her power (*shakti*), but it *marks*, and gives a context for, its expression. The difference is subtle but important.

Examining the exchange of *talis* between *matammas* and the goddess makes more explicit what is only suggested in the puberty rite and marriage contexts of the *tali*. Receiving a *tali* from the goddess, instead of from a man, openly questions the dominant societal need for marriage as a context for the expression of a woman's *shakti*. More specifically, it highlights the control implied by the marriage *tali* tied by a man on his bride, in contrast to the freedom of movement permitted by the *tali* of the goddess. Govindamma narrates a very different mandate than that of marriage to a man when she tells of the goddess ordering her to wander from village to village, "I keep going around every *uru*. I don't know when she'll stop me and where she'll allow me to build [a permanent place]."

The Goddess's *Tali*

While, traditionally, women need the context of marriage within which to express their auspicious powers (of fertility), the goddess is not bound by this human context; she wears the *tali* and has children without a husband. The *talis* of many forms of the goddess Gangamma and her village sisters are usually very visible, in contrast to married women's *talis*, whose chains or threads are visible at the back of the neck, but whose pendants are usually modestly tucked under their saris, not to be put on public display. Some of Gangamma's and her sisters' forms are just a head, with no torso or body, but around the neck is still a *tali*.

Gangamma takes two primary forms in Tirupati, as an older and younger sister (Pedda Gangamma and Cinna Gangamma, respectively). The story is told of the older sister having children whom she tried to protect from the envy of the younger, childless sister by covering the children with a basket when Cinna Gangamma came to visit her. In anger, the younger sister turned the children into chicks. Pedda Gangamma then offered to give some of her children to her sister if Cinna Gangamma would turn the chicks back into children. This story was told when I asked the temple attendants who were the small rock forms that were lined up on each side of Cinna Gangamma. It then occurred to me, if the goddess had children and was wearing a *tali*, who was her husband? When I asked this question during the 1992 *jatara*, the flower sellers and temple attendants said she had no husband. When I returned to Tirupati for a year in 1999–2000, these same women answered without any hesitation that Siva was her husband. The conceptual presence of a husband may be a recent development, a way of bringing Gangamma into a more Brahminic world view, as there is no mythology of her and Siva being married, and he is iconographically and ritually absent from her temples and shrines.

In her description of river goddesses in Maharashtra, Ann Feldhaus describes a similar phenomenon of goddesses who wear the auspicious signs of a bride (bangles and the wedding necklace [*mangalsutra*]) but who have no husbands; she calls them "husbandless wives." A husband may be implied, but "no one seems particularly bothered about the question of his identity" (1995: 53, 55). One woman told Feldhaus:

> "There is no husband. She's Krsnabai, isn't she? And Krsnabai has no husband. Krsnabai is a river. She's understood to be a river, isn't she? Then, doesn't this river finally join the ocean? So that makes the ocean her husband. That's how you should understand it." And then she added, "If there *has* to be a husband!" (1995: 54)

When I asked Veshalamma who tied Gangamma's *tali*, that is, who is her husband, she answered:

> It's actually a vow [*mokku*]; people make a vow that if they get married, have children, or if something good happens to them, they'll give her a *tali*.[8] It doesn't mean that she [the goddess] got married. She's Adi Shakti [the primordial goddess]. Who would be able to bear her by getting married to her? Even my own husband keeps telling me that after getting married to me, he's not able to bear me.

Veshalamma: The *Tali* as Protection of the Goddess

Veshalamma's independence and mobility for a married woman in her thirties were immediately striking, especially given her advanced state of pregnancy (about seven months) at the time of the Navratri festival when I first met her. While there were other women who worked on the temple grounds as flower sellers, sweepers, and attendants to the goddess, Veshalamma rarely engaged in conversation with them or other devotees. When I asked the flower sellers who she was—if she was associated with the temple—they answered that she simply performed various tasks as service (*seva*) to the goddess. Later, there were some whisperings about her having exchanged *tali*s with the goddess. I learned only gradually over the next few months about the institution of *matamma*s and then realized that Veshalamma was so identified.

While others may have whispered about this identity, the relationship with the goddess was not one about which Veshalamma was ashamed. When I met with her to ask more about her relationship with the goddess and elicit her life story, we (and the tape recorder) were immediately surrounded by a group of curious onlookers. When I suggested that we move out of the central temple courtyard to a shaded spot under one of the temple gates, she asserted boldly, "Whatever I have to say is by the grace of the goddess. I'll speak here." (After only a few minutes, however, when the children became too noisy even for Veshalamma, we moved from the covered courtyard to sit under one of the *gopurams*.)

The flower sellers had told me that Veshalamma had spent the previous week sleeping at the temple. When I asked her why, she answered, "I was feeling depressed [lit. my mind was not good], so I slept here. At my place, I felt like I was being crushed [suffocated] but now I'm feeling reinvigorated [*usharuga*; lit. active]." And then she began her story, which she characterized as one full of "troubles, troubles, and more troubles."

> I was born at Manchala Vidhi [Main Street] and matured [reached puberty, while living in the neighborhood] behind Jyoti Theatre. Then they took me to Madras. My parents thought I wouldn't learn any housework, so they took me to Madras and put me in a hostel, but I refused to stay there. Why should I be put in a hostel when I have parents? They themselves took me to the hostel. They called me an adopted child; they called me "sister's daughter." I cried, but they still took me there. . . .
>
> When I was small, I had to face so many troubles, so they brought me to Veshalamma Gangamma [whose name Veshalamma the woman has taken as her own] temple and married me to her. They said, "We're going to give her to you [the goddess]," so they got me married [to her]. They did this in a respectable way [with sufficient grandness]. After that I had to sell coconuts and dry fish; I did all the household work. I sold *idlis* to the hospital. I went to Nagiri, Nagalapuram, Esalapuram to sell pickles. . . . I worked hard and looked after them [my parents], but still they didn't look after me. So I have only her [pointing to the goddess]; I don't have any parents. I've experienced only troubles, troubles, and more troubles.

Veshalamma later elaborated some of her early troubles: she was adopted and never knew who her birth parents were; and as a baby, she had difficulty drinking and her parents thought she would die. Because of this, she said, her parents offered her to the goddess; but, she continued, her adoptive mother never took care of her and cared only for the son to whom she herself had given birth. At another point in her narrative, in the middle of a description of her mother dressing her up like the goddess when she was a little girl, Veshalamma suddenly shifted topic, "They [her parents] actually showed some interest in me before I reached puberty, but once I reached puberty they began to trouble me." Veshalamma bemoaned that she never found out who her birth parents were: "If I had been told, I would have gone to look for them, to see who they were. When anyone [new] like you comes to the temple, I always hope that they might be my parents. I want to see and talk to them."

Veshalamma said that her parents first wanted her to get married to an old man (seventy years old), when she was just sixteen years old. She rebelled, "How could I get married to such an old man! I wouldn't marry him. So I loved and got married to my [current] husband [a marriage of choice rather than an arranged one]." When I asked her how a man feels when he gets married to a woman who is already married to the goddess—was he afraid of her in some way?—she answered:

> Yes, he's afraid of me; he doesn't even smoke in front of me. . . . He's afraid because I might become possessed by the goddess. Twice, when I was possessed, I beat him; that's why he's afraid of me. [When I'm possessed] he's very respectful of me. But when he's been given trouble outside, he comes home and beats me. He asks me to leave the house or chases the children out.

On another occasion, Veshalamma said that she did not like to become possessed unless she knew that there would be someone there to serve the goddess (which she implied may not happen at home): "Someone should give me turmeric water and camphor. Who will do that for me? When she comes into my body, she asks for neem leaves, turmeric water, camphor, and whatever else she likes. Who will give all this? No one; everyone will just stand there and look at me."

Her husband first became physically abusive after she gave birth to a baby girl: "He hit me because I gave birth to a daughter, and I didn't give birth to a son." She later described the abuse in more detail, saying that her husband left wounds on her and broke her hand. She says that this is when she began to come to the temple regularly, telling the goddess, "You are my mother." At another point in her narrative, when she told of the death of her mother, the rejection by her own brother, and the harassment of her mother-in-law, she rather matter-of-factly stated, "I have no one. If I want to go to my native place [i.e., maternal home] and stay for a few days, no one is there for me. I have no one. Whenever I feel sad, I come here to the temple and stay. She [the goddess] is my mother and father, and my mother-in-law, too." Although she was married to the goddess at a young age, it seems to have taken time and the experience of multiple troubles before Veshalamma learned to turn to the goddess for her dependable protection. The goddess conceptually protects and cares for Veshalamma, but the temple is also a physical refuge. She often sleeps at the temple, sometimes for days at a time, when she is physically sick, when her husband is abusing her, or when she is simply sad. No one at the temple asks why she is there, no one bothers her, and no one from her home comes looking for her.

In the absence of a caring, protective mother, Veshalamma finds refuge only in the goddess, and the exchange of *talis* has created and signifies this protection. Ironically, Veshalamma says that her mother took for herself the *tali* and silk sari that had been given to Veshalamma at the time of her marriage to the goddess; but, Veshalamma maintains, for this transgression, her mother's hand and leg were paralyzed (presumably caused by the goddess).

Veshalamma told me that the same day that she first told me her life history, Gangamma herself came to her in the guise of a Brahmin woman (a woman possessed by the goddess):

> She [Gangamma possessing the Brahmin woman] gave me a blouse piece and said, "You don't have to be afraid; I am with you. . . . If you hadn't come to the temple, you would have died. I am protecting you." . . . The goddess came to me earlier, too. I had cooked everything for her, dried fish and eggs, and fed her. Gangamma told me she was satisfied that day, "That day, you filled my stomach, so I'll see to it that your stomach, too, is full. I'll not harm you. Don't cry." She called my husband and warned him, "If you hurt her, I'll kill you." My husband trembled. [The goddess said,] "If she as much as cries, I won't allow you to live any more."

Veshalamma says she never just "sat and ate," but worked hard as a little girl, going from place to place in Tirupati neighborhoods selling pickles. This is the primary reference in Veshalamma's narrative to the mobility enabled/required by the goddess. But the motif is strongest in her own observable actions: she walks to Cinna Gangamma's temple almost daily, sometimes staying there for days at a time (leaving her children at home or bringing them with her) and periodically also makes the rounds to other Gangamma temples all around Tirupati. One morning, she offered to take my fieldwork assistant and me on a round of temples and shrines on the outskirts of the north side of Tirupati. Her pace was brisk and deliberate as we walked for several hours under the heated April sun, but she did not tire and after several hours even seemed invigorated.

As mentioned earlier, both Veshalamma and Govindamma did marry human males, and in this way they may not be typical of many *matammas*. Govindamma exchanged *talis* with the goddess *after* she had married her husband and had children, while Veshalamma underwent a more formal marriage ritual to the goddess in the temple upon reaching puberty and before her human marriage. It is significant that both women chose their own husbands, rather than entering arranged marriages. Govindamma was already independent from her family (and had moved around a lot) when she met her future husband while working at a construction site. Veshalamma simply states that she chose her own husband, without giving further details.

After Veshalamma had gotten married to her husband, her family called her a prostitute, saying that she was already married [to the goddess], and presumably a second marriage was adulterous. She described their opposition: "My brother pushed me out of the house, saying 'we don't have any connection with you any more, so leave.' They troubled me a lot. If I think of it now, I feel sad and feel like crying. When my mother was alive, she didn't take care of me; now, too, my stepmother doesn't. My brother, too, isn't in a position to care for me." As mentioned earlier, Veshalamma's husband, too, provides no protection and abuses her: "After getting married, I haven't been happy. I don't get along with my in-laws. Only if I work and bring in money will my husband talk to me. Otherwise, he beats the children and me. Because I can't face these problems, I come to Amma [the goddess]."

Veshalamma's story of troubles with parents, husband, and in-laws may be commonly shared by other women and are not unique to *matamma*s. And many of these women, too, outside of a *tali* relationship with the goddess, may come to her for protection from these troubles. But what makes a *matamma* different is that this protection/relationship is formalized, and with it, she assumes the freedom to move, to be independent. It is this freedom of movement that is the dominant motif in Govindamma's life story. Not only is she free to move, but she feels she *must* move, at the command of the goddess.

Govindamma: Wandering with the Goddess

As a widowed mother of two grown sons, Govindamma is at a very different stage of life than is Veshalamma, and they also have different kinds of relationships with the goddess. Unlike Veshalamma, who exchanged *tali*s with the goddess at puberty and only after that married a man, Govindamma got married to a man first—a marriage that she says the goddess herself initiated. Further, Govindamma's narrative actively negotiates her unusual position of being married to a man *and* the goddess; she directly addresses the issue and justifies her unusual position.

Govindamma's life story is most striking for its repeated images of moving from place to place at the direction of the goddess, a restlessness that does not permit her to settle down in any traditional way. In response to the question of where she was born, she said:

> In Kolar [Karnataka]. I was there until I was five. My mother's place was Ambur [near Vellore]. From there [Kolar] they brought me to Ambur. When I was twelve [presumably after reaching puberty], the goddess took me all around the world; she didn't allow me to stay in one place. Even now, I keep moving around. Even now, she makes me go to old temples, to powerful goddess stones, *shakti* stones [*shakti rayi*]. Wherever people are having problems, she takes me there....

FIGURE 2.1. Govindamma invoking the goddess Gangamma to possess her. Photo by Joyce Burkhalter Flueckiger.

> The goddess keeps taking me from hill to hill, valley to valley, village to village. . . . I go wherever she calls me. Even if I go to Hyderabad or Vijayavada, wherever I go, she doesn't allow me to stay more than ten days. She says, "Get up," and she brings me back. . . . I keep going around from village to village. I don't know when she'll stop me and where she'll allow me to build and what she will do.

In another conversation when I asked Govindamma if she were afraid of the potentially destructive power (*ugram*) of the goddess, Govindamma used the same image of wandering/moving that had somehow empowered her, "No, no, I'm not. It's because I've been wandering from hill to hill, valley to valley, since I was young; so I'm not afraid."

Govindamma did not want to get married to a man, but said that "the goddess married me off. Then the children came." She then suddenly shifted her reference for the agent of the marriage from the goddess to the god Vishnu, who came to her in a vision, giving her reasons that she should get married:

> One Friday at twelve o'clock, I sat for *puja* [worship of the deity]. I thought that I don't need a husband, and so I came [to the temple of the goddess]. That day he [the god] came lying on a five-headed serpent, and the wall became a sea. He said, "If you don't get married, you won't achieve release, liberation [*moksha*]. You should get married, have children, and experience both suffering and happiness. You can't avoid this. For the good of the world [*loka*], the drama of marriage cannot be avoided. For twenty-five years, he [her husband] will beat you, cut you, poke you, hit you, and cause you to bleed. You have to experience all of this. This is inevitable. This is the way of the world [*samsaram*], and you have to overcome it." He [the god] gave me this boon [*varam*] and went off. . . . I sat down at twelve o'clock for the *puja*, and he gave me this vision [*darshan*] at 3 p.m.
>
> I used to do *puja* at Cinna Gangamma's temple, and I used to sleep there before I was married. But now, after marrying, she asked me to sleep somewhere else: "You're now living in the [social] world [*samsaram*], so you should live separately and serve me [lit. do *kollavu*]. . . ." Next to this temple, there's Nerelamma's temple. She came at one o'clock at night, along with Gudiamma and all the others [sister goddesses]. I thought to myself, "How should I talk to them [the goddesses]?" I came here thinking that I shouldn't get married, but even then, he [the god] brought me a match [potential husband]. I said to the goddess, "If you like the match, then get me married." And the flower garland came down from the [image of] the goddess. They [others in the temple] asked, "What did you ask Amma, for

which she's given you flowers as an answer?" I only answered, "Give me the flowers. Amma knows what I asked for." And I brought the flowers back home. I came back home at one o'clock at night.

It is noteworthy that in this account it is the god Vishnu, and not the goddess, who tells Govindamma that marriage (and its accompanying suffering) is necessary for her to achieve liberation. His presence, particularly in his cosmic form, lying on the serpent in the ocean (rather than through one of his incarnations on earth, such as Venkatesvara), represents a more textual, Brahminic tradition than that of the village goddesses and is a tangible manifestation of the multiple discourses (Sanskritic/textual and nontextual) that Govindamma is negotiating through her narrative and vision. The concept of liberation, *moksha*, itself is a Brahminic concept not commonly articulated in relationship to Gangamma traditions. While Govindamma had moved about from place to place as a pubescent girl—with and at the order of the goddess—only after she was married and had children did the goddesses give her the *tali* and *pasupu/kumkum* that mark her special relationship with and obligation to Gangamma. The goddess then told her that she had been with her husband long enough; now she should move about with *her*:

> One hundred and one Ammavarus [goddesses] came to me. They took me to the Gangamma temple. They bathed me, applied *pasupu/ kumkum*, and put bangles on me. They told me, "All these days you were with your husband; now you're our own. Wherever we are, you should come there." This was like twenty-five years ago, after all the children. This is because I asked Ammavaru to make me like Avvayar [an old female devotee who served the god Ganesh]. I don't need my exterior form [*rupam*]; I don't need my beauty; make me Avvayar." ... I haven't removed my *bottu* and *kumkum* even though my husband is dead. Because 101 Ammavarus put on my *kumkum/ pasupu*, I haven't taken it off.

In another later conversation, Govindamma elaborated that she was twenty-five years old when she got married to the goddess, after her three children were born, "It was to keep me as a *kanya pilla* [virgin girl; i.e., she did not have sex with her husband after receiving the *talis* of the goddesses]. The goddesses tied the *talis*. Now if the goddess comes on me and speaks, everything she says will happen." Govindamma's narrative expresses some of the tension among ideologies of marriage, gender, and women's auspiciousness that may be present in the traditions of *matammas* and of middle-class Brahminic rhetoric and practice.

While, for Govindamma, her marriages to a husband and the goddesses were sequential, in the case of her daughter, there was a struggle between human and goddess marriages. As a young girl (virgin; *kanya*), Govindamma's daughter had lived with her two maternal, childless aunts; she was thought to have brought fertility into the house, and both women had their own children. Thereafter, her relatives wanted to marry the ten-year-old girl to Govindamma's brother (an acceptable marriage partner in conventional South Indian cross-cousin marriage). Govindamma tried to resist this marriage, however, because of the age difference; and the groom, too, was not interested in marrying someone who would "become possessed just like her mother." The goddess Ammavaru concurred, "No, let her remain a *kanya*. When her mother becomes old, we'll come to her." However, the relatives prevailed and took the girl "uphill" to Tirumala (site of the temple of the god Venkatesvara) and dressed both her and her groom in yellow wedding clothes and garlanded them (it becomes clear later that this was a "mock" wedding). However, as they were coming down the hill, a monkey tore the girl's sari, grabbed the flowers, and ran off. When the family returned home, they found that the picture of the god on the hill, Venkatesvara, and his wife, Padmavati, had fallen down and broken. And the daughter lost her sight at the same time.

The narrative sequence is not clear, but it seems that the girl had some kind of pox even at this time. The goddess told Govindamma that if the daughter did get married, not only one pox (*ammavaru*, a manifestation of the goddess) would come, but seven different poxes would come. The goddess was literally fighting for the girl in dramatic ways, but the relatives proceeded with the mock marriage. Govindamma narrates, "The goddess [who is also the pox] peeled off the skin and ate it. The girl's hair came off like a wig comes off. The skin from her hands and legs came off just like that. And the goddess ate it." The girl died after a twenty-five-day battle between the poxes (the goddess) and the humans who wanted her to marry their brother. The goddess prevailed. This is the powerful goddess who gave Govindamma her *tali* and who orders her to move with her from village to village, hill to valley. Govindamma responded to the comment that it was unusual that she could "bear" the demands of a relationship with such a goddess, when most people were so afraid of her:

> You must be born for this in order to bear [Telugu, *bharincu*] her. Most people can't even bear pictures of her. Ask them to keep these pictures and bear her. Let's see if they can. They'll get scared and take them to a temple. I was born for this, and I've faced all these difficulties, without any house, without any stable home village [*uru*]. I wander around from village to village, between tree and snake hole. If it was anyone else, they would have left the goddess and gone off. Because I was born for this, even after having faced all these problems, I'm not worried that I don't have a house, that I don't have this, that I don't have that. Whatever will happen, let it happen. Why should I have what the goddess herself doesn't have? I'm not both-

ered that I don't have jewels or property. Let it happen as it should. I was supposed to face difficulties along with the children, and I've experienced all of it. I've faced things with my husband, too. I'm serving the public. People tease me, "Ankalamma [one of the seven sisters] hasn't given you a house or a plot of land." They've teased me like this. I don't let it bother me. They say, "This *talli* [mother] is making you roam about like this." But I don't let this bother me. If I'm born like this, this is what should happen.

Conclusion: Responsibilities to and Manifestations of the Goddess

A *tali* relationship with the goddess does not come freely, but comes with responsibilities toward the goddess and other humans who must interact with her. The relationship with the goddess is not simply a private one; both Veshalamma and Govindamma also serve as intermediaries between the goddess and the human world by regularly getting possessed by Gangamma on Tuesdays, Fridays, and/or Sundays. The goddess speaks directly to people who come to her with questions and to have their futures discerned. Further, both *matamma*s are regularly called upon to visit persons in whom the goddess has manifested as poxes (measles, chickenpox, rashes, and in earlier times, smallpox) and to perform rituals for/to them. Govindamma concludes one of her narratives:

> Now I've come to the end of my life. I don't own a house. Up until now, I haven't asked Amma for this or that. I just keep going around and coming back. I don't go and earn money; I don't engage in fraud and earn money that way. When people come [to the goddess, through Govindamma's possession], she heals them. People who are childless, she gives them children. Those who are unmarried, she gets them married. This is the drama of my life.

Govindamma has also taken up an unusual ritual responsibility: to take *garega* (a bamboo temple-shaped structure tied to the top of her head) to various goddess temples in order to bring them prosperity. Govindamma says that her presence with the *garega* blesses run-down temples, and they "rise up" and become active and prosperous. Note here that Govindamma speaks of permanent structures for the goddess, unlike the traditional locales at the edge of villages where the goddess resides under open skies—another sign of shifting village traditions in urban contexts such as Tirupati.

The oral narratives that we have been considering in this chapter were told by two (albeit atypical) *matamma*s in a contemporary context that is multilayered and rapidly shifting. The narratives reflect and negotiate some of the pressures on the tradition and the individual women participating in it, pressures created, in part, by shifting patronage, early twentieth-century and contemporary reform movements, growing middle-class sensibilities, and the "upward" mobility of the Gangamma tradition in Tirupati.[9] However, the narratives also provide us with hints of what *matamma* tradition may have provided (and potentially may still provide) to women: protection, freedom to move, and agency.

Each context in which the *matamma* tradition is represented provides a different interpretive frame for the social/ritual institution, and to address all of these social-historical perspectives is beyond the scope of this brief chapter. Here I have focused on rituals and narratives of the goddess and the narrative voices of the women themselves, voices frequently lost in the dominant discourse about *matamma*s in the press, in institutions such as universities and development organizations, and in middle-class conversational discourse. The narratives of Govindamma and Veshalamma suggest that the *tali* relationship with the goddess has provided them a social-ritual institution of refuge, in which they are protected by the goddess. It is also one that enables them to be independent from reliance on husbands and sons. These narratives suggest that the *tali* of the *matamma* may mark her female agency and auspiciousness in ways similar to that of the *tali* of the goddess. The *matamma* tradition offers an alternative context to that of marriage in which a woman's powers and auspiciousness may be marked and expressed. Govindamma's and Veshalamma's narratives also make clear, however, that a *matamma*'s agency and auspiciousness do not necessarily translate into a trouble-free life. But as they negotiate these troubles, their *tali* relationships with the goddess give *matamma*s freedom (even compulsion) to move beyond the social and physical constraints often imposed by *tali*s given by husbands and give them a site of refuge and protection.

NOTES

1. The fieldwork upon which this chapter is based was conducted in Tirupati, Andhra Pradesh, between September 1999 and June 2000. I gratefully acknowledge the support of an American Institute of Indian Studies senior research grant for this research.

2. See Vasudha Narayanan's chapter in this volume for more on temple dancer *devadasi*s, associated with Sanskritic male deities.

3. These women sell flowers and coconuts to worshippers to offer to the goddess. They have been a constant presence over the years that I have been visiting Tattayagunta Gangamma temple.

4. I use the ethnographic present narrative tense; however, the ethnographic research upon which this chapter is based took place in 1999–2000.

5. Navratri is a newly introduced festival to Gangamma's temple; that is, it is not a festival traditionally associated with this level of village goddess. One could interpret its introduction as a "Venkatesvarization" of the temple, indicating its move "up" into the range of Brahminic rituals associated with the god Sri Venkatesvara, whose Tirupati temple is the wealthiest in India and a site to which thousands

of pilgrims come each day. However, I would suggest that in this case, the pan-Indian goddesses were, in the minds of Gangamma's traditional worshippers, simply an expansion of the set of seven sisters—that is, they were "Gangamma-ized."

6. In Indian languages, "jungle" connotes uninhabited space, not necessarily forested space. The phrase *konda-kona*, while literally meaning "hills-valleys" also connotes this kind of *jungli*, uninhabited space.

7. I was able to observe this ritual at the Telugu wedding of an Emory University women's studies graduate student, Yamini Atmavilas, in September 2004 in Atlanta. Yamini's mother tied the *tali* just before the bride performed Gauri *puja*, in an antechamber to the public stage upon which the groom and the bride's father were performing Ganesh *puja*. Yamini's mother told us that her own mother-in-law had become very upset when, upon the death of her husband, she was expected to stop wearing *kumkum* and jewelry and to start dressing simply. She angrily declared that "all this" had not come to her simply because she was married; after all, "didn't my mother tie the *puttininti tali* before my husband did?"

8. Leslie Orr's chapter in this volume documents similar vow making and giving the goddess ornaments, including *talis*, as early as 1000 c.e. A key difference between offering the goddess a *tali* as an act of devotion or fulfillment of a vow (an offering still common in contemporary Hindu practice in South India and in South Indian temples in the United States) and offering a *tali* as a *matamma* is that in the latter case, the human woman also *receives* a *tali* from the goddess.

9. In 1992, the traditional female attendant to Gangamma in her largest Tirupati temple was replaced by Brahmin male priests, who began to recite Sanskrit verses to the goddess, introduced several Brahminic rituals, and strongly discouraged animal sacrifice.

REFERENCES

Egnor, Margaret. 1991. "On the Meaning of Sakti to Women in Tamil Nadu." In *The Powers of Tamil Women*, ed. Susan S. Wadley, 1–34. Syracuse, NY: Maxwell School of Citizenship and Public Affairs, Syracuse University.

Ewing, Katherine Pratt. 1997. *Arguing Sainthood: Modernity, Psychoanalysis, and Islam*. Durham: Duke University Press.

Feldhaus, Anne. 1995. *Water & Womanhood*. New York: Oxford University Press.

Gentes, M. J. 1992. "Scandalizing the Goddess at Kodungallur." *Asian Folklore Studies* 51: 295–322.

Handelman, Don. 1995. "The Guises of the Goddess and the Transformation of the Male: Gangamma's Visit to Tirupati and the Continuum of Gender." In *Syllables of Sky*, ed. David Shulman, 283–337. New Delhi: Oxford University Press.

Kersenboom, Saskia C. 1987 [rpt. 1997]. *Nityasumangali: Devadasi Tradition in South India*. Delhi: Motilal Banarsidass.

Marglin, Frederique Apffel. 1985. *Wives of the God King: The Rituals of the Devadasis of Puri*. Delhi: Oxford University Press.

Narayanan, Vasudha. Forthcoming. *The Hindu Traditions: An Introduction*. New York: Oxford University Press.

Reynolds, Holly Baker. 1991. "The Auspicious Married Woman." In *The Powers of Tamil Women*, ed. Susan S. Wadley, 35–60. Syracuse, NY: Maxwell School of Citizenship and Public Affairs, Syracuse University.

Wadley, Susan, ed. 1991 [1980]. *The Powers of Tamil Women*. Syracuse, NY: Maxwell School of Citizenship and Public Affairs, Syracuse University.

3

Lovesick *Gopi* or Woman's Best Friend? The Mythic *Sakhi* and Ritual Friendships among Women in Benares

Tracy Pintchman

Studies of Hindu women's social bonds in North India tend to focus on women's place in the domestic sphere and the relationships women share with natal and conjugal kin. By way of contrast, scholars have tended to relegate to the margins women's extra-domestic ties with other women, including friendships forged in both natal and affinal households. There are good reasons for this in many cases. Kirin Narayan, for example, has observed that in Kangra, North India, where she does her research, close female-female friendship tends to be confined largely to youth, especially adolescence; once women marry, family ties become the all-consuming focus of women's emotional energy. She notes that many women feel the intimacy friends share is not even accessible to married women (1986, 66).[1] Joyce B. Flueckiger, however, has recorded the existence in Chhatisgarh (middle India) of ritualized friendships among both unmarried girls and married women (Flueckiger 1996, 40; cf. Jay 1973). My own research among women living in the city of Benares in North India suggests that at least some Hindu women living in this part of North India also cultivate close, lifelong friendships with other women—friendships that are ritually sealed, highly valued, and self-consciously maintained, even after marriage.

My observations are based on research that I undertook in the city of Benares in 1995, 1997, and 1998. I did not set out to investigate women's friendships. My work during these years focused instead on women's devotions to Krishna during the month of Kartik (October–November). Krishna is widely worshipped in contemporary India in his forms as both divine child and playful lover. He is said to have been raised in a community of cowherds, and stories about his youth emphasize his special relationship with the many cowherdesses, called *gopis*, of Vrindavan, the region where he grew up. In his child form, it is said that Krishna is irresistible to the *gopis*, who take great delight in his boyish charm. As he matures into adolescence, Krishna becomes an irresistible young man, and the cowherdesses fall deeply in love with him, eager to enjoy his erotic embrace. In this role, Krishna is the divine lover of women. One of the most famous images of Krishna situates him in the *rasa-lila*, the famous "circle dance," where Krishna, surrounded by a circle of *gopis* in the forest, not only dances with them, but also multiplies himself many times over so that he can make love to each and every one of them. While early texts focus on Krishna's dalliance with all of the *gopis*, subsequent traditions pair Krishna especially with one consort, Radha, and portray Radha as the chief *gopi* and Krishna's primary partner in love. Krishna eventually leaves Vrindavan to take up residence in Dvaraka, where he leaves Radha and the cowherdesses behind, acquiring a vast number of wives and assuming the rulership of the Yadava clan.

During Kartik, many Benarsi Hindu women perform a collective daily *puja*, a form of ritual worship, in which they raise Krishna from infancy to adulthood, culminating in his marriage to the plant-goddess Tulsi toward the end of the month.[2] During this *puja*, women assume the devotional stance of the *gopis*. Just as the *gopis* are believed to have gathered around Krishna in a circle in the original circle dance, so Kartik *puja* participants gather in a circle around icons of Krishna and other deities; and just as the *gopis* of long ago adored Krishna with song and dance, *puja* participants worship him with song and devotional offerings. Popular Krishna traditions equate the *gopis* with the faithful female servants, known collectively as the *sakhis*, who accompany and serve the divine couple Radha-Krishna. *Sakhi* means "female friend," and in Kartik *puja* circles, women are enjoined to refer to themselves and to each other only with this term.

In the course of discussing the meaning of the term *sakhi* with Kartik *puja* participants, I found that participants tended to define it first in terms of human friendship, bringing up the term's connection to Krishna mythology only at my prompting. When I probed further, I was told also of a ritual of becoming (*banana*) or tying (*bandhana*) *sakhi*, in which women exchange vows of lifelong friendship. Once I learned of the existence of this ritual, I began to ask informants about it explicitly. About twenty of the thirty-six women I formally interviewed in the course of my research confirmed its existence and described for me both the act of ritually becoming *sakhi* and the bond that is thereby established, including the meaning of the relationship and the obligations that it entails. Almost all of these women claimed the authority of experience, contending that they themselves had established ritually sealed *sakhi* relationships that they value and strive to maintain.

I have never witnessed the ritual that women described to me. The reports tended to be consistent, however. Furthermore, Edward Jay recorded the existence of ritual friendships among women, including ritual *sakhi* relationships, in Chhatisgarh more than thirty years ago (Jay 1973), indicating that the tradition exists beyond the confines of Benares and has been around for a while. Several of my informants lamented that the practice of creating ritual friendships between female friends was a tradition in decline and that girls and younger women were not preserving the practice to the same degree as the previous generation. This may be true, although I did talk to some young women who had entered into ritual *sakhi* friendships. I suspect that in their conversations with me, informants tended to idealize the *sakhi* relationship and gloss over ways in which their own *sakhi* ties may deviate from the ideal, so one certainly ought to exercise caution regarding informants' reports about what has actually transpired in their own *sakhi* relationships.[3] What especially interests me in this context, however, is the way that ritual friendships performed among the women I interviewed seem to appropriate the mythic *sakhi* of Krishnaite sacred history as a model for extra-domestic human female-female social and emotional bonds that women choose for themselves.

Six informants explicitly described the *sakhi* bond among women as one that imitates or replicates divine models. All six invoked the relationship between Radha and her *sakhis*, or the relationships that Radha's *sakhis* shared with one another, as the root (*mul*) or role model (*adarsh*) for the *sakhi* bond. One woman, for example, proclaimed, "My relationship with my *sakhi* is like the relationship of Radha and her *sakhis*. And we hope that we will be together in the same way for our whole lives." Another invoked as a model the relationship shared by Radha and Krishna as well, noting, "The way Krishna used to love Radha and the kind of deep affection that the *sakhis* have for each other, similarly we also become *sakhi*."

This seeming collapse of an erotic, male-female relationship—that between Radha and Krishna—with the relationships of deep friendship attributed to Radha and her female friends adumbrates a larger issue surrounding *sakhi* relationships as they were described to me: the *sakhi* bond in many ways imitates or echoes some of the social and emotional aspects of the marital bond. Like marriage, the *sakhi* relationship is considered unique, deeply intimate, and entailing specific rules and obligations. I would argue that the *sakhi* bond that informants in Benares described to me deploys religious and marital imagery in ways that sacralize ongoing relationships among female friends, according them social and even religious legitimacy and establishing a socially valid place for them in women's lives. Although these relationships exist only at the margins of patriarchal social discourse, which defines women largely in terms of male-centered kinship relationships, they are reported to be of great importance to many of the women who enter into them.

All but one of the women who spoke with me about the *sakhi* bond affirmed the existence of a ritual whereby the bond is sealed. The essential elements of this ritual practice include an exchange of gifts and food, the swearing of an oath, and the presence of a deity, who acts as a witness.[4] This is how one informant, Gita,[5] described the process of becoming *sakhi*:

> You buy bangles, *bindi*, hair ribbons, clothes, and some ornaments—
> like earrings—to give. By giving these, this is tying *sakhi*. If the
> girls are unmarried, then they give each other these gifts and
> go to the Sakshi Vinayak temple and say, "Considering you as a
> witness, we will remain *sakhi*." And they take an oath that "we will
> remain friends with each other, participate in each other's auspi-
> cious and inauspicious functions, in birth and death, marriage, and
> so forth. And at the time of death, I will be with you."

The gifts exchanged most often include those like the ones Gita described: clothes, makeup, jewelry, *bindis* (the decorative dots that Indian women place on their foreheads), and *sindur*, a bright red or orange powder that married women place in the part of their hair. Two informants described the items exchanged as "stuff for marital auspiciousness" (*suhag ka saman*). Other women stressed the exchange of food, especially sweets and *pan*,[6] as crucial to the sealing of the bond. *Sakhis* not only feed one another, but they also self-consciously exchange with one another food polluted by their saliva. One elderly informant described the process as follows:

> In the ritual of becoming *sakhi*, there are some *puja* things—sweets,
> yogurt, *pan*—and the *sakhis* feed each other these things.... For ex-
> ample, if you and I were becoming *sakhi*, then I would feed you
> sweets, you would feed me sweets, and then you would bite off some
> *pan* and I would chew it; and I would bite off some *pan*, and you
> would chew it. And they say to each other, "Everyone may leave
> us, whether it is husband, or mother, or father, or brother, but we
> will never leave each other!"

The exchange of such polluted food signals both intimacy and lack of hier-archy, indicating that both parties are willing to accept the other's pollution into their bodies. Equality is an essential component of the *sakhi* relationship. Jay stresses the nature of ritual friendships as a means to transcending social difference; he notes that the ritual friendships he observed in Chhattisgarh never occurred within the same caste in the same community, claiming that the very hallmark of ritual friendships is their ability to legitimize close per-sonal relationships across caste.[7] Similarly, the women I interviewed insisted that there should be no hierarchy between *sakhi*s, even though one's *sakhi* may come from another caste, religion, or nationality. One informant, for example, proclaimed, "Sometimes we even make *sakhi* with a Harijan.... we are never aware of caste after making *sakhi*." It is difficult to know to what extent such claims are true: none of the women I interviewed claimed to have a Dalit or Muslim *sakhi*, although one informant did claim that her *sakhi* is Christian. Nevertheless, the rhetoric of equality is very important in women's descriptions of their *sakhi* relationships. Other informants described the *sakhi* bond as one of choice based solely on strong mutual affection. As one put it, "*Sakhi* means that you should have true love [*saci priti*]."

Regarding the types of foods exchanged in the *sakhi* bonding ritual, Ved Prakash and Sylvia Vatuk have noted that sweets play an important role in all kinds of ritual activity and in cementing social ties between individuals and groups; they are associated with pleasure, celebration, and rejoicing (Vatuk and Vatuk 1979, 182). Bride and groom also exchange sweets and yogurt— which some informants mentioned explicitly as items exchanged in the *sakhi* bonding ritual—at the time of marriage (usually as yogurt mixed with brown sugar, *gur*), suggesting parallels between the *sakhi* relationship and the marriage relationship. Such parallels are also evident in naming conventions. About half the women who spoke with me about the *sakhi* bond insisted that one should never refer to one's *sakhi* by name, claiming that this is an essential rule (*niyam*) governing the relationship. One informant, Lilavati, drew an explicit parallel to the marriage relationship in this regard, noting, "The way we don't call our husband by his name, similarly, we don't call our *sakhi* by her name. We call her '*sakhi*' or 'mother of so-and-so.' " Whereas husband and wife are unequal partners, however, *sakhi*s are not; hence one informant described the importance of using the term *sakhi* as reflecting the special closeness and feelings of equality that are characteristic of the relationship, signaled in the mutual feeding that takes place in the *sakhi* bonding ritual.

Like marriage, too, the *sakhi* relationship is also a bond that informants generally described as lifelong and unbreakable. In her research on this topic, Flueckiger notes that married women who enter into ritual friendships assume ritual obligations similar to those of kin (1996, 40).[8] This also seems to be the case among the women I interviewed. Here is how one informant, Hem Kumari, responded to my questions about her *sakhi* relationship:

> My *sakhi* and I have always been friends. We were brought up
> together. When I was a child, we used to play together, run
> around the village, and bathe together in the village tank.... We used
> to work in the fields together. So that's how our friendship started.
> Then when we got older, we decided we should become *sakhi*. I
> became *sakhi* with her on the day of Makkar Samkranti—women
> often make *sakhi* on that day. So that is how we became *sakhi*, and

then we started giving each other gifts. When I got married, she gave
me a gift; when she got married, I gave a gift to her. And since we are
sakhi, if she is in trouble, I can help her, and if I am in trouble, she
can come help me. Even though we are now married and living in
our husbands' place, we send each other letters, and we keep in
touch. My *sakhi*'s husband died. She has two daughters and one son;
so I occasionally call her here. Whenever there is a marriage in
my family she will come over here (to Benares) because she still lives
in my (natal) village. And whenever I have a chance to go and
visit her, I also go and visit her. Whatever we have to feed each
other, we feed each other. This is what we do.

Hem Kumari's description points to the obligations that several informants
described as intrinsic to the relationship: attending one another's important
family functions, making an effort to spend time together even if one has moved
away, exchanging gifts, feeding each other, and sharing resources. Of course,
the ability to fulfill such obligations is contingent on the cooperation of parents, husbands, or in-laws. But when permission is granted, *sakhi*s are obli-
gated to maintain the tie through such specific behaviors.

Another characteristic of the relationship that informants stressed was
complete honesty and trust, especially in keeping one another's secrets. One of
my informants, Ramavati, noted:

When two *sakhi*s sit down with one another, they will obvi-
ously talk about their sorrows and pleasures [*dukh-sukh*]. . . . And
whatever one *sakhi* tells the other, she must keep it secret. They must
not tell one another's secrets to anyone else because the rules of
the *sakhi* relationship are very strict. You must always keep to your-
self all the things you hear from your *sakhi*.[9] There are lots of things
about which *sakhi*s only tell their *sakhi*s. There are lots of things a
woman cannot say to her husband but can say to her *sakhi*.

Narayan has also noted the importance among female friends of sharing
secrets. She quotes one informant named Veena, who claims, "With a female
friend [*saheli*] you can share those things that can't be shared with others, you
can say things that you shouldn't say to our husband's sister [*nanad*] or to the
sister [*bahen*] made there" (meaning, in the husband's village) (Narayan 1986,
66). Another of Narayan's informants, Kamal, is quoted on the same page:
"Only a *saheli* can be counted on to keep secrets. A woman you know later
might tell anyone."

Among the women I interviewed, some also described the special bond of
honesty and trust that exists between *sakhi*s as surpassing that of a woman
and her husband or kin. Lilavati, for example, noted, "When we become *sakhi*,
then we will not hide anything from one another. . . . you never lie to your *sakhi*.

You may lie to your husband sometimes, but you never lie to your *sakhi*. This is how pure [*shuddh*] the relationship with the *sakhi* is." Another woman volunteered, "After the joining of *sakhis*, no one is as trustworthy as your *sakhi*, not even your brother, sister, anyone from the in-laws' house, like mother-in-law or father-in-law; no one is as trustworthy as your *sakhi*." Yet another informant explained, "In Hindi, there is a phrase: 'relatives are left, but one doesn't leave one's friends [*hit chut jate hain, lekin mitr nahin chute*].' Friends are always friends. Women have their *sakhis* like this; if you have made a *sakhi*, it is your duty [*dharma*] that you should never leave your *sakhi*."

Informants repeatedly stressed the need to keep up the *sakhi* relationship and refrain from violating the rules and obligations perceived to be intrinsic to it. Most agreed that this is difficult, and for this reason several informants cautioned against taking more than one or two *sakhis*. Seven of the women I interviewed urged that there should be only one *sakhi*, usually taken during childhood and maintained throughout one's lifetime. Four women allowed for two *sakhis*, one in the natal home and one in the home into which one marries. Others claimed there is no restriction on how many *sakhis* one may have, but one must maintain each and every *sakhi* relationship and fulfill all the obligations that are entailed in the relationship—and for that reason, it is important to limit the number of one's *sakhis*.

The existence of ritually bonded *sakhi* friendships among the women I interviewed raises two important issues I wish to stress here. First, the *sakhi* bond affirms Susan Sered's observation that even in religious traditions that accord institutional authority primarily to men, women may appropriate and reshape religious traditions in ways that are uniquely meaningful to them (Sered 1992, 1994). As noted, many women consider the bonds of friendship between human *sakhis* to be modeled on the intimacy enjoyed among Radha's *sakhis*, between Radha and her *sakhis*, or between Radha and Krishna. The *sakhi* relationship integrates aspects of Krishna mythology in ways that support and strengthen women's social bonds with one another rather than with deities or human males. The love between Krishna and the numerous *gopis/sakhis* is often interpreted as sexual and hence transgressive, transcending earthly, human morality. For many Benarsi women, however, the *sakhi* represents an earthly female-female bond characterized by ties of mutual trust and caring, and it may imitate or even surpass blood or marital kinship bonds in terms of its professed emotional valuation in women's lives.

Second, the *sakhi* bond provides an alternative to predominant social constructions that locate women's important social ties solidly within the domestic sphere, especially within the conjugal home. Gloria Raheja has argued that Indian women's songs may question the discourse of patriliny, challenging its claim to exclusive authority and constructing alternative readings of kinship (Raheja and Gold 1994, 105). The *sakhi* bond offers another kind of alternative construction. It mimics the husband-wife bond in significant ways (ritually sealing the bond, not using each other's names, feeding one another, entailing lifelong obligation, and so forth). Yet it is a tie in which the two parties are equal, and both affection and obligation are understood to be mutual. It is also a relationship over which women have control. Generally, Hindu women living in this part of India do not freely choose their husbands; but they can, and do, choose their *sakhi*s.

Susan Seymour notes that, in Indian contexts, love tends to be experienced as a "deep sense of emotional connectedness," which she calls relational love. Seymour maintains that feelings of relational love may be extended to non-family members as well, including friends. With respect to her own experience among Indian women, she remarks that even married women expect and value feelings of love among friends. She writes that her friends Mita and Sita "frequently spoke to me of their affection for and friendship with me and their fear that I would one day go away and forget them. They wanted to build into our relationship some sense of *dharma*—some agreement that I would take the friendship seriously and, after leaving India, would continue to communicate with them" (Seymour 1999, 85). I had a similar experience when I was preparing to leave Benares in 1998 after spending many months over the course of four years conducting research among a group of women. I had grown very close to a few women, and it was hard for all of us to think about saying goodbye without knowing when I might be returning to the city. This is what I recorded in my journal during the final days of my stay:

> I went to do some last follow-up interviews today with Krishna Devi and Kusumlata, who loaded me down with gifts of necklaces. I took pictures of Kusumlata's whole family and promised to bring them by on Friday. She wanted to tie *sakhi* with me. When I went there today, as she was giving me all the necklaces, she said, "This is for us to become *sakhi*." She was saying that this was her way of tying *sakhi* with me, but I didn't have anything to give her. I felt so bad. As she put me on the Rickshaw, she said that "it is as if half my body is leaving and going to America."

As I look back on that moment, difficult for both Kusumlata and me, it now seems obvious that the image of friendship Kusumlata invoked in expressing her feelings about my departure—that it was like half of her body leaving for America—evokes the image of *jori*, meaning something like "united couple" or two persons joined together in a harmonious oneness, a single being embodying two persons. The ideal of the *jori* is captured in the image of Ardhanarishvara, Shiva in his form as half-male, half-female, god and goddess fused together in the same body. Sudhir Kakar contends that the "wished-for oneness of the divine couple" is especially important to Indian Hindu women and represents their idealized image of marriage (Kakar 1990, 83–84).

Narayan observes, however, that in Kangra, North India, where she has conducted field research, the same term, *jori*, is used for the relationships between unmarried girlfriends and between bride and groom. Narayan contends that the shared use of this term might indicate that a husband is expected to psychologically replace a group of girlfriends (Narayan 1986, 68). While this may be true, it is also possible that the image of two beings sharing the same body points to an underlying conception common both to deep friendship and to marriage of an ideal, unbreakable, and transformative bond between persons, forged of intimacy and affection, that transcends mere social convention in its significance and claims to mutual obligation. This may be the longing that Seymour notes for "some sense of *dharma*" in female friendships. And the longing for a sense of *dharma* is precisely what is addressed in the *sakhi* relationship—through the deployment of religious and marital symbolism, ritualization, and the elaboration of rules and obligations entailed in forming and maintaining the bond.

NOTES

1. Ursula Sharma, another researcher who has worked in Kangra and whom Narayan cites (Narayan 1986, 66–67), also concludes that married women's relationships with other women tend to revolve primarily around female kin living in the husband's household. Sharma also notes that the term for friend (*saheli*) "is not much used among rural women except to express the relationship among unmarried girls of the same village" (Sharma 1980, 185). Instead, the married women Sharma studied tend to use fictive kinship terms to describe all nonfamily women, including those with whom women share a close emotional relationship (1980, 185–190).

2. For more on women's performance of Kartik *puja*, see Pintchman 2003, 2005a, and 2005b.

3. Many thanks to Kirin Narayan for bringing to my attention the need to clarify this point.

4. Three informants insisted that the ritual must take place in front of a Tulsi plant, but other women cited other divine witnesses, including Satyanarayan, Ganesh, the Ganges, and Shiva. See Flueckiger 1996 and Jay 1973 for their descriptions of friendship-bonding rituals in Chhattisgarh.

5. I have changed the names of all informants to conceal their identities.

6. *Pan* is a mixture of betel nut, spices, and other additives rolled up in a betel leaf and chewed for enjoyment.

7. Jay notes (1973, 154), "Ceremonial friendships are a means of bridging the gap between castes when two individuals wish to establish a dyadic relationship other than the normal one characteristic of members of different castes."

8. Jay (1973) describes ritual friendships of all sorts as essentially fictive kin relationships.

9. Literally, "you must always digest" all the things you hear from your *sakhi*.

REFERENCES

Flueckiger, Joyce B. 1996. *Gender and Genre in the Folklore of Middle India*. Ithaca, NY: Cornell University Press.

Jay, Edward. 1973. "Bridging the Gap between Castes: Ceremonial Friendship in Chhattisgarh." *Contributions to Indian Sociology* 7: 144–158.

Kakar, Sudhir. 1990. *Intimate Relations: Exploring Indian Sexuality*. New Delhi: Penguin.

Narayan, Kirin. 1986. "Birds on a Branch: Girlfriends and Wedding Songs in Kangra." *Ethos* 14, no. 1 (Spring): 47–75.

Pintchman, Tracy. 1999. "Karttik as a Vaisnava *Mahotsav*: Mythic Themes and the Ocean of Milk." *Journal of Vaisnava Studies* 7, no. 2: 65–92.

———. 2003. "The Month of Kartik and Women Ritual Devotions to Krishna in Benares." In *The Blackwell Companion to Hinduism*, ed. Gavin Flood, 327–342. Oxford: Blackwell.

———. 2005a. *Guests at God's Wedding: Celebrating Kartik among the Women of Benares*. Albany: State University of New York Press.

———. 2005b. "Domesticating Krishna: Friendship, Marriage, and Women's Experience in a Hindu Women's Ritual Tradition." In *'Alternative' Krishna Traditions: Krishna in Folk Religion and Vernacular Literature*, ed. Guy Beck, 43–63. New York: State University of New York Press.

Raheja, Gloria Goodwin, and Anne Grodzins Gold. 1994. *Listen to the Heron's Words: Reimagining Gender and Kinship in North India*. Berkeley: University of California Press.

Sered, Susan Starr. 1992. *Women as Ritual Experts*. New York: Oxford University Press.

———. 1994. *Priestess, Mother, Sacred Sister: Religions Dominated by Women*. New York: Oxford University Press.

Seymour, Susan C. 1999. *Women, Family, and Child Care in India: A World in Transition*. Cambridge: Cambridge University Press.

Sharma, Ursula. 1980. *Women, Work, and Property in North West India*. London: Tavistock.

Vatuk, Ved Prakash, and Sylvia Jane Vatuk. 1979. "Chatorpan: A Culturally Defined Form of Addiction in North India." In *Studies in Indian Folk Traditions*, ed. Ved Prakash Vatuk, 177–189. Delhi: Manohar.

4

Words That Breach Walls: Women's Rituals in Rajasthan

Lindsey Harlan

This chapter contemplates some ways that Hindu women's rituals expand, dissolve, interrogate, reconfigure, and challenge the conceptual space and normative value of domesticity. It focuses on Rajasthani women's performance of *ratijagas*, celebratory night wakes that women perform in conjunction with important rites of passage, especially births and marriages, and refutes the premise that the impact of women's rituals performed at home is contained and circumscribed by location. Investigating ways in which women's ritual utterances exert influence, it agues that women's domestic ritual performances influence praxis in other domiciles, which constitute realms exterior to them, but also in nondomestic public space, often conceptualized in India, as elsewhere, as primarily the sphere of men.[1] Attended by women traveling between households and audited by familial men who inhabit public spaces more conventionally and routinely than do women, women's *ratijagas*, like other women's rituals, breach walls and influence social life in realms beyond their domiciles.

Women and Domiciles: On Location and Orientation

Because many of the rituals that women perform are performed at home, we tend to think of them, and to encode them, as "domestic" rituals. These include daily *puja* (worship) of household deities, *vrats* (weekly, monthly, annual, or ad hoc "vows" that please deities and generally entail some kind of fasting), other calendrical rituals (such as Navratri, the semiannual celebration of "Nine Nights" of devotion to the goddess Durga), and rites of passage (birth rites, weddings, etc.). Women's performance of these rituals in homes is too easily identified with the space of enactment. Conceptualizing the rituals as essentially locative conveys various troublesome assumptions, including the notion that their efficacy is limited to the home and that they are expressions of women's desires that are normatively bounded or defined by domestic space. In this simplistic equation of space and purpose, women's rituals are deemed to be designed to promote the welfare of the family members, including men, women, and children living within the homes in which women live and so sharing walls that separate immediate family from others: other relatives and nonrelatives.

It would be an error to dismiss the locative dimension of many women's rituals: the place in which women perform them, the place that women inhabit, is important. It literally grounds identity. Various scholars have argued that locus, whatever its dimensions, is a significant and vital ingredient in the formation and expression of identity. Valentine Daniels has shown the extent to which location, with its own soil and water, is key to these processes.[2] Joyce B. Flueckiger and Peter Gottschalk, inter alia, have argued that identity is influenced not only by one's village, but also by larger areas, whether regions or village nexuses, which incorporate nearby locations or settlements into one's understanding of self and social location.[3] Identity is, then, at least partially constructed by notions of residence, which are tangibly and multiply referenced by indices such as the water brought into and drunk at home and the soil that becomes the mud and dust traipsed into homes, later to be swept up by women performing domestic duties.

For many women in India, the domicile is not simply a place of residence or grounding, but also a location that they leave or enter as brides and that designates some degree of confinement. For women in different parts of India and from different social locations in the same part of India, there are varying degrees and modes of restriction that bind women to their natal or conjugal homes and discourage or prohibit their participation in public life beyond the domicile. I say "public life beyond the domicile," because there are public activities in which women engage within the domicile, and, as we shall see, this fact should prevent any facile contradistinction between domestic and public, or between "female" and "male" realms.

Among Rajput women, about whom I have written over the years, spatial restrictions have been among the strictest in India. In the past few decades, however, the institution of *parda* has become increasingly elastic, at least for those women living in and near towns and cities. In and around Udaipur, where I have conducted much of my research, many of the young women whom I came to know well in the 1980s are now mothers-in-law who have decided to loosen or dispense with some or all of the strictures of *parda* for their daughters-in-law. It is now not uncommon to see Rajput women shopping in town. Moreover, many women no longer veil at home in front of senior family members and visitors.[4] That said, women who do not observe *parda* in the cities often do observe it when they return to their country residences in the erstwhile *thikanas* (estates) that their families once ruled.[5] Their family status among villagers remains tied to a code that is largely antiquated in town, especially a town like Udaipur, which has become a trendy destination for tourists, who often rent rooms in guesthouses owned by Rajputs.

It would be easy, but naive, to imagine that in the "olden days" of *parda*, when women's movement was highly restrained, the rituals performed by women would have been faithfully passed down from mothers-in-law to daughters-in-law and therefore would have stayed strictly within domestic perimeters and so remained uninfluenced by what they learned in their natal homes. Such a segregated imaginative construct would unrealistically limit the influence and impact of rituals to the domicile where they were practiced at one particular place and time.[6] It is important to emphasize that women's rituals have always been subject to change, which should not be linked simply with modernity. The so-called traditional has always changed, and so "traditional" ritual has changed with every performance. It has been filtered through the sieves of performers' diverse improvisational strategies and inspirations. It has also been apprehended and interpreted variously by those who participate in it, even if "only" as attendees or auditors, whose presence, expression, bearing, and commentary are, in any case, noted by and reacted to by performers, whose actions are not only influenced by audience but also, at least partially, motivated by a desire to impress those who attend. This is so even if performers' utmost desire is limited to impressing upon people, including children, the importance of the particular (albeit ephemeral) incarnation of ritual that they enact.

Apart from this objection, which insists on the diachronic nonfixity or fluidity of traditional ritual praxis, there is the objection about the limitation of women's rituals to domicile. However constrained women have been to designated parameters, they have regularly traveled between domiciles—as brides or as wedding guests—and so observed variant practices. Fertile opportunities for encountering variation are provided by women's *ratijagas*, for which women invite relatives and friends, as they do all the deities worshipped by members of the hostesses' households. Women's movement across household borders for *ratijagas* has introduced visiting individuals to novel constellations of deities, some of whom various women may not have worshipped in their homes. Occasioning discussion of worship, blessings, and miracles, night-long wakes have allowed women to exchange information about *bhakti* (dedication to deities) and enabled women to take away with them new impressions of practice and even, perhaps, new commitments to self-chosen deities (*isthadevtas*).[7] Thus the performance of *ratijagas* for marriages and other rites of passage requires and promotes a kind of transportation of women and ideas that functions inevitably as a source of information, inspiration, and creativity.

The close connection between travel and transformation is not, of course, limited to the case of Rajput women attending rituals. It is, for example, a dominant theme in Fatema Mernissi's book *Scheherazade Goes West*, which argues that travel is a source of power for women. Discussing this book about harem life in Morocco with some students, I recalled a conversation I once had with an elderly Rajput woman in Udaipur. She told me that when she was growing up, her father prohibited all females in the home from reading newspapers.[8] Although as a child she must have overheard men's conversations about important political events, she, along with others observing *parda* in that household, would have been relatively sheltered from politics and so relatively uninformed, for example, about conditions under which women (and men) live elsewhere. Traveling to different homes, however, she and other women sheltered by household codes and strictures would be able to sample the experiences of women living beyond their domestic borders by observing what goes on, absorbing directions and narratives, and learning from other women about what they had learned from other travels and other sources, including newspapers.

That sampling must have always been the source of great enrichment and the impellent cause of some alternative thinking and doing. Here it should be noted that in arid and rocky Rajasthan, where villages, towns, and kingdoms have typically had long distances between them, even populations living in relative proximity have varied in surprising ways: popular wisdom has it that the language (*boli*) in Rajasthan changes every few miles.[9] With the change of language comes differences in idiom, expression, and so on. For many women married into Udaipur families, the Mewari tongue that their husbands have spoken since birth is a dialect to be learned. In-marrying brides in Mewari homes have created an insurgence of language and of notions that language constructs.

Thus marriage has been followed by a period of transition with words and ideas surely being exchanged or loaned, perhaps even on a long-term or permanent basis. Add to this circumstance the tradition of high social status families making alliances with other important families from erstwhile kingdoms, which are inevitably distant (both inside and outside of Rajasthan), and there arises the opportunity for fluid, if perhaps at times slowly seeping, accommodation, both to new and old ways, among cohabiting women. When these women stream into and out of the homes of other women, who have their own diverse natal dialects/languages and upbringings, there is often much to talk about. Exchanging news, gossip, and recipes and perhaps discussing films and television shows, women learn about lands and customs far beyond the borders of domicile, and even of region.[10]

On a macro level of analysis, the movement suggests that women's practice of rituals in their individual homes has surely, if often subtly, altered the religious terrain inside and outside their dwellings. Emblematic of this change in Mewar is the legendary *bhakti* poet Mira Bai, who upset Mewar's ruling family when she arrived as a bride with an unshakable commitment to her *isthadevta*, Krishna.[11] Treasuring her worship and considering it more important than her in-laws' familial goddess worship, she affronted members of her *sasural* by according Krishna priority. Eventually she abandoned *parda*, domicile, and kingdom to wander the roads and forests while praising Krishna before ultimately taking refuge in his temple at far-away Dvaraka. There, many devotees believe, she miraculously merged with his icon when her natal family tried to retrieve her to Mewar.

Whatever the impact that Mira's legend of rebellious devotion may have had on women throughout the centuries, it is clear that she is understood today as having had tremendous clout: there is a well-visited Mira temple at the great fortress of Chittor, where her devotion is celebrated. Residents and visitors know of patronage of the "Mira Bai temple" (as the Vaishnava temple has become known) by the royal family, which originally rebuked her for her insolent worship and departure, then ultimately and futilely demanded her return. This shows a tacit, even implicit, recognition of a prominent instance of a bride bringing with her a devotional agenda.

Mira is patently exceptional in her rebelliousness: a brides expects, and is expected, to tour and pay respect (*dhok*) at the prominent temples in her husband's village or estate (*thikana*) and to honor all deities installed there, as well as the other deities worshipped in her *sasural*'s shrine or shrines. Brides typically conform to expectation but are not, however, asked to forswear all prior theological commitments and ways of worshipping. Moreover, women's narratives about ancestral women's importation of their natal family's goddesses parallels and complements men's narratives of goddess procurement through icon seizure, a feature of the spoils of war. Victorious kings often demanded brides and icons. That the two might come together and so directly import ritual at times seems reasonable and is supported by indigenous narrative.[12]

In short, brides arriving at their *sasural* bring with them a new wind that may stir the course of religious thought and praxis. Women singing at *rati-jaga*s for weddings and other occasions receive exposure to new religious acts and ideas, as well as tidings of divine blessings and miracles at various people's domestic shrines or temples, to which pilgrimage may later be made on subsequent visits that also, of course, allow for recreational visiting. Thus women, who are often represented as conservators of tradition, are also agents of change, who usher in new influences that may alter praxis at home and beyond.

Before offering some specific ideas about how this takes place, I pause to frame this discussion with a non-Indian allusion. Briefly thinking through some of the dynamics in the film *Chocolat* will help to connect the erosive and etching winds of change in India with those effected by women elsewhere. Realizing that not all readers will be seasoned Indologists, I offer the example to demonstrate that some myth and ritual can be construed as revealing the influence of women on religious praxis and the power of women not only to bring others into their domestic realm, and so render and exert nonprivate, nonfamilial influence, but also to influence what goes on beyond their space, in the homes of others and in the institutional practice of religion outside all domestic spaces.

Chocolat

In the opening scene appears a sunny, medieval-looking French village. Almost immediately, however, the sunshine vanishes and a snowstorm hits. Blown into this town by the blustery north wind are two female travelers in Red Riding Hoodish red capes, which offer the only visual relief from the village's stony architecture. With their vibrant attire, so evocative of fairy tale, they foreshadow the infusion of enlivening change—of novel and alien customs, heretical ideas, and transgressive *joie de vivre*—that their residence is soon to effect. The foreshadowing is not subtle. As soon as the hooded travelers arrive in this town, which has been rendered lifeless and deserted by the unanimous church attendance of the town's Catholic denizens, the church doors blow open with a bang and disrupt the solemnity of the service, which, we are to understand by the wriggling and dozing of the attendees in their pews, is uninspiring.

Most visibly upset by the wind's disruption is the Comte de Reynaud, represented in the film as emblematic of solemn religious devotion and as stalwart in upholding and enforcing Catholic morality, with its sharply gendered division of space and duties. After learning of the arrival of the newcomers, mother and daughter who have just rented a defunct and dusty *patisserie*, he greets them and invites them to attend church. The mother, Vianne Rocher, declines. Visibly dismayed by her unabashed announcement that they do not attend church, and by her revelation that she is an unwed mother, the count departs abruptly.

Further provoking the count is Vianne's opening of a *chocolaterie* during Lent. Outraged, he forbids churchgoers to patronize the shop, with its vibrant Mayan decor. He informs Vianne that one of his ancestors, a previous count, whose grimacing statue guards the square outside the church gates, routed the Huguenots and that, as his heir, he should have little trouble shutting her down and driving her out.

The count is wrong. He is no match for Vianne, who verily incarnates the winds of change. Raised in Central America and belonging to a group of nomadic healers, her mother married a French apothecary on his mission to seek new cures. Having returned with him to France and given birth to Vianne, she ultimately eschewed settled life with him and took off with Vianne to travel and to vend cacao remedies. Vianne, in turn, had a daughter and took up a peripatetic life selling curative and exquisite chocolates, laced with exotic chili pepper.

Although forbidden by the count and by Catholic Lenten tradition to buy Vianne's chocolates, which the count images as the work of the devil, some of the villagers most afflicted by stagnant social norms and unyielding expectations of conformity to rules about proper gardening, husband maintenance, and courtship succumb to the allure of Vianne's inviting establishment. Admiring the luscious chocolates in her window, they heed Vianne's plea to enter and accept, albeit at first tentatively, her overtures of hospitality and friendship. Gifting samples, she initiates the process of rescuing them from loneliness, shyness, timidity, sexual lethargy, and domestic abuse. Consuming Vianne's carefully formulated and soothing sweets, the socially alienated villagers find themselves altered and strengthened in their sense of worth and purpose.

At Vianne's urging, these deviating townsfolk enter, and thrive in, the building housing both Vianne's shop and her living quarters: the *chocolaterie* is literally "where she lives," a slang expression economically conveying the connection between domicile and identity. Having rented the room above her shop, she lives where and as she heals. Moreover, by the end of the film, her patients have become apprentices occupying Vianne's inner sanctum, her kitchen, where she exerts nurturing power. As a much maligned and besieged Vianne ponders whether to leave them to wander away with the wind, they staff her kitchen and wield the tools of her trade as they concoct chocolates to take into town for a planned chocolate festival. Having learned her craft, they take Vianne's ways and their influence to the streets, where they can visit change on, and bring happiness to, the previously uninitiated.

Whether or not one is willing to see Vianne and her followers as practicing a "religion of chocolate," one should easily recognize that there are aspects of their practice that are evocative of, or at least similar to, the religious. The count represents her praxis as heretical. Moreover, she deploys ritual divination: she asks customers to gaze at a spinning painted disk and then to tell her what they see. According to their responses, she discerns "their favorites" and fills their divined prescription with healing morsels. Moreover, the chocolate festival, heralding the arrival of spring and employing street performers resembling those abounding at contemporary May Day celebrations, implies benign, if paganesque, transgression. Thus the chocolates created in Vianne's kitchen by her disciples ultimately make their way into the town square, just outside the church gates and directly under the nose of the memorialized defeater of Huguenots. What began in the kitchen of the exotic woman and daughter who blew into town proceeds outward and onward into the town square, the quintessentially public place.

Among the attendees at the festival is the vanquished count. Having starved himself during Lent, he becomes possessed by an uncontrollable craving for chocolate. That his transformation, his acceptance of desire, is not ephemeral is suggested by his decision to date his secretary now that he realizes that his wife has completely abandoned him, and also by his withdrawal of his unwelcome influence over the town's young priest, who now preaches to parishioners tolerance and acceptance of some nomads, "river rats" anchored in the river bordering the town. The breezes blown from Vianne's kitchen thus continue to move outward and so affect not just the center, but the periphery, of the community.

The change visited on the town is sufficiently transformative that the town now exerts a boomeranging influence on Vianne: it tempts her to abandon her perpetual roaming and abide in one location. Because her actions have transformed the place where she lives by altering its perspectives and conventions, she is now free and able to live there and to resist the urge to wander. Having changed the town, she can, as her travel-weary daughter puts it, live like a normal person.

What are we to take away from this exotic story in order to understand better the wind blown by, and as, women in India? There are many possible things one could take away, but for the purpose of this chapter, let me focus on three.

1. As a traveler, a woman can be understood as incarnating, as well as experiencing, change. In the context of ritual, as in life generally, she serves as an agent shaping to some extent her environment even as she adjusts to it. This agency may or may not take the form of what is generally called "everyday resistance."[13] A woman may or may not understand the implementation of change as subversive even though it does, in effect, transform the household, which is so often too easily conceptualized as tranquilly reproducing generations in a stable and conservative patriarchal culture.

In *Chocolat*, the circumstances of the radical catalyst Vianne, who is, after all, a fictional figure, are atypical: they little resemble those of postwar French women, and they certainly diverge from those of Rajput women in whatever time period. Vianne has no man. This heroine is a "loose woman," unsupervised, and so unbound by male authority. It is therefore unsurprising that she will transgress the town's mores by having sexual relations with a nomadic boatman. She is blown by the wind, but she also is the wind, blowing away what is stagnant even if by the end, also adjusting, that is to say, being calmed and soothed by the rhythm of settled life in a small town.

2. The domestic location of women is not inherently private. Access may be "by invitation only," but women incorporate outsiders into the bodies of their households and exert their influence on others in these bodies in a way that renders their apparently private worlds at least intermittently public. At the

same time, of course, their exposure to outsiders influences them and so modifies their domestic social body and praxis. Familial and nonfamilial guests come and go, but their influence, like the influence of incoming brides, leaves non-ephemeral impressions.

In the film, Vianne makes chocolates that lure others into her cafe/home and, through the influence she wields within the walls of her living space, manages to alter radically the lives of those she feeds, who ultimately learn to make her recipes in her kitchen. Influencing the behavior of consumers, who eat her food but also take in her sparse but powerful advice, she effects changes that produce both familial cohesion and discord. Consumed by the coarse and unappealing husband of one consumer/patient, the chocolates cause him to desire his wife, even as she cleans their toilet: in later scenes, he appears to be attentive and supportive of her as she attends a transgressive chocolate soiree catered by Vianne for her landlady. After eating Vianne's chocolates, Josephine, a key character whose nervousness and kleptomania portend imminent breakdown, is emboldened to leave her physically and mentally abusive husband, Serge. Thus what comes from Vianne's kitchen is radically transformative. It strengthens, creates, or, in certain circumstances, destroys domestic social bonds in other domestic spaces.

3. The influence of women's praxis overflows the bounds of domesticity and seeps into, or even floods, quintessentially public dynamics and institutions. This is true, of course, in realms other than religion. Note an example from economics: European women's utilization of sugar in their recipes once supported the institution of slavery in Caribbean islands.[14]

In *Chocolat*, this point is best represented in Vianne's radical transformation of the count, who is also the mayor. When he attends, along with the priest, the paganesque chocolate festival, we know that the townspeople are now liberated from his dogged interference, which he justifies as enforcing Catholic morality. By the end of the film, the town is no longer bound by the moribund ethos it calls *tranquillité*.

With these three points in mind, let us turn to *ratijaga*s to see how they belie domestic boundaries and wield influence on other places and institutions.

*Ratijaga*s and Their Spheres of Influence

We begin with point one. As a traveler, a woman incarnates and experiences change: she is an agent shaping her environment even as she adjusts or assimilates to it. As we have seen, women coming into a household, as guests or brides, are influenced by what they encounter, while the women in the household into which they come are influenced by them and will also be further exposed to alternate ways and things when they visit other women in their domiciles. This occurs when women perform *ratijaga* rituals. Playing for hostesses and guests, the musicians (harmonium players and drummers) typically sing songs that facilitate identification, and even substitution, of one deity for another. Identification can, of course, effect temporary ritual homogenization, which may counteract or balance, rather than effect, differentiation. But familial deities, whether *kuldevis* (familial goddesses) or locative, cultic deities, are worshipped and conceptualized in situ—in their (household or temple) shrines—as discrete deities with local and cosmic identities.

Let us take the example of *kuldevis*. Singing songs to invite and honor the familial *kuldevi*, a goddess with whose identity many singers may not be familiar, musicians strategically employ generic names, such as Mata, Bhavani, and Amba. In one such song, there is a common and recurrent invocation of the goddess Amba, yet identified with her, in the very first verse, is the well-known Mewar cultic deity Avadi Mata (Avadi Mother), invoked also simply as Avada and as Avadi Rani (Queen Avadi):[15]

> Reveal yourself again and again, O Amba.
> Reveal yourself again and again.
> Bhavani, reveal yourself again and again.
> When you reveal yourself, I am happy, Avada.
> When you reveal yourself, I am happy.
> Amba, reveal yourself again and again.

The next two verses identify Amba also with Yogmaya, a well-known epithet with a pan-Indian range of recognition. But in the verse following them, this goddess is identified specifically with the Sisodiya Rajput *kuldevi*, Bayan Mata (Bayan Mother), who is invoked here as Bayan Rani (Queen Bayan):

> Amba, the necklace on your breast is beautiful.
> Your earrings are fully inlaid, your earrings, Avadi Rani.
> Your earrings are inlaid, inlaid, Oh Bayan Rani.
> Reveal yourself again and again.
> Oh Sukh Devi, reveal yourself again and again.

This verse invoking the family *kuldevi*, who specifically watches over family members and protects them against outsiders, also summons Sukh Devi, whose shrine in Bedla *thikana* (a tributary estate in the erstwhile Mewar kingdom), is well known and much visited by people from various nearby places and caste backgrounds. Given the invocation of well-known or transfamilial deities, as well as the one *kuldevi*, one should note that the generic epithet Ambaji surely also, and more specifically, references for those living in the erstwhile Sisodiya-ruled kingdom of Mewar, the Ambaji temple in Udaipur, which is patronized by the royal family.

Thus, this song identifies all deities and so allows everyone to relate to an inclusive deity belonging to no one particular place or no particular set of persons. Nevertheless, while centrifugally stating that these goddesses are "the same," the verses also centripetally retain discrete names and epithets differentiating all goddesses with their sets of devotees. I have written at length about the homogenization and differentiation of goddesses traveling between residences with brides.[16] In the context of *ratijagas*, it should be emphasized that exposure to the *kuldevis* worshipped by women in different families is made through the lyrics of *ratijaga* songs. The same principle holds for locative, cultic goddesses, such as Mewar's Avadi Mata.

Moreover, in songs such as this one, musicians invoking and pleasing particular goddesses and identifying them with other deities map a constellation of divinities with complex relations, including identification, but also homology and other forms of association. Together with songs sung for other divinities, such as Bheruji, Satimata, heroes (*jhumjharjis, bhomiyajis*, and ancestors (*pitrs* or *purbaj*), the *ratijaga* singers convey significant local knowledge, which expands the horizons of any traveling women's information and allows for the diverse construction and absorption of various divine identities, with their geographical (dwelling and shrine) referents and their associations with outside (hostesses') occasions.[17] These associations infiltrate/inform theology and ritual performance in different domiciles.

Women, then, inform their own and others' understandings of divinity with ritual experiences and discussions in their homes. They inform their in-laws' conventions when they arrive as brides. Traveling to one another's homes to participate in *ratijagas*, they see familiarity in the *ratijaga* observance of others, while learning about ritual practices and divinities who may be imported to help them back in their homes.

By this time, it should be clear that, as point two contends, the home in which a *ratijaga* is performed is not simply a family's private space and that the realm in which women perform the ritual is not simply private or domestic, as opposed to public, space. Women living at such a house temporarily, but repeatedly, render their home public when they exert the power of invitation. Whereas Vianne attracts guests and changes/is changed by guests with the lure of chocolate, Rajasthani women attract *ratijaga* participants—outsiders, whether human or divine—with promises of hospitality. This sets the terms of mutual influence and, perhaps, endearment.

In the days before printed invitations, these promises were typically made with grains of rice, in other words, food, one of the most basic elements of hospitality and, in this context, a metonym. In the Rajasthani epic *Pabuji*, the songs sung by performers as Rajput women's *ratijaga* songs at the weddings of the heroes Pabuji and Gogaji (who has an independent cult but who also appears in Pabuji's epic) describe the invitation of various familial deities via rice grains delivered to each god by the goddess Amba. Thus with women singing praises for deities and the goddess also summoning all divine participants, the point is driven home: females, divine and human, are responsible for drawing outsiders inside. They are represented as bringing into the household others, travelers whose evanescent presence as guests blesses the family and reflects/produces its social capital.

Thus we see the conjoint power of women and goddesses to attract and to bring together guests from other realms, including the divine. One might ask, of course, what sort of power is this power of divinities, whose existence may be challenged? Attributing to women the power to attract and make use of divine power in this connection might be deemed to be simply crediting them with the illusion, rather than the exercise, of power. And yet, few would doubt the power of Brahmins, whose status and influence are mostly unquestioned because of their perceived control over powers unseen. In the case of both Brahmins and women, power is claimed, but also perceived, by others: men, children, and women.[18] Women are expected to perform rituals that benefit not just themselves, but others, including men and children. Furthermore, in matters religious, women's knowledge is often considered authoritative. I have noted that women typically defer to men when it comes to matters they deem to be historical (itihasik), but men often defer to women when it comes to matters of theology and ritual.[19]

Women's power to invite outsiders is not absolute—men often wield substantial influence when it comes to determining which men will be invited to visit during the ratijaga and so whose wives must accompany them. Moreover, like women, men worship isthadevtas, chosen deities, whom women are expected to please for their own good and for the benefit of the family.

Despite some sharing of power, it is primarily women's responsibility to organize and to invite other women to attend ratijagas, and women traveling to ratijagas are understood as having been invited by the women who host them. During this time in which women host women, hostesses effectively construct an overwhelmingly female space by excluding household men (though not children) from their vicinity and so claim authority for the division of social space.[20] Barring men, women assume control and define their physical and personal boundaries.

Denying men access when outsiders visit is an exertion of moral authority that effectively removes men and relegates them to the position of blind audience. Men outside the women's space can hear the songs women sing but cannot access or influence immediately the women who sing. Thus, for example, during a ratijaga I attended, when a middle-aged man from the hostesses' household peeked around the corner for a moment to see what was up, he was quickly banished by women, albeit gently and with much gaiety.

The power of women to shape the social world through their activities as hostesses inviting, arranging, and managing guests is much observed by writers with diverse agendas, including, for example, Stephanie Jamison, writing about Vedic ritual, but also Virginia Woolf, whose fictional hostesses make it clear that even a nonreligious party is an expression of self, truth, artistry, and power, particularly the power to create and guard social order.[21] Through invitation and hospitality, women construct a social sphere for themselves and their families: they build, break, and renegotiate alliances by including and honoring some while excluding and degrading others.

In this ephemeral world of women, which encompasses worlds exterior to it, *ratijaga* ritual enacts the passage of time in such a way as to shape the future for the holders of the *ratijaga*, by securing blessings but also by instructing others, including the household's daughters, who are often termed "guests" in, and who will marry out of, their natal households. Inviting both deities and other women, often accompanied by their children, women map and configure their social world, which exists both inside and outside their domiciles. In mapping, which both reflects and shapes or charts social interaction, women's rituals encompass and exclude certain people and deities and so define both social and theological realms.

The mapping of social relations is an explicit and common feature of *ratijaga* songs. Let us look, for example, at one *ratijaga* pamphlet's song for the hero Tejaji, whose name or history is not even mentioned in the song, except for the indexical, printed title, "Tejaji." This song lists various relations, such as sister and sister-in-law. Each is said to be a "big flower," though the role of conjugal flowers takes precedence over the natal flowers. Thus, the sister might give one a blouse, but a blouse's sleeve rips easily. By contrast, a sister-in-law gives one a blessing, and a blessing "lasts forever." The song goes on to map other familial relations and, while affirming the importance of natal ones, maintains the superiority of conjugal ones.[22]

Another song, which I heard at a *ratijaga* at the home of a girl who described her family as "little brother Rajput" (i.e., a family tracing its line from a younger brother of a ruler or nobleman and so not inheriting parental property according to the principle of primogeniture), clearly maps the social world represented and created by the performance of *ratijaga* ritual.[23] Naming participants and describing their participation, women count themselves present and render themselves responsible for the ritual that so many divinities are attending. The song reads as a veritable register of sociability in which everyone works together for the mutual procurement of blessings:

> Bhagvat Kanwar put the wick in the lamp.
> Mahavir Singh's wife filled it with butter.
> Light the lamp for the four watches of the night.

In this song, as in the *ratijaga* ritual, women are featured as agents with a shared purpose and an espoused cohesion that bonds family to family in terms of hospitality and responsibility. The song represents women as coalescing with other women to effect good fortune for the host family and also for the participants, who share in the benefits of ritual placation.[24] Like Amish men together building a barn for a recently married couple, these women conspire to give beneficiaries what they need for a bright future.

This social mapping could be construed to be inherently conservative. It could be seen as enforcing a code of cooperation that preserves patriarchal norms and so the status quo. And yet, by invoking names, it inscribes individual people onto the social map, and these individual people are not simply substitutable units. Named persons with discrete identities and histories, they are agents who presumably would not always agree with each other nor accept each other's lives uncritically. Furthermore, the song includes various people who perform the same function, whatever their relations to each other. Thus sisters and sisters-in-law are joined in purpose, even as social code, including code conveyed in the lyrics of *ratijaga* songs, may put these in tension.

Having argued that the world of women performing *ratijaga* ritual is far from private and that what goes on in one household has a charge or force that affects and helps to define other households, I turn to the final point: women's ritual praxis saturates the boundaries of domesticity, including multiple domiciles, and penetrates overtly public dynamics and institutions. In *Chocolat*, one woman making chocolates and selling them out of her home-cum-shop transforms the mayor, the church, and ultimately the entire town, whose members congregate joyously in the town square. Recalling that this is dramatic fiction, we might ask, are there any parallels?

There are many. Think about the fact that the epic *Pabuji*, which is performed publicly by Nayaks (often by a male-female pair), incorporates representations of Rajput women's songs into its episodes (*parvaros*) treating Pabuji's and Gogaji's marriages. Performing this epic in public places for diverse audiences, Nayak performers represent Rajput women as singing songs that summon the gods, as *ratijaga* songs do.[25] True, the Nayak singers may be viewed as co-opting the voices of Rajput *ratijaga* singers, but co-optation is often an act of power recognition and appropriation. Nayak performance of these songs represents Rajput women as having power, even as singers deploy power by representing them according to their performance agendas in songs that stand for, but in their dense narrativity little resemble, the *ratijaga* songs that Rajput women sing in their homes.[26]

Another example is the exportation of women's songs into various cultic contexts. In hero shrines, women, typically musicians but also women from diverse communities, sing *ratijaga* songs for Rajput heroes. One female musician, whom I watched perform many such songs in Udaipur, regularly sings *ratijaga* songs for the murdered prince Surtan Singh in a small, satellite temple.[27] During the annual festival for Surtan Singh in his imposing, main temple in Udaipur, other drumming and harmonium-playing women musicians come to sing songs for him and summon him to the festival, which culminates in a public *ratijaga*, attended by both men and women.

A similar situation is found at shrines for Bheru Singh, who was murdered by his relatives because he insulted them when he wore too fancy a coat for his status. Bheru Singh's memorial pavilion (*chhatri*) is to be found at Mewar's royal cremation ground in Ahar. There is also a temple for him in the mansion (*haveli*) once owned by Bheru Singh's family. Both shrines for this hero, who, like Surtan Singh, was murdered by order of the royal family, draws women singing songs that Rajput women sing in *ratijagas*.[28] Having taped and transcribed the songs, I showed the lyrics to a Rajput woman, who immediately recognized them and noted that they were "sexy." Like the lyrics sung for many other heroes, they describe the hero as exceedingly alluring.[29] The singing in a cultic context of songs that are sung by descendants of Rajput heroes at home surely represents Rajput women's ritual tradition as authoritative and invests Rajput women with the power to enact and claim authenticity in a culture that is heavily influenced by Rajput norms and values.[30]

Before leaving this discussion of lyrics sung by women in the homes of Rajput heroes' descendants but also performed in cultic shrines, let me note that the participants in such cults are of exceedingly diverse origins and so the dispersion of *ratijaga* songs is wide.[31] In cultic worship, people form impressions of Rajput heroic history and authority that are filtered through women's songs of praise and adoration.[32]

To Bheru Singh's Ahar shrine come men and women from various communities, including some Muslims and many Jains, among them the main *bhopa* (medium), who is regularly possessed by Bheru Singh. As Lawrence Babb has observed, Jain families have adopted martial heroes as emblematic of valorous conquest, even as they have transformed the image of these heroes from violent to virtuous warrior by investing them with Jain values, particularly, non-injury.[33] At the cult of Bheruji, this process occurs among Jain women, who worship at the shrine of a Hindu hero while espousing Jain identity and norms. Equally intriguing is the veneration at Bheruji's shrine by a young Muslim woman with whom I struck up a conversation while doing fieldwork. I asked her how she squared her veneration of a Hindu hero with her practice of Islam. She said that she was forbidden by Islam to worship an image and that she would not bring an image of Bheru Singh into her home, but that she can, and does, light a devotional *diya* (oil lamp) for him at home. This ritual act, she said, does not violate Islam or trouble her in-laws, whose welfare she aspires to promote through ritual veneration. In effect, she could perform her aniconic worship for the cultic hero at home, having taken from the cult her mental impression, based on his icon, the *bhopa*'s possession, and depictions in *ratijaga* songs.

Thus we see that the songs that women sing for their ancestral heroes at home are integrated into cultic praxis and help to represent, through verbal icons and descriptions of veneration, Rajput heroism in diverse cultic milieus. The impressions that women attending cultic rituals take away from their communal worship at shrines and bring back into their homes are a creative admixture formed from elements of *ratijaga* songs, other songs (such as *bhajans* and *aratis*), public worship of adorned images, and possession manifestations. Together, these impressions influence both cultic theology as construed by devotees (note the Muslim informant's theologizing) and also the form and nature of their individual domestic practice (in the Muslim woman's case, her deployment of a *diya* in lieu of an icon).

To conclude: women's *ratijaga* rituals are not simply a family affair. They are scenarios enacting public praxis. When guests are invited in, as they are for *ratijaga*s, the putative division between private and public space is suspended. Granted, not all of the public is allowed in, but that is true for many other public spaces, including businesses operating in public space but regarded as "private enterprises." Moreover, traveling between households, women witness ritual devotion and trade experiences: they exchange news, influence one another's views, and so color the lenses through which travelers will apprehend their own praxis and social interaction when they return to their own domestic spaces. Finally, the views and actions of women at home inform and influence what goes on outside the home. The words of women singing *ratijaga* songs in their homes are expressed, even as they are adapted, in the very public veneration of their culture's heroes, who in various ways reflect and shape cultural ethos. The words of women singing *ratijaga* songs at home breach walls to permeate public culture, with its fluid assumptions about and assessments of divinity and value.

NOTES

1. On this division elsewhere, see Buchanan 1996.
2. Daniels 1984.
3. Gottschalk 2000 and Flueckiger 1996.
4. For further reflections on the elasticity of *parda* see Harlan 1992.
5. My trip in 2002 provided many opportunities to discuss *parda* and its morphing into an increasingly multiform phenomenon, with individual families making increasingly liberal decisions about women's confinement, concealment, and mobility.
6. On the problematics of "tradition," see Appadurai et al. 1991.
7. On women's importation of goddesses, see Harlan 1992 and 2001.
8. See Harlan 2003, 41.
9. I have also heard the expression used with kilometers.
10. On the impact of television, see Steindorph 2004.
11. There are many variations of this legend. The account I employ here is one familiar in many of its elements to women living in Udaipur. For a discussion of variants of the Mira legend, see Harlan 1992, Mukta 1997, and Martin (forthcoming).

12. See Harlan 2001 and 1992.

13. For classic works on "everyday resistance," see Haynes and Prakash 1991, 1–22; and Scott 1985.

14. See Sussman 1994, 48–69; and 2000.

15. Her name also appears in English as "Avara" or Avari.

16. Harlan 2000 and 1992.

17. On the associations among these various deities in song, see Harlan 2003, ch. 5.

18. On the ritual complementarity of and the tension between women and Brahmins, see Harlan 1992 and forthcoming (b).

19. On this phenomenon and *itihas*, which often blends history with myth, see Harlan 2003.

20. In effect, they temporarily reestablish the *zanana*, the women's quarters of a traditional Rajput home in centuries past.

21. See, for example, *Mrs. Dalloway*; "The New Dress," esp. 64; and *To the Lighthouse*, esp. 94–97. I thank Julie Rivkin for instructive comments on Woolf's parties as "aesthetic moments" countering disorder, February 2002.

22. *Ratijaga Ku Git*, n.d.

23. Some of the Rajputs said they were reluctant to accept the claim of "little brother Rajput" without genealogical proof and presumed what they call "Daroga" provenance, that is to say, descent tracing back to a union between a Rajput man and a woman of another caste. See Harlan 2003.

24. For further reflection on this song and others, see Harlan 2003 and 1995.

25. For detailed analysis, see Harlan 2003.

26. On this appropriation, see Harlan 2000.

27. This woman refers to herself as a *rajgahak*, "royal singer," to dispense with any impression that she was ever merely a musician for hire by just anyone. Others refer to her as a Dholhin, a member of a "drummer caste"; she contests this designation.

28. On heroes, death, and agency, see Harlan 2003.

29. On lyrics, see Harlan 2003, ch. 5.

30. Harlan 2003, ch. 2.

31. It is not necessary to establish where such songs were composed originally; what matters, in terms of authority and as in the case of the songs in *Pabuji*, is the perception that the songs are ancestral songs.

32. Extensive analysis of the cults of Surtan Singh, Bheru Singh, and other Rajput heroes is to be found in Harlan forthcoming (a).

33. Babb 1996.

REFERENCES

Appadurai, Arjun, Frank J. Korom, and Margaret A. Mills. 1991. "Introduction." In *Gender, Genre, and Power in South Asian Expressive Traditions*, ed. Arjun Appadurai, Frank J. Korom, and Margaret A. Mills, 3–20. Philadelphia: University of Philadelphia Press.

Babb, Lawrence A. 1996. *Absent Lord: Ascetics and Kings in a Jain Ritual Culture.* Berkeley: University of California Press.

Buchanan, Constance. 1996. *Choosing to Lead: Women and the Crisis of American Values.* Boston: Beacon.

Chocolat. 2001. Directed by Lasse Halstrom. Miramax.

Daniels, Valentine. 1984. *Fluid Signs: Being a Person the Tamil Way.* Berkeley: University of California Press.

Flueckiger, Joyce Burkhalter. 1996. *Gender and Genre in the Folklore of Middle India.* Ithaca, NY: Cornell University Press.

Gottschalk, Peter. 2000. *Beyond Hindu and Muslim: Multiple Identity in Narratives from Village India.* New York: Oxford University Press.

Harlan, Lindsey. Forthcoming (a). *Lasting Impressions: Representing Heroism in Contemporary Hero Cults.* Manuscript under preparation.

————. Forthcoming (b). "Nala and Damayanti's Reversal of Fortune: Reflections on When a Woman Should Know Better." In *Nala and Damayanti*, ed. Susan S. Wadley and Joyce Flueckiger. New Delhi: Chronicle Books.

————. 2003. *The Goddesses' Henchmen: Gender in Indian Hero Worship.* New York: Oxford University Press.

————. 2001. "Battles, Brides, and Sacrifice: Rajput Kuldevis in Rajasthan." In *Is the Goddess a Feminist? The Politics of South Asian Goddesses*, ed. Kathleen Erndl and Alf Hiltebeitel, 69–90. Sheffield, England: Sheffield Academic Press.

————. 2000. "Heroes Alone and Heroes at Home: Gender and Intertextuality in Two Narratives." In *Invented Identities: The Interplay of Gender, Religion, and Politics in India*, ed. Julia Leslie and Mary McGee, 231–251. Delhi: Oxford University Press.

————. 1995. "Women's Songs for Auspicious Occasions." In *Religions of India in Practice*, ed. Donald Lopez, 269–280. Princeton, NJ: Princeton University Press.

————. 1992. *Religion and Rajput Women: The Ethic of Protection in Contemporary Narratives.* Berkeley: University of California Press.

Haynes, Douglas, and Gyan Prakash. 1991. "Introduction: The Entanglement of Power and Resistance." In *Contesting Power: Resistance and Everyday Social Relations in South Asia*, ed. Douglas Haynes and Gyan Prakash, 1–22. Berkeley: University of California Press.

Martin, Nancy. Forthcoming. *Mirabai Manifest: The Many Faces of a Woman Poet-Saint in India.* New York: Oxford University Press.

Mernissi, Fatema. 2001. *Sheherazade Goes West.* New York: Washington Square Press.

Mukta, Parita. 1997. *Upholding the Common Life: The Community of Mirabai.* Delhi: Oxford University Press.

Ratijaga Ka Git. n.d. Edited by Sarasvati Devi Bhensali and Jnandevi Teli. Ajmer: Sarasvati Prakasan.

Scott, James. 1985. *Weapons of the Weak: Everyday Forms of Peasant Resistance.* New Haven, CT: Yale University Press.

Steindorph, Sally. 2004. "Missed Messages: TV Producers and Rural Viewers Discuss the Representation of Villages on Indian Television." Paper delivered at the 18th European Conference on Modern South Asian Studies, Lund, Sweden, 6–9 July 2004.

Sussman, Charlotte. 2000. *Consuming Anxieties: Consumer Protest, Gender and British Slavery 1713–1833.* Palo Alto, CA: Stanford University Press.

———. 1994. "Women and the Politics of Sugar, 1792." *Representations,* no. 48 (Autumn): 48–69.

Woolf, Virginia. 1973. "The New Dress." In *Mrs. Dalloway's Party,* 61–73. New York: Harcourt.

———. 1927. *To the Lighthouse.* New York: Harcourt.

———. 1925. *Mrs. Dalloway.* New York: Harcourt.

5

Threshold Designs, Forehead Dots, and Menstruation Rituals: Exploring Time and Space in Tamil *Kolam*s

Vijaya Rettakudi Nagarajan

We make the *kolam* to indicate auspiciousness and to prevent ritual pollution.

—Janakimami, Tirunagar village

The *Kolam* on the Front Stoop and the Red Dot on the Forehead

Throughout the Hindu cultural and religious world of Tamilnadu, India, women's ritual drawings called *kolam*—ground rice-flour designs in white—mark space, including the thresholds of homes, the edges of streets, and trees. These women's ritual designs also mark time: dawn and dusk; the month of the winter solstice, or Markali; and the abundant rice harvest festival called Pongal. Sometimes outlined in red clay, and sometimes a matrix of dots circled by one curvaceous line, these *kolam*s are ubiquitous, drawn daily in public places by millions of Tamil female hands, and visible to everyone (figure 5.1).[1] Also abounding in everyday life is the visible ritual marking of the red dot floating in the middle of Tamil women's foreheads, the *pottu* as it is called in Tamil, or *bindi* in Hindi or Sanskrit. The design is usually a filled circle of red, or shades of burnt sienna, a reflection of its mercury oxide

FIGURE 5.1. A Tamil girl making a labyrinth *kolam*, Mayiladuthurai, Tamilnadu. Photo by Vijaya Nagarajan.

nature. Alongside these more traditional shades of dark red, *pottu* colors nowadays vary from parrot green to magenta, bright yellow, or colors that match the sari or the outfit one is wearing.[2]

It took me many years to realize that these two kinds of ritual designs are more intimately connected than I would have first imagined. They form a kind of kinship with each other; they mirror and echo each other as parallel ritual expressions of complicated and nuanced concepts, such as auspiciousness and inauspiciousness, purity and pollution (Carmen and Marglin 1985; Marglin 1985). These keywords are central to the understanding of the inherent ambivalence of expressive ritual power in Tamil women (Williams 1983).

As Mangalapatti from the village of Rengalachetty once said to me, "The *kolam* is the *pottu* of the house; the *pottu* is the *kolam* of the house. Do you understand how that is so?" Lakoff and Johnson have observed, "The essence of metaphor is understanding and experiencing one kind of thing in terms of another" (1980: 5). The visual presence of the *pottu, kolam,* and other forms of ritual traces of worship indicates that a space has been initiated for ritual purposes. A comparison of the *kolam* with the *pottu* can deepen our understanding of the way visual signs function metaphorically and spatially in Tamilnadu.

This chapter is an exploration of how ritual marks on the thresholds of homes and bodies mean what they mean. In my many conversations with Tamil women over the years, one of the leitmotifs was that the *kolam* on the front stoop "indicates auspiciousness and prevents ritual pollution." This binary encoding of meaning, presence indicating one state of being and absence another, is at the core of these domestic rituals. Their *presence* and *absence* enable *kolams* to carry meaning. The *pottu* on the forehead, when present, similarly communicates a state of auspiciousness. The absence of a *pottu*, on the other hand, may reflect a state of being which is soaked through with ritual pollution. I see these ritual marks now as a form of communication, a way of letting what is or what is not happening on the inside of the house or the body be visible to the outside world, akin to a silent but very visible announcement. Sometimes these binaries become indicative of the deeply ambivalent valences of women's ritual power, sometimes alluding to a woman's responsibility for death, primarily the death of her husband. These ritual markers act as a binder of sorts, bringing together a multitude of strands of local vernacular thinking of what it means to be a Tamil house, a Tamil woman householder, or a Tamil woman (Hart 1973, 1975; Daniels 1984; Wadley 1980).

This chapter explores two Hindu women's rituals that mark time and space in Tamilnadu. They are, in one case, a household ritual and, in the other, a ritual performed on the body. I argue here that these two public rituals embody Tamil Hindu women's interior states of being auspicious householders and, simultaneously, function as active vectors for sending forth positive intentionalities or activated blessings for the day, on the surface of both the home and the woman's body. This chapter expands the realm of the "domestic" to include the householder's physical body and the community beyond the threshold of the domicile by mapping correlations and correspondences between domicile and householder. The *kolam* and the dot become vehicles of communication beyond the threshold and have implications across the interiority and exteriority of thresholds by articulating in ritual time and space moments of emotional and physical transformation. This chapter knits together theories of auspiciousness/inauspiciousness and ritual purity/pollution with the appearance and the disappearance of the *kolam* and *pottu*.

How do the *kolam* and *pottu* define and articulate these differing axes of value, that is, auspiciousness/inauspiciousness and purity/pollution (Carmen and Marglin 1985; Marglin 1985)? The *kolam* functions as a key semiotic indicator on the Tamil cultural landscape, not only mapping the individual's passage from degrees of ritual purity and auspiciousness to those of ritual pollution, but also articulating the nonlinearly punctuated contours of a cosmology soaked through with auspiciousness and ritual pollution in ritual time and space; that is, sometimes one object may be auspicious, and another next to it inauspicious, and so on.[3] The *kolam* is linked to these categories in three important ways. First, its presence or absence prescribes social relationships, determining the boundaries of appropriate interactions between auspicious and inauspicious people, places, and objects. Second, its location marks several types of thresholds, both spatial and temporal, indicating the boundaries between auspicious and inauspicious worlds. And finally, discourse related to the *kolam* conjoins the notions of *mangala* (auspiciousness) and *amangala* (inauspiciousness), *mati* (ritual purity), and *turam* (particularly menstrual pollution of ritual distance) or *teetu* (generalized ritual pollution).[4] In this chapter, I focus on the active, fluid, and porous folk notions of auspiciousness and ritual pollution as they shape and constrain the domestic interactions of Tamil women.

Presence and Absence of the *Kolam* on the Front Stoop

The presence or absence of the *kolam* on the front stoop is equivalent to announcing that a household is open or closed to the world, a cultural category that sends off a capacious sense of hospitableness or hospitality, specifically, the willingness and ability to feed a stranger. By looking immediately at the front stoop, if I see a *kolam*, then I can imagine that a woman is functioning at a high level of open hospitality. If I were a wandering *sadhu* (an ochre-dressed holy man or woman), a minstrel, or a beggar, I could perhaps hope for a meal or some uncooked or cooked rice in my begging bowl. I could hope for and imagine a possible site of hospitality, an "open" household—healthy, functioning, perhaps holding a surplus of food, which can overflow outward into the community. Telegraphing receptivity and hospitality, the presence of the *kolam* indicates the ability of the household to serve as a welcoming, "feeding" host to strangers, visitors, and guests.

The presence of the *kolam* also indicates the sense that women's power to create a sphere of "positive intentionalities" moves in two directions: outward, to the world beyond the threshold, and inward, to the household. The auspicious power travels from women's hands through the *kolam* and upward into the bodies of those passing through its energy field, as they step over, around, or through the *kolam*. This capacity is especially significant during moments of women's ritual life-cycle ceremonies, articulating how and why the household may be seen as open. At particularly important life-cycle ceremonies, an overflow of generosity is imagined, required, and enacted. It is through the capacity of generosity that auspiciousness is generated.

Yet another way that the *kolam* communicates its presence is to infer the "good, auspicious" news from the inside of a woman's body, layered on the outside "skin" of the house itself. As one Tamil Brahmin woman, Padma, from the village of Aiyappur said:

> Listen, Vijaya, in the time before phones and telegraphs, the
> *kolam* was the way we found out what happened in the house dur-

ing the night. If there was a huge, *vishesham* [special] *kolam*, and
we knew that there was no wedding planned that day, then,
we may guess that the girl in the house has come of age or a
baby has been born.

It is clear from this that these huge *kolams*, reflecting either the birth of a child
or the first menstruation of a girl—events that are both auspicious and ritually
polluting—are, then, celebrated and announced publicly.[5]
 At the most visible level, the presence of a *kolam* on the threshold both
signifies and invites auspiciousness while keeping ritual pollution at bay. The
kolam, though announcing auspicious yet polluting events, also has the power
simultaneously to alleviate the pollution caused by the event. It indicates that
the woman of the house is "in" and that the household is successfully maintaining its everyday rhythm. In the words of an eighty-three-year-old Tamil
Brahmin Iyengar woman, Padma, in Srivilliputtur: "If someone dies, then, one
should not put the *kolam* for one year. Otherwise, you have to put the *kolam*
every day. If you do not put the *kolam*, it is *akkiyanam* [spiritual ignorance].
That means someone will die in your house. You should not not do the *kolam*.
You have to put the *kolam*." So, if the presence of the *kolam* is a generous
invitation for the outside world to come in, its absence indicates a closed
household—a site of suffering, death, or other ritually polluted or polluting
states of being. Usually during menstruation, after childbirth, if she is ill, or
when there has been a death in the family, a woman is not expected to make
the *kolam*. All of these ritual practices and their rules are not universally
applied but may shift and change, depending on the caste, class, and degree of
modernity adapted by the household. In some communities, childbirth is not
necessarily announced by a *kolam*, but in others it is. And so on.
 In Tamil culture, suffering is accepted as an inevitable part of everyday life,
and the *kolam* helps to structure the experience of suffering. As it was put
succinctly by one Tamil woman, whose family had migrated generations ago
to Kerala and still amazingly drew the *kolam* every day, "The *kolam* is done to
prevent future suffering, to be able to manage our current suffering, so, we
know when it is happening around us, to reduce tension, and a kind of meditation." The lack of a *kolam* announces a household's suffering to the community as a whole. The continued absence of the *kolam* signifies the gradual
ebbing of suffering in the family; the reappearance marks visually the end of
the period of suffering and ritual pollution. Veena Das's understanding of ex-
ternally oriented suffering, that is, suffering that originates from the outside, is
relevant here:

> [The external orientation] holds suffering to be accidental...
> holds existence to be blameworthy but points to the capriciousness
> of the gods, the inexplicability of the world, and the contingency of

life as the reasons for suffering. It does not make the sufferer inter-
nalize her suffering, nor does it posit a meaningful world or a just
god or a comprehensive scientific discourse within which suffering
can be made comprehensible. Dare one say that it gives irresponsi-
bility a positive sense? (1995: 139–140)

As part of the larger context of the experience of suffering in Tamilnadu,
the presence of the *kolam*, too, affirms a normal, well-functioning existence
and affirms the suffering person by its absence. In a world where both happiness and suffering are equally inexplicable, the ephemeral *kolam* represents
the capriciousness of the gods and the contingencies of life, and it helps to
attract neighbors and strangers to assist those in need. Besides indicating death,
a lack of a *kolam* on the stoop could indicate a menstruating woman under-
going a period of incapacity and, therefore, the possibility of a woman experiencing pain and suffering during her menstruation.

In conclusion, the presence or absence of a *kolam* on a threshold visually
cues people about what to expect and how to behave; for example, the absence
of the *kolam* may catalyze looking in on the household and bringing gifts of
food, clothing, or comfort. By its absence, the *kolam* prescribes a supportive
response to suffering, engendering a responsibility to enter the ritually polluted
household in an empathetic emotional state. In this way, the *kolam* alleviates
suffering by structuring the community's response in situations of grief, pain,
and loss. The Hindu concepts of auspiciousness and ritual pollution and their
reflection within the *kolam* on the stoop make possible the recognition and
celebration of joy and the detection of and support for suffering. It might be
said that the visual sign of the *kolam* affirms life by its presence and affirms
suffering by its absence. As Clifford Geertz observes, "[T]he problem of suffering is, paradoxically, not how to avoid suffering, but how to suffer, how to
make of physical pain, personal loss, physical defeat, or the helpless contem-
plation of others' agony something bearable, supportable—something, as we
say sufferable" (1973: 104). Therefore, one can say that the *kolam* may be a
sign of a community's perceptive control over chaos, pollution, and suffering
(Hart 1973, 1975). By providing an orientation to the emotional state of the
household, the *kolam* imposes a pattern on the community landscape that reveals the contours of satisfaction, happiness, and suffering in each individual
household.

The *Pottu*, or Dot on the Forehead

Commonly consisting of one or two red dots and occasionally a black line, the
pottu is actually a multitude of signs that telegraph relevant cultural information to informed viewers. The *pottu* varies in frequency, style, and color,

according to caste, religion, class, and marital status. For example, the *pottu* reveals whether a woman is old or young, maritally available or unavailable. The *pottu*'s communications function to guide people's behavior in relation to a woman, letting them know whether they can tease her as a sister or must bow down with respect.

When the Dot on the Forehead Is Present

If a girl wears a red *pottu*, this signifies that she is past her first menstruation and is therefore eligible for betrothal and eventual marriage. The red color of the *pottu* has both a literal and metaphorical significance. In Tamil culture, red is usually worn after a girl has passed the stage of "blood magic," or puberty (Buckley and Gottlieb 1988). One of the key colors of the sari worn during the wedding ceremony, red also symbolizes the potential and actual power of sexuality. Among certain subcastes, if a woman is wearing two red *pottus*—one in the center of her forehead and the other at her hairline—this signifies that she is married. Stella Kramrisch has observed a similar significance for the color red in the *kolam*, too, pointing out that the threshold zone is "protected by the design traced on the floor in an unbroken line forming loops and enclosures, each marked by a dot in its center, the dot being a symbol of the seed, the source of life. Sometimes the threshold is dressed in red dots, similar to the red dot commonly seen on an Indian woman's forehead. The dot is a symbol of blood, the source of life" (1985: 105; 1983).

The woman of the household is well aware that her power stems from her ability to create auspiciousness, and she wears indicators to acknowledge this fact, such as the *pottu* (or *bindi*), *tali* (wedding necklace), toe rings, or henna on her hands and feet (Reynolds 1980). Each morning, after her "purification" bath and before she puts the new *pottu* on her forehead, a woman may offer a prayer for the longevity of her present or future husband. Indeed, some Hindu women believe that placing the *pottu* on their forehead has a positive impact on the length of life of their husband, present or future. A woman is considered to have the ability to keep her husband alive, and therein lies some of her power as the bearer and container of auspiciousness. After her bath, she is also considered to be in a nonpolluting state, capable of personal and household generosity to the community. Red dots may be placed on the foreheads of both men and women to signal a recent visit to a household or temple shrine. Red powder may also be smudged onto new clothes in gratitude to the goddess Lakshmi, for her generosity. It is important, however, to note that these signifiers have less importance in contemporary times as these kinds of markings have shifted from an emphasis on ritual meanings to an emphasis on beauty. Therefore, these signifiers have come, increasingly, to transcend caste, class, and religious affiliation.

When the Dot on the Forehead Is Absent

A black line on the forehead generally indicates a prepubescent girl, who is still considered a child. This status implies that she is "tease-able" and able to receive gifts from anyone in the community with no special meaning attached. If an adult Hindu woman is not wearing a *pottu*, it is likely that she is a widow. However, if other signs do not corroborate this (such as wearing a beige or white sari and no jewelry), then the absence of a *pottu* could indicate that a woman is menstruating, in a state of mourning, or perhaps just too busy working to put on a *pottu*. Christian or Muslim women do not usually wear the *pottu*, although some do so as a fashion statement.

Two Memories of Absence

I have a personal interest in the concept of ritual pollution, which stems from a lifelong awareness of its multifaceted nature within Indian culture. I am especially intrigued by practices associated with menstrual pollution. To some, women's isolation during the state of menstrual ritual pollution may seem like an inconvenience or insult, a perspective with which I partially agree. But I would suggest that this isolation can also be simultaneously and paradoxically a period of welcome rest and conviviality. The positive or ambivalent aspects of practices associated with ritual pollution are rarely reflected in fieldwork accounts of childbirth, menstruation, or death. I will share two personal stories that hint at the underlying emotional paradoxes of rituals informed by this concept.

One of my earliest encounters with the idea of ritual pollution took place in our ancestral village, Rettakudi, when I was nine years old in 1970. Our family had just returned to India from a four-year hiatus in America and had quickly resettled in Rettakudi for the summer. I adapted easily to the Tamil language and culture, which were integral to our home life in both India and America. A few weeks after we arrived, however, a strange event happened to me: I lost my mother. Whenever I asked my father or grandparents where she was, they would look away as though I had asked a very embarrassing question. Curious and sad, I thought my elders were hiding something from me. I searched everywhere but couldn't find her, so I concluded that my mother must have either run away or died.

The next day, I decided to follow my grandmother all around the house, at a discreet distance. After we had eaten in the afternoon, and all the family members were moving to their respective corners for napping, I noticed my grandmother putting together a simple meal of rice and vegetables, wrapping it carefully in banana leaves. She walked out the back of the house, through the cowshed that circled the house, and on toward the front. I followed her, wondering whom she was on her way to feed so surreptitiously. Standing behind the door of the cowshed, I watched her walk across the dusty wayside path and place the small bundle before the threshold of an adobe hut that I had never noticed before. Her gestures were distant, as if she were making an offering to a goddess or an Untouchable.

To my surprise, she called out my mother's name and announced, "The food is here! Is everything going well?" My mother's voice, restful and contemplative, answered softly with a faint ring, as if from a distance, "I'm fine, *amma*, thanks. How is everything out there?" My grandmother replied in an amused tone, "Your eldest daughter, Vijaya, is giving us trouble. She keeps thinking you have disappeared. She doesn't at all understand what is going on. Don't you teach her anything useful in America?" I was deliriously happy to hear my mother's voice at last. "She is alive after all!" I thought. "I hear her voice, and now I must see her. Or maybe she is just a ghost from the dead."

As soon as my grandmother returned to the main house, I saw my mother's bangled hand reach tentatively across the threshold to pick up her food. The shadow of her form appeared and disappeared so quickly that I wondered if I had only imagined it. Leaping across the threshold of the hut, I felt as if I were on a dangerous mission to rescue my mother and return her to the main house. I pushed open the heavy wooden door into the very dark room and was about to dash into her lap, crying out with joy, laughing. But, barely seeing my mother's form lying in a shadow-laden, dusty corner through the light of the kerosene lamp, I hesitated, disturbed by what I saw. My mother was frowning and seemed angry with me, and I noticed she had no *pottu* on her forehead. She looked different, with her hair unbound and in disarray, and relaxed, away from the prying eyes of a dense household community.

On seeing me, she said sharply, "Shoo! Get out, you silly monkey child! You shouldn't be here."

"But, *amma*, I thought you had died!" I blurted out, jumping happily into her lap. "Why are you here? Is this where you have been all this time? Nobody would tell me where you were. I am so happy you are still alive! Can I take you back to the main house now?"

"No," she replied:

> Don't touch me. I hope no one saw you. I am *turam* [distant]; no one can touch me now. Listen: don't tell your grandmother you came here. She would be very upset if she knew. But it is probably all right; you're still a child so it shouldn't affect you. But don't tell anyone you have seen me. I am *turam*. . . . later I will tell you what that means. I promise to be back tomorrow. Just think that your mother didn't have to work for three days, and she's having some quiet resting time. So, run off my foolish little monkey—and be sure to wash your hands and body wherever it touched mine. But don't go in through the front door of the house. Enter the backyard through the

cowshed at the side of the house, and wash at the water pump. Then wait awhile before you touch your grandmother. She is *madi* [pure], you know.

Puzzled and disturbed by her behavior and her stern tone of voice, unusual in my mother's normally indulgent self, I rose out of my mother's lap, walked backward out of the mud hut, and washed as she had instructed. Then I ran into the main house and immediately demanded of my grandmother, "What is my *amma* doing in that other house? Why have you put her there?"

She replied with the mysterious word *turam* again. She added, "For three days your *amma* will be in the other house, and then she will come out and join us on the fourth day, after she's washed her hair. Then she can eat with us again."

From that day onward, I began to notice the sudden disappearance and reappearance of other women to and from the small huts scattered throughout the village, set apart from the houses. The neighboring women would bring food to these huts for each other, and a few days later the mothers, wives, and daughters would return with glistening wet hair, once again considered "touchable." And then they would go back to work hard in the domestic chores of an extended household.

As I spent my childhood traveling between India and North America, two overlapping, yet distinct, codes of ethics, attitudes, and world views trailed me from one dislocation to another. I was in one place, then the other, each place continuing to mark me even when I was not there. Then, when I was a teenager, we settled down in suburban Maryland. Whenever American friends crossed the threshold to our home, their first comments were invariably about the *kolams* that my mother created on the threshold each morning. "What is that?" "Can I step on it?" they would always ask. Of the *pottu* I wore most days on my forehead, my friends would ask "whether it was blood," with an echo of disgust and disbelief. Or, if I were discovered to be indeed wearing a red dot with intentionality, the questions would inevitably come: "Why was I wearing it? Did I have to put it on every single day? What does it mean?" and so forth. I struggled as best as I could to answer their questions. I kept on wearing it, as I could not imagine doing otherwise.

If one of the women in our house was *veetil illai*, or "not in the house" (menstruating), or if we all were "not in the house," my astonished and puzzled friends would witness my father walking briskly back and forth between the kitchen and the living room serving all of us tea, sweets, and the cooked food he had prepared. He would discreetly set the food down at a suitable distance from himself; we would wait until he moved away, and only then would we proceed to eat. We had become *turam*.

Whenever I think of menstrual time, an amusing image comes to mind: my father backing away from us when we stretched playfully our hands to him over the threshold of our ritually polluted spaces and encroached upon his ritually pure space. He would retreat, beseeching us to stop, saying with fear and annoyance, "Do not touch me, do not come closer!" as if even the intersection of the ritually pure and impure would cause him enormous pain or destroy him in some way. The look of terror in his eyes was not a look we saw often. As a teenager, it made me feel powerful to think that I could make my father fear me because I was a woman who had become *turam*. That "touch" was itself dangerous somehow intrigued me; yet I also questioned daily the very basis of the distinction between pure and impure. So what if women were menstruating; why couldn't they still be priests in the temple? What had menstruation to do with purity? I wondered to myself and argued with others, including our local Hindu temple priests, often. Why was menstruation celebrated and honored the very first time it occurred, then hidden underground, like a golden, auspicious spring which was named temporarily "untouchable"?

Since menstruating women are not allowed near spaces where gods and goddesses are housed (in temples and kitchens), my menstruating sisters and I could not touch anything in the kitchen and consequently could not do much housework. I remember the times spent "not in the house" as restful, unruly, indulgent, and playful—periods when we were permitted to be lazy and to reflect on our lives in America. All three of us were treated particularly well; we were served tea, food, and sweets and our wishes were fulfilled. When the fourth day arrived, we would take our head baths and become ritually pure again, losing our special space of quiet and rest.

Reflecting on this experience, it is not difficult to see that this kind of bodily experience of ritual pollution has its mix of positive and negative valences in terms of women's sacredness and ritual power. The emotional and cultural ambiguity and paradox of women's ritual domestic power plays itself out through these kinds of lived experiential and bodily narratives, a subtle weaving of power and powerlessness, a valorizing of female auspiciousness, on the borderlines of temporary "untouchability" and "touchability," in the Indias and Americas of my own and other Indian women's pasts, resurrected only in memories, a series of nodes and experiences, in tandem and counterpoint to sealed theories and understandings.

In conclusion, we can draw the following analogy: the *pottu* is to the body as the *kolam* is to the house. So, the *house:kolam::body:pottu*. Just as the *kolam* marks the threshold between the interior of the household and the community outside, the *pottu* on the forehead marks the threshold between the internal body/soul and the external world. The same visual metaphor can be observed in the red henna applied to the hands and feet as ritual markers of ceremonial time and space, as in marriage ceremonies. The significance of the literal and metaphorical edges of the body is elaborated in folktales, proverbs, notions of hospitality, and the many stories about the inauspicious consequences if a woman does not put a *kolam* on her threshold or a *pottu* on her forehead.

Marking Thresholds of Space and Time

In addition to its presence and absence, another way the *kolam* articulates concepts of auspiciousness/inauspiciousness and purity/pollution is through its location in space and time. The thresholds on which the *kolam* appears are both spatial and temporal, indicating the boundaries between auspicious and inauspicious realms and periods.

Spatial Thresholds

The spatial threshold is a powerful metaphor in Indian secular and ceremonial life, a charged location between ritually pure and impure or between auspicious and inauspicious places. The *kolam* is created at three types of spatial thresholds: (1) the household shrine in the kitchen, (2) the entrance to the main house, and (3) the entrance to village temples.

The *kolam* at the household shrine in the kitchen marks the women's domain, creating a threshold between the kitchen activities and the separate and sacred space of the divinities that inhabit the shrine. The gods face the worshipper from the east (the most highly valued sacred direction), and the worshipper prays toward the glancing gods. In relation to the rest of the house, the kitchen is considered to be the abode of the gods and goddesses in the secular world of the householder. The place where the food is prepared is the center where all the family's ritual activities are commenced, maintained, and completed. In fact, the entire women's cooking area is the literal and metaphorical hearth—the spiritual and psychological core of the household and the most valued site for the production of auspiciousness. Architecturally, the kitchen is also the most protected part of the household. One of the few fully walled and bounded rooms, it is the most distant from the outside world (Blier 1995).

The second type of *kolam* is created on and beyond the threshold of the main body of the house, facing the village path and dividing inside and outside, known and unknown, safe and unsafe worlds. As we have seen, the key site for a *kolam* is the front entrance to the house, distinguishing inside from outside, household from commons, and private from public. *Kolams* on household shrines and interior thresholds mark the movement of family members from the inner sanctum through all the interior doorways to the front door—the place where the house meets the exterior world. Proceeding down the village street, one can observe that each household in an auspicious state of being is marked with a *kolam*. Between sacred and profane, auspicious and inauspicious, controllable and uncontrollable, the threshold guards the house from the chaos of the outside world. The *kolam* on the front of the house demarcates the ritually polluted commons from the private, domesticated household space.

Shulman has eloquently referred to the *kolam* as a protective, invisible, three-dimensional screen in front of the house, which is seen through its visible, two-dimensional form. He points to the threshold area as the "point at which it [the *kolam*] emerges into form—a complex form at that, carefully planned and executed, a reflection of some inner labyrinth externalized here at the boundary, the line dividing the inner and the outer, the pure from the chaotic" (1985: 3). This type of *kolam* may also be seen as a visual metaphor for the division of the commons, the shared public civil space, from the controlled and contained space of the home and, therefore, metonymically, the woman of the house.

The third type of *kolam* is made at the village temple, where it carefully delineates each temple threshold from the preceding one and from the world outside. Approaching a South Indian temple, one observes that a *kolam* marks each threshold for the advancing worshipper, from the outer entrance to the innermost "womb chamber" of the divinities. This sequence of *kolams* marks the passage of worshippers as they travel to the interior shrine to visit the gods and goddesses and to receive *darshan*, or blessing (Eck 1985). At the edge of the village community, the temple may be conceptualized as a giant, three-dimensional *kolam* marking the threshold where the village ends and the "outside" world begins. Here again, the *kolam* maps the journey from a ritually polluted space to a ritually pure space.

The designs of *kolams* drawn in the kitchens, doorways, and temples reflect symbolic *tirthas* (crossings)—that is, spaces to be crossed with a consciousness of the sacred (Eck 1981). When a space has been sacralized, this affects people's behavior in ways that are characterized by ritual hospitality and auspiciousness. *Kolams* at the front entrance to the house are made as an offering and blessing, to be stepped on and erased slowly under passing feet. In the words of one Tamil woman, "Stepping on the *kolam* is like stepping into the Ganges River."

Another woman said emphatically, "Stepping on the *kolam* is akin to taking a bath in the sacred Ganges River, an act that purifies body and spirit." But, it is important to point out that not everyone steps on the *kolam*; many walk around it, so they do not step directly on it and smudge it, revealing its increasing presence as more and more a symbol of beauty, rather than its many ritual aspects. On the other hand, a *kolam* should not be stepped on if it is located at the center of a sacred space, such as a household shrine or a temple before a deity, because it is believed to be highly charged with divine energy. *Kolams* made at household shrines function as porous boundaries between earthly and divine realms, while those made at temples are part of a continuum of sacrality.

Temporal Thresholds

It is crucial that the *kolam* be created before the sun rises every day, when darkness is transformed into light, at a time of betwixt and between. Dawn exercises a particular sort of ritual imagination. The time between four and five-thirty in the morning is called *brahma-murti* or *brahma-muhurtam,* "the time of God's face," when the deities turn their faces toward humans. The *kolam* is a visual, aesthetic signal designed to attract the gaze of the divinities. Thus the *kolam* marks the temporal threshold between night and day.

Perhaps the *kolam* could be considered a parallel version of the male yogic positions of the *surya asana,* "the worship of the sun." In fact, the ritual practice of drawing a symbol on the ground to worship the sun is mentioned in the Rig Veda. According to the art historian Stella Kramrisch:

> The most ancient Sanskrit treatise on Indian painting pre-
> scribes the worship of the sun god through an eight-petaled
> lotus flower drawn on the ground. Several Puranas speak of
> the art of drawing the sun on the ground and that the sun was
> worshipped in a circle in early days. However, this practice was
> not sanctioned by the Vedas; it belonged to those outside the
> Vedic pale. The drawing of a magic diagram on the floor, how-
> ever, became essential in building a Hindu temple. (1983:
> 105–107)

Madan, a social anthropologist, points out one of the congruencies be-tween auspiciousness and temporal location:

> There are many auspicious and inauspicious moments in
> one's life, just as there are in a day. The most auspicious mo-
> ment of the day is the rising of the sun. It fills the earth, the sky,
> and the heavens with light and brings with it the promise of good
> works and wisdom for men. . . . Sunrise manifests the glory of
> God, enlivens our intelligence, and purifies the whole earth.
> (1987: 48)

In addition to demarcating the boundary between night and day, the *kolam* serves another important temporal function. The month of the winter solstice from mid-December to mid-January (Markali) is the time of year when the sun travels at its lowest point in the sky. At this time, *kolam* making marks both the sun's nadir and the zenith of the Tamil agricultural cycle. Markali is considered to be the month that spans one day in the life of a divinity. In other words, if one year in human experience is equivalent to one day in the community of gods and goddesses, Markali is the beginning of the new divine day.

At the end of the Markali month and the beginning of the Thai month is a threshold period that is celebrated with the Pongal festival, the most popular festival across castes and classes. This is a highly auspicious time for the community, signifying the abundance of the fields during the harvest. In the village Krishnagudi, Chellamma, a young *dalit* ("Untouchable") woman who lived in a lovely home with beautiful squash plants gracing the side and roof of the house, expressed the sense of joyful anticipation at this time of year:

> The *ammans* [goddesses] are coming.... We feel this is when everything good is coming. The happiness ... is coming. Food is coming. Children are coming. Wealth is coming. Beauty is where the divine comes. Rice is turned in. The fields are brimming over with the harvests. It is when we are at the wealthiest time of our year and most hopeful of financial security.

Because of its beauty, the *kolam* is the focalized site where the divinities are hosted by the woman of the household.

Kolam making reaches its annual peak during Markali and its monthly peak during the Pongal festival, when the best and most elaborate *kolams* are created. Drawing the *kolam* in rice flour becomes the event of the day, creating in the end a sense of fine white lace cloth draping over every surface imaginable. The month of Markali is an auspicious time for honoring divinities but an inauspicious time for human celebrations. As one elderly Tamil woman put it:

> The reason we create such elaborate *kolams* during the month of Markali is because the threshold, the doorway between heaven and earth, is the most open during this time. It is the time to communicate with the gods and goddesses. That is why we go on pilgrimage during that time. It is also a great time to die, because you automatically go to heaven. It is a bit like dying on the banks of the Ganga.

On the other hand, Markali is considered to be a highly inappropriate time for getting married because one's energies should be devoted to spiritual rather than material matters.

The *kolam* also signals the temporal rhythms of families, communities, castes, regions, and religions. Certain castes and religious traditions may have family or lineage commitments to particular astrological calendars, and the elaboration and density of the *kolam* patterns indicate special days of celebration. For example, Christian families might make substantially larger and denser *kolams* on Christmas Day. Or, Hindu orthodox castes may mark the period between mid-July and mid-August with dense *kolams*, and other families or castes may mark the festivals of individual saints or animal deities such as snakes.

Mapping Auspiciousness and Ritual Pollution

While the degree of ritual pollution can be inversely related to the degree of auspiciousness, the demarcations between ritually polluted and auspicious states are complex. As mentioned earlier, menstruation and childbirth are auspicious, life-affirming conditions, though paradoxically they are situated in a ritually polluted state of being (Marglin 1985; Das 1995; Madan 1987; Carmen and Marglin 1985). Additionally, death is usually considered to be inauspicious and ritually polluting—although even this state is ambiguous because it is linked to the reproduction of the family lineage. For example, days of worship that commemorate the dates of ancestors' deaths are considered to be ritually polluted *and* auspicious, since these occasions focus on both the loss of family members and the continuation of blood kinship ties. In most cases, the *kolam* reflects the conjoining of states of being that are auspicious and "pure," that is ritually nonpolluting. That is why the *kolam* is *not* made when women are menstruating or when there is a death in the family, to show that the household is presently not hospitable. There are two exceptions, however. First, when a girl attains her first menstruation, a huge feast is made, a giant *kolam* is created, food is served, and so forth. And second, when a child is born, then, too, a huge *kolam* is made, though in this case food is brought in by neighbors, because childbirth is considered to be a state of incapacity and closed hospitality.[6]

The Role of Domesticity in Hindu Everyday Life

One of the most critical ways to understand the role that ritual pollution plays in Tamil Hindu women's social spaces is to understand the role and ideology of the householder in Hindu traditional life. Female householders may in some circumstances hold an equivalent, complementary, ritual importance to male householders in Hindu everyday life. Especially when we look at them from the perspective of women's narratives of their own rituals, these women's rituals become charged with an intense celebration of women's sense of their own female importance and vitality. It is also important to note the ideology of the householder and its hold on women's ritual lives.

The Ideology of the Householder

The state of the household, the pragmatics of everyday life, and the concern for material existence are all part of the making of the *kolam*, the affixing of the *pottu*, and the performance of many of the rituals that signify the life of the householder. The importance of the householder has been eclipsed by the ascetic in scholarly treatises. In the West, there has long been a fascination with the *sadhu*, the wandering monk who renounces the world in search of pure truth and understanding. By contrast, the householder, a worldly character, is a much more realistic and popular expression of Hindu personal conduct and moral life.

Madan's detailed and wonderful ethnography, a landmark study of nonrenunciation in the community of Kashmiri Brahmin men, may apply here. He notes:

> The figure in the centre of the stage is a rather homely character, namely, the householder [*grhastha*]. If not exactly cast in a heroic mould, he is not the "phantom-like" man either that Dumont (1966: 48) considers him to be. It is the ideal of his life to "live in the world" but to do so in the light of the renouncer's philosophy (see Dumont 1970: 12, 41, et passim). Translated into the householder's idiom, renunciation becomes the twin ideals of self-possession and detachment in the midst of worldly involvements, which are not considered by him evil in themselves. What he seeks to resist is being enslaved by such involvements. He hopes to mediate between total indulgence and total renunciation. It is, indeed, all a matter of relations. (1987: 2–3)

In the idiom of the nonrenounced realm of the householder, the *kolam* ritual can be seen as an "affirmation of a disciplined this-worldly life as the good life" (Madan 1987: 3). It expresses everyday concerns, hopes, and desires, such as good health and prosperity within the family. Many women with whom I spoke articulated the view that the *kolam* brings not only auspiciousness and goodness, but also the orientation of disciplining earthly desires. The householder must always be aware of binding her or his desires, constantly incorporating ascetic values into daily life. This relates to Madan's interpretation of the religious ideology of the householder as one who "acknowledges the sovereignty of good: the desired must be brought under the regime of, and encompassed by, the preferred" (3). The continuity of domestic life is at the heart of the notion of auspiciousness.

Lakshmi is the goddess of auspiciousness, or *mangala*, which includes good luck, wealth, wakefulness, alertness, quickness, and abundance. When Lakshmi is invited in by the woman of the household, a portion of the divine auspiciousness is transferred to the earthbound realm of the woman householder. Indeed, the woman of the household is often referred to as the Lakshmi of the house. Like the goddess, the woman has the power to attract wealth and prosperity into the household and to prevent poverty from crossing the threshold. Since the householder is seen as the creator of *mangala*, when domestic life is interrupted, the flow of auspiciousness also comes to a halt. This interruption in the flow of auspiciousness from the goddess Lakshmi to the woman of the house-hold, and its further effect, to the household itself, is usually attributed to her generally unbeloved sister, the goddess Mudevi, or Jyestha. Mudevi is the god-dess of sleep, restfulness, laziness, ill luck, poverty, and scarcity (see Leslie 1991; Nagarajan 1993).

Within the domain of the *kolam*, domesticity reigns in the model of the woman householder as the source of the flow of auspiciousness throughout the community. Creating the *kolam* is an active way for Tamil women to ar-ticulate their desires daily. It is a form of prayer in which the women of the household directly communicate their intentions to Lakshmi, the goddess of prosperity, beauty, and good fortune. Madan discusses the nature of this type of intentionality:

> The distinction between the state of auspiciousness and the crea-tive agent . . . is most important as is the relation between the two. . . . The point to note about these usages and similar others is that it is not the person himself or herself who is auspicious but rather his or her intentions, actions, or even merely the pres-ence (and witnessing the same), which are so and are, therefore, expected to have happy consequences. The ultimate source of aus-piciousness is, of course, the divinity. (Madan 1987: 53–54)

Therefore, the notion of auspiciousness is itself bound with positive inten-tions, actions that are themselves expected to be seething with goodness, and is likely to spread all around (Nagarajan 2000: 565–566).

The Moral and Good Life

In conclusion, the *kolam* then is a sign that proclaims a Tamil woman householder's moral status, separating the woman of the house from those who have chosen not to take the householder path. It helps to give us a clue perhaps to the puzzle of why a Hindu woman does not need to do any puri-fying rituals before she makes the *kolam*, as she would in most other rituals. The *kolam* celebrates the female body in its potential or actualized sexual state, rising directly from the marital—or, perhaps, premarital—bed, and it an-nounces this bodily state directly through its material form. The lack of need to purify the body to make the auspicious *kolam* makes sense, for it is not purity that the *kolam* embodies, but rather the auspicious, sexually satisfied or po-tentially satisfied woman who is within the moral and cultural social bounds of householder life. As one municipal sweeper woman in the medieval town of Thanjavur shouted out to me as she swept up the dirt of the day before, "Hey, I hear you are asking everyone why we are doing the *kolam*. I will tell you why. It shows you slept in your own house that night, that you woke up there."[7] She grinned and laughed, with great merriment. And all of the women sitting around me on a porch also laughed. When I looked up to find her, to continue our conversation once I had gathered my work supplies, she had swirled out of my line of sight. And I could not find her again, though her voice rang in my head for years to come. What did she mean by that statement?[8]

The ritual principle of auspiciousness is embedded in cultural notions of morality, value, and the meaning of life. Madan observes that the notion of auspiciousness is bound with the life worth living: "For the common Pandit, the life of the man-in-the-world—epitomized in the role of the householder—though arduous, is the moral and good life. It is a life worth living" (1987: 47). Tamil female householders equally substantiate their desires for a "moral and good life" through the daily practices of banishing laziness and attracting status, wealth, material possessions, health, children, good fortune, and other forms of auspiciousness. The *kolam* and its ritual parallel, the *pottu*, or red dot, according to many Tamil women with whom I spoke, are visual and aesthetic statements that "we are living in the world and experiencing life fully; we want to be free from poverty and ritual pollution and have a life worth living." The assumption is that weaving thoughts and words into designs has the power to shape reality.

NOTES

An earlier version of this chapter was presented at the Annual Meeting of the American Academy of Religion in Kansas City in 1991. I want to thank my mother, Pichammal Nagarajan; Alan Dundes; Elizabeth Collins; the Fulbright-Hays Dissertation Research Award (1992–1994); Frederique Apffel Marglin; and Harvard University's Women's Studies in Religion Fellowship (2001–2002) Program and all the wonderful fellows. I want especially to thank the editor of this volume, Tracy Pintchman, for inviting me to present this paper on the panel "Women's Rituals, Women's Lives" in 2002 at the University of Wisconsin South Asia Conference and for inviting me to contribute to this book, and I thank the careful and thoughtful anonymous reviewer at Oxford University Press for making a dense web of wonderful suggestions, some of which I took and all of which made me think hard about what I was trying to do, though I alone am responsible for any errors.

Most of all, I thank my husband and companion for these many years, Lee Swenson, and our two children, Jaya and Uma, who have been eagerly pressing for the *kolam* work to come forth.

1. For a broader view of the *kolam* and an exploration of other related aspects, see Nagarajan 1993, 1998a, 1998b, 2000, and 2001, among others; and Kramrisch 1983.

2. The *pottu* has counterparts for men, although they take different forms and reveal different kinds of knowledge.

3. For example, a large *kolam* outlined in red *kavi* (from a reddish soft powder) signifies the highest degree of auspiciousness (first menstruation, marriage, childbirth, and so forth) in an upper-caste household.

4. These terms mostly apply to upper-caste households; further research is needed to understand how these categories would work from the position of multiple-caste households.

5. Marglin 1985, Carmen and Marglin 1985, and others have argued that events and bodies may be both auspicious and polluting, including acts of menstruation, sexuality, childbirth, and certain kinds of auspicious deaths.

6. For some other critically important texts on the complex valences with which to read menstrual and ritual pollution practices around the world, see Buckley and Gottlieb 1988; Douglas 1984.

7. See Nagarajan 1993 for a fuller explanation.

8. There are numerous stories of the powers of chaste Tamil women. The classical Tamil texts of the *Shilapadikaram* and *Manimekalai* come to mind.

REFERENCES

Blier, Suzanne Preston. 1995. *African Vodun: Art, Psychology and Power*. Chicago: University of Chicago Press.
Buckley, Thomas, and Alma Gottlieb, eds. 1988. *Blood Magic: The Anthropology of Menstruation*. Berkeley: University of California Press.
Carmen, John, and Frederique Apffel Marglin, eds. 1985. *Purity and Auspiciousness in Indian Society*. Leiden: Brill.
Daniels, Valentine. 1984. *Fluid Signs: Being a Person the Tamil Way*. Berkeley: University of California Press.
Das, Veena. 1995. *Critical Events: An Anthropological Perspective on Contemporary India*. New York: Oxford University Press.
Douglas, Mary. 1984 [1966]. *Purity and Danger: An Analysis of the Concepts of Pollution and Taboo*. London: Ark.
Dumont, Louis. 1966. *Homo Hierarcchicus: Essai sur le systeme des castes*. Paris: Gallimard.
Eck, Diana. 1981. India's *Tirthas*: "Crossings" in Sacred Geography. *History of Religions* 20, no. 4: 323–344.
———. 1985. *Darsan: Seeing the Divine Image in India*. Chambersburg, PA: Anima.
Geertz, Clifford. 1973. *The Interpretation of Cultures*. New York: Basic.
Hart, George L. 1973. "Woman and the Sacred in Ancient Tamilnad." *Journal of Asian Studies* 32: 233–250.
———. 1975. *The Poems of Ancient Tamil: Their Milieu and Their Sanskrit Counterparts*. Berkeley: University of California Press.
Kramrisch, Stella. 1983 [1968]. "Unknown India: Ritual Art in Tribe and Village." In *Exploring India's Sacred Art*, ed. Barbara Stoler Miller, 85–120. Philadelphia: University of Pennsylvania Press.
———. 1985. "The Ritual Arts of India." In *Aditi: The Living Arts of India*, ed. Robert Adams and Rajeev Sethi, 247–270. Washington DC: Smithsonian Institution Press.
Lakoff, George. 1987. *Women, Fire and Dangerous Things: What Categories Reveal about the Mind*. Chicago: University of Chicago Press.
Lakoff, George, and Mark Johnson. 1980. *Metaphors We Live By*. Chicago: University of Chicago Press.

Leslie, Julia. 1991. "Sri and Jyestha: Ambivalent Role Models for Women." In *Roles and Rituals for Hindu Women*, ed. Julia Leslie, 107–127. New Delhi: Motilal Banarsidass.

Madan, T. N. 1987. *Non-Renunciation: Themes and Interpretations of Hindu Culture.* Delhi: Oxford University Press.

Marglin, Frederique Apffel. 1985. *Wives of the God-King: The Rituals of the Devadasis of Puri.* Delhi: Oxford University Press.

Nagarajan, Vijaya. 1991. "The Kolam and Ritual Aesthetics: Gender, Ritual Pollution and Rice Paintings in Tamil Nadu." Paper presented at the Annual Meeting of the American Academy of Religion, November 23–26, Kansas City, Missouri.

———. 1993. "Hosting the Divine: The Kolam in Tamil Nadu." In *Mud, Mirror and Thread: Folk Traditions of Rural India*, ed. Nora Fisher, 192–204. Middletown, NJ: Grantha Corporation, and Santa Fe: Museum of New Mexico Press.

———. 1998a. "The Earth as Goddess Bhudevi: Towards a Theory of Embedded Ecologies in Folk Hinduism." In *Purifying the Earthly Body of God: Religion and Ecology in Hindu India*, ed. Lance Nelson, 269–298. Albany: State University of New York Press.

———. 1998b. "Hosting the Divine: The Kolam as Embedded Ritual, Aesthetic and Ecology in Tamil Nadu, India." Ph.D. diss., University of California, Berkeley.

———. 2000. "Rituals of Embedded Ecologies: Drawing Kolams, Marrying Trees and Generating Auspiciousness." In *Hinduism and Ecology: The Intersection of Earth, Sky, and Water*, ed. Christopher Chapple and Mary Evelyn Tucker, 453–468. Cambridge, MA: Harvard University Press.

———. 2001. "(In)Corporating Threshold Art: Kolam Competitions, Patronage and Colgate." *In Religions/Globalization: Theories and Cases*, ed. Lois Lorentzen, Dwight Hopkins, David Batstone, and Eduardo Mandieta, 161–186. Durham, NC: Duke University Press.

Reynolds, Holly Baker. 1980. "The Auspicious Married Woman." In *The Powers of Tamil Women*, ed. Susan Wadley, 35–60. New Delhi: Manohar.

Shulman, David. 1985. *The King and the Clown in South Indian Myth and Poetry.* Princeton, NJ: Princeton University Press.

Wadley, Susan, ed. 1980. *The Powers of Tamil Women.* New Delhi: Manohar.

Williams, Raymond. 1983. *Keywords: A Vocabulary of Culture and Society.* New York: Oxford University Press.

PART II

Beyond Domesticity

6

Domesticity and Difference/ Women and Men: Religious Life in Medieval Tamilnadu

Leslie C. Orr

In recent scholarly examinations of women's ritual activity, there has been an increasing appreciation and valorization of the "domestic." This analytic category, which has been utilized with particular success by Susan Starr Sered in her research on elderly Jewish women's religious lives, has afforded investigators the opportunity to explore new contexts, to abandon an exclusive focus on formal and public expressions of religiosity, and to consider also the religious activities that take place outside of these frameworks and in arenas where women are more likely to be found (Sered 1992, 139–140). But the conception of "domesticity" implies not only a rethinking of the location of religion; even more important is the fact that it prompts us to pay attention to the interpretation of religious activities by those who engage in them. As Sered says, domesticity "is not an inherent characteristic of any particular ritual, place, or event," but is above all a matter of intent, in which "the ultimate concerns of life, suffering, and death are *personalized*— domestic religion has to do with the lives, sufferings, and deaths of *particular*, usually well-loved, individuals" (Sered 1992, 32). The acknowledgment of the validity and significance of such an ori- entation seems particularly helpful in the study of women's religious lives within the Hindu tradition, whose institutional structures generally exclude women from publicly recognized roles as re- nunciants or ritual specialists and whose textual traditions focus largely on men as the central religious actors and on transcend- ing attachment as the primary goal of religious activity.

I propose in the present chapter to explore whether a domestic religious orientation, engaged with the personal and the particular, can be discerned in the context of precolonial South India. My focus is on the period of the ninth to thirteenth centuries in that part of India today known as Tamilnadu, and I draw on the resources provided by the thousands of inscriptions composed in the Tamil language and engraved in stone on the walls of Hindu and Jain temples during this period. These inscriptions record actions, particularly the making of gifts to temples, that were undertaken by a wide variety of people. These people—who sponsored building projects and gave land, money, livestock, ornaments, and images to the temple—included kings and queens, merchants and shepherds, Brahmins and temple women, and local "lords" and their wives and daughters. There is, of course, a great deal that the inscriptions do not tell us; religious activities carried out in the home and in other contexts apart from the temple were rarely documented. Further, the inscriptions' accounts are restricted to the undertakings of people who had both the means to commission the engraving of such records and the desire that their actions should be known to posterity. But despite these limitations, the inscriptional corpus represents a discursive and social space in which both men and women participated, and it gives voice to particular individuals whose goals and motivations in undertaking various religious activities can be glimpsed in the records they have left.

Vows and Self-Offering

Perhaps the quintessentially domestic religious activity with which contemporary Hindu women are engaged, and which is attracting increasing scholarly attention, is the "vow" or, in Sanskrit, *vrata* (Reynolds 1980; Robinson 1985; Peterson 1988; McGee 1991; Tewari 1991; Pearson 1996; McDaniel 2003). Women's observance of *vrata*s typically involves worship, the creation of ritual designs, fasting or other austerities, and the recitation of stories concerning the origin and power of the vow. These rituals are usually undertaken annually, on days sacred to the particular deity whose blessings are sought, and almost invariably have as their overt aim the well-being of children, brothers, or husbands. Hindu women throughout India observe such vows, and in contemporary Tamilnadu, they are referred to by the term *nonpu*. It is therefore a matter of great interest to discover this word in the medieval Tamil inscriptions in the context of women's religious activities. Three stones set up in front of the temple dedicated to the goddess Mariyamman in Kandachipuram (a small place in South Arcot district), with short inscriptions in tenth-century characters, record the observance (*nol*) of *nonpu* by three women, all of them identified with reference to their fathers (ARE 57, 58, 59 of 1935–1936); another stone found in a field in the nearby village of Ariyur documents the *nonpu* in the Durga temple of a woman who is nameless but is identified as someone's wife (ARE 234 of 1936–1937).[1] Another four stones from Gangayanur, in the same area and evidently inscribed in the same period, bear very similar inscriptions; here the term *parani* is used instead of *nonpu*, but the verb *nol*, which is related to *nonpu* and means "to endure, suffer, do penance," is applied to the action of the four women—each of whom is identified both as a daughter and as a wife (ARE 458, 459, 460, 461 of 1937–1938).[2] As these eight inscriptions are so few and so terse, we may find it useful to turn to Tamil literary sources for a greater understanding of the meaning of the term *nonpu* and the possible contexts for women's votive practices a thousand years ago.

An obvious starting point for such an examination is with two ninth-century devotional works, *Tiruppavai* and *Tiruvempavai*, the first composed by the female poet-saint Andal, a devotee of Vishnu, and the second by Manikkavachakar, whose poems praise Lord Shiva. Both of these hymns frame their expressions of praise and self-dedication within the context of a women's ritual in which a group of young women wake up early in the morning during the month of Markali in the cold season and go together to bathe in a pond or river, with the object of being granted a good husband. Andal's *Tiruppavai* is particularly detailed and informs us of the terms of the vow: the girls refrain from consuming ghee and milk, they bathe in the cold water and keep themselves unadorned, and they distribute alms. Following this period of self-denial, the girls dress up, feast on rich milk-rice, and take part in a procession featuring music, drums, singing, lamps, flags, and banners (*Tiruppavai* 2, 26, 27).

The *pavai* rituals outlined in these two ninth-century devotional hymns may possibly be linked to the temple festivals in the month of Markali that are described in inscriptions of the eleventh to thirteenth centuries. Although the inscriptions do not mention any special observances undertaken by women, or austerities as part of the proceedings, there are processions and feasting and even, at the temple of Tirupampuram (Tanjavur district), arrangements made for the singing of *Tiruvempavai*.[3] It is difficult, however, to see any connections between the *pavai* observances of the poems and the practices commemorated by the tenth-century *nonpu* and *parani* stones. For one thing, Andal and Manikkavachakar do not use the term *nonpu* to refer to the girls' ritual, which is called simply *pavai* or *markali niratal*, "Markali bathing," in the poems. When we do encounter this term in the Tamil devotional literature— for example, in the hymns praising Shiva (composed in the sixth to ninth centuries) that are collected in *Tevaram*—it consistently refers to severe ascetic practices. In fact, those who most often perform *nonpu* in these texts are Jain monks, who are castigated by the Shaiva poets for their excesses (e.g., *Tevaram* 2:121.10; 3:103.10; 5:32.9). In the sixth-century Buddhist text *Manimekalai*, the word also refers to austerities, which, again, are presented in negative terms, as selfish and vain, when undertaken by Jains (3.75, 90, 120; 21.98), although the text displays admiration for others who practice *nonpu*—including the Buddha himself (3.60; 5.99) and other sages and ascetics.[4] Twice in the *Manimekalai*, *nonpu* refers specifically to fasting, and in one case this is a fast to death; neither of these fasts is disparaged, nor identified as a Jain observance (14.95; 17.42).[5]

In light of the literary evidence, the tenth-century *nonpu/parani* stones would seem to commemorate the achievement of women who had carried out rather extraordinary acts of self-discipline—more along the lines of the *nonpu* of renunciants than the votive ritual of the young women in the *pavai* poems. In contrast to those who observed the *pavai* ritual, hoping to attain the auspicious state of marriage, the women who undertook severe ascetic practices would have done so with intentions similar to those of renunciants, seeking detachment from the realm of relationship and desire—a manifestly nondomestic goal. The inscribed stones, perhaps set up by their fathers or their husbands, may have honored them for having completed an especially lengthy and rigorous fast, of the sort that is undertaken by Jain women today and celebrated by their families at its conclusion (Reynell 1987).[6] Or perhaps these women died in consequence of their austerities—since this is what is usually implied by the existence of a commemorative stone, in medieval South India as in contemporary North America.

For example, what is called in Tamil a *nicitikai* memorial was established in honor of Jains, both laypeople and renunciants, who undertook a fast to death (*sallekhana*). In contrast to the many such inscriptions from the medieval period that one finds to the west, in what is today the state of Karnataka (Settar and Korisettar 1982; Orr 1999), there are only a handful of these in Tamilnadu. Of the Tamil records, there is only one (from Coimbatore district, in the western part of Tamilnadu) that commemorates the fast to death of a woman, and her name, Pullappai, indicates that she was originally from Karnataka (ARE 597 of 1905). It appears that the practice of fasting to death as a means of purification—avoiding harmful behavior and the accumulation of bad karma, striving for transcendence of one's physical state and liberation from this world—was less common, or in any case less commonly commemorated, by Jains in Tamilnadu as compared to their cousins to the west. But in the Tamil country, these observances may not have been exclusive to the Jain community: it is possible that such practices and such motives are precisely those celebrated in the *nonpu/parani* stones.[7]

Another type of memorial that, again, is more commonly found in Karnataka (Settar 1982, 196)—and, even farther to the west, in Maharashtra (Sontheimer 1982, 277–281)—is the *sati* stone. Indeed I know of no inscribed *sati* stones in Tamilnadu (cf. Srinivasan 1960, 6–7). There are, however, at least four inscriptions of the medieval period that have been engraved on temple walls in various parts of the Tamil country that record women's self-immolation: a tenth-century inscription from Allur, in Tiruchirappalli district, that records the gift of gold to the temple by a woman named Gangamadeviyar "who was entering the fire" (SII 8.690); an inscription from Dharmapuri district, dated A.D. 1017, in which a wife is said to have "entered the fire" following her husband's death (*Avanam* 12, 21);[8] the grant of land, recorded at Cheydunganallur in Tirunelveli district in the mid-twelfth century, for the merit of Puricanti, who "entered the fire" (ARE 363 of 1959–1960); and the gift of lamps by Vikrama Kampan for the merit of two persons who had died as a result of his attack—a warrior whose home had been ambushed and his wife, Vampu, who had subsequently "entered the fire"—the donor having been ordered by the elders of the community to make this gift to the temple at Tirukalakkunram (Chingleput district) so that the brother of the dead man should desist from further vengeance (ARE 162 of 1932–1933).[9] What is interesting is that two of these four inscriptions make no reference to the woman's status as a wife or a widow. In the absence of the mention of a husband, we may question whether these acts of self-immolation were *satis* at all, and I suggest that these women's self-sacrifice was not motivated by the desire to be reborn again with the bond of marriage preserved and to maintain the web of personal and particular familial ties even after death. That the first of these inscriptions records the woman's own gift to the temple, rather than arrangements made by others to honor her or make expiation for her death, indicates that the relationship being solemnized by her renunciation of life was that with God rather than with man. Thus this act of self-giving appears to be inspired by an impulse to transcend one's specific human and social condition.

In the Tamil country, and especially in the northwest parts of this region, the type of memorial we encounter most frequently is the hero stone. It is clear from the Tamil "Sangam" literature of the early centuries of the first millennium that the setting up of hero stones for men who had fallen in battle or in cattle raids was a long-standing tradition (Srinivasan 1960, 3–6; Soundara Rajan 1982, 59–75; Settar 1982, 184–187). The hero stones from the period we are considering—the ninth to thirteenth centuries—generally bear an image of an armed man and a Shiva *linga*, and about half of them are inscribed with a short statement telling how the hero met with death. Often he was engaged in combat on behalf of a lord and is referred to as his servant (*cevakan*); sometimes the person or group who erected the stone will also be mentioned (see, e.g., CN 56). As is the case for *nicitikai* and *sati* memorials, hero stones are much more abundant in Karnataka than in Tamilnadu, and there they are adorned with more elaborate relief sculptures, including images of the hero ascending heavenward in the embrace of celestial maidens (Settar 1982; Rajasekhara 1982). Although the hero stones found in Tamilnadu lack such narrative depictions of the hero's postmortem destiny, the sculpting of the Shiva *linga* on many of these memorials suggests that the hero in death is consecrated to Lord Shiva, and will attain his divine abode—or, perhaps, that the hero's courageous protection of his community and loyalty to his chief are equated with the acts of self-sacrificing devotion performed by the worshipper.[10]

Another kind of self-offering recorded in the medieval Tamil inscriptions—and one with which women as well as men were involved—is the vow of the servant (fem. *velaikkari*, masc. *velaikkaran*) not to survive her or his master. There is a group of more than thirty records of such oaths of fealty by both women and men inscribed on the temple walls of Arakandanallur, in South Arcot district—a place very near to the sites where the *nonpu/parani* stones have been found (ARE 122–126, 136–150, 153–160, 162, 187, 188 of 1934–1935). Another such record is found in the temple at nearby Elvanasur (SII 22.156): here we read of the vow made by the *velaikkari* Tevapperumal that she die together with her lord. Although these vows express the same values of faithfulness and self-dedication that are manifest in the hero stone inscriptions, they lack any explicit reference to religious motivations and expectations, devotion to a deity or anticipation of a heavenly reward; these records resemble other oaths engraved on temple walls in this part of South Arcot district, which solemnize political alliances among clans and agreements of mutual defense (see Orr 1998b).

Although we do not hear of any cases where the *velaikkari* or *velaikkaran*'s promise of self-sacrifice in allegiance to a human lord was actually effected, devotion to the cause of a divine lord did result in acts of self-immolation. There is an inscription of the twelfth century from Punjai, to the south, in the Kaveri delta region, where we see a group of servants (*velaikkarar*) loyal to the trident of Shiva, who gave up their lives—by entering the fire—in support of the temple's contention of ownership of certain properties. The rival claimants to the land had to concede to the temple and were required by the local assembly to set up metal images of those who had died and to make a donation to provide for worship of these images (ARE 188 of 1925). At Paiyanur in Chingleput district, an inscription of uncertain date records another land dispute, evidently between the temple and the Brahmin assembly, in which two ascetics gave up their lives (ARE 108 of 1932–1933). Finally, we might add to these examples of self-sacrifice a couple of cases in which the interests of the temple deity were furthered by the offering of one's head. At the temples of Jambai and Arakandanallur—in precisely the same area of South Arcot district where we find the *nonpu/parani* stones and the *velaikkarar* oaths of fealty discussed above—inscriptions of the thirteenth and fourteenth centuries record land grants to the families of men who had cut off their heads in order that the temple *mandapa* might be completed (SII 12.178; ARE 197 of 1934–1935). It may be significant that, in both cases, these men were the relatives of temple women, but such extreme acts of self-dedication do not seem to have been undertaken by temple women themselves. It is unclear how precisely such acts were efficacious in advancing temple building projects; perhaps the self-sacrifice exerted moral pressure on the people of the community who were in a position to provide financial support to the temple, in the same way that the deaths of Shiva's servants at Punjai forced local landowners to submit to the temple's demands. A further possibility, however, is suggested by the wording of another memorial of a head offering: this is a stone, with a representation of a man having decapitated himself with a sword, which bears a tenth-century inscription recording the man's offering of his head to the goddess and the granting of land to his relative, in recognition of this superior asceticism (*me tavam*) (SII 12.106).[11] The use of the term *tavam*, equivalent to the Sanskrit *tapas*, suggests that this act is equivalent to the austerities of sages and renunciants—performers of *nonpu*—and generative of a spiritual energy capable of bringing about a desired goal.

In the case of the *nonpu/parani* stones and several of the records of women entering the fire, the aims of the performers remain obscure, yet all of the self-sacrificing acts we have considered here seem to have a similar quality: the virtues displayed by women cannot be distinguished from those of the men whose deaths are commemorated in medieval Tamil inscriptions. These extraordinary acts and the fashion in which they were recognized and celebrated reflect the value placed on valor and self-sacrifice, whether that of women or of men. Within this group of activities, the undertaking of austerities is apparently the focus for some of the observances, while elsewhere loyalty and allegiance are stressed. In most cases, both aspects are present, as are both domestic and transcendent elements. Ironically, perhaps, women's acts of self-discipline and self-offering, documented in the records of *nonpus* and *satis*, point less consistently toward a domestic orientation, with their lack of reference to beneficiaries of the observance and their suggestion that it is the woman herself who attains her religious goal by renouncing her connection with the world. The self-sacrifices represented in the hero stones, in the *velaikkarar* oaths of fealty, and in the self-immolations and self-decapitations performed for the sake of the temple deity are motivated by this-worldly goals and are highly personalized, and thus domestic. The sense of relationship with and service to one's community, lord, or local deity—concern for "*particular*, usually well-loved, individuals," in Sered's words—is much more vividly presented in these cases, which refer for the most part to men's actions, than in the records of *nonpus* and *satis* carried out by women. But even here, in the absence of an explicit reference to a divine power or to a future existence after death, a transcendent dimension is invoked—by the celebration of the devotion, mastery of the self, and fearlessness that have allowed those whose acts are commemorated to rise above the ordinary sphere of human conduct.

Gifts to Gods and Goddesses

The vast majority of medieval inscriptions concern much more mundane activities, but they do have another type of connection to the transcendent inasmuch as they record gifts to the divine beings enshrined in the temple. Overall, the kinds of gifts that women and men made were identical in substance and in purpose. But closer examination reveals subtle differences, in terms of preferences and emphases in donative activity. To get a more precise sense of what these differences are, I surveyed a group of more than 2,000 inscriptions, of the ninth to thirteenth centuries, from six study areas in different parts of the Tamil country.[12] About 1,200 of these inscriptions are the records of gifts from individuals where it is possible to determine the sex of the donor: 161, or a seventh of these, concern the gifts of women. Most of the gifts of both men and women were for lamps to be burned in the temple (42 percent of women's gifts; 35 percent of men's) or for various worship services and festival observances (16 percent of women's gifts; 25 percent of men's).[13] But a number of the inscriptions record the setting up of images of deities—and this is a type of endowment that was apparently of considerable interest to women. While overall only one-seventh of the inscriptions recording gifts by individuals present women as donors, nearly a quarter of the 100 or so inscriptions documenting the establishment of new images in the temple identify women as their sponsors. Of the 25 goddess images newly consecrated, a third had been set up by women. This pattern seems to indicate a special affinity of women for the patronage of goddesses, and this is borne out in other ways: in the case of the 40 inscriptions recording arrangements for worship and special gifts for goddesses already established in the temple, a quarter identify women as sponsors, a proportion that is about twice what one would expect given the number of female donors. Women's visibility in the establishment of images and the patronage of goddesses is all the more impressive when we consider that in inscriptions of the ninth to thirteenth centuries, half of all the images were sponsored and half of all the goddess-related donations were made during the thirteenth century—a period when the proportion of all gifts that were made by women had dropped to its lowest point, just over 10 percent (see Orr 2000b).

Apart from the quantitative patterns that this survey of study areas reveals, we find in inscriptions recording women's donations from all parts of Tamilnadu certain predilections with respect to the kinds of gifts they chose to offer goddesses. Very often they donated jewelry to adorn the goddesses' images. We see this even in the case of a Jain religious woman, identified as the disciple of a male sage, who presented gold ornaments to a Jain goddess at Chitaral in Kanniyakumari district at the end of the ninth century (TAS 1.194–195). Around the year 1000, there are many records of gifts of ornaments made by women of the royal court to goddesses enshrined in the temples of the Kaveri delta (see Venkataraman 1976, 52–58, 66–71, 130–136). Among these donations, it is interesting to find in several instances the gift of an adornment referred to as a *tali*. Judging from the Tamil literature of the period, the word *tali* could simply mean a particular type of necklace, but beginning in the eleventh century, it began also to designate the emblem of marriage worn by women so long as their husbands remained alive (Jayadev 1960, 50–51). In A.D. 981, a *tali* was presented by the

Chola queen Cempiyan Mahadevi to the goddess Uma at Vrddhachalam (SII 19.302); a decade later, a palace woman in the service of one of Rajaraja's queens gave to the goddess Uma at Tiruvidaimarudur a gold *tali* set with a double row of gems and a pearl necklace (SII 23.278); and, in 1015 at Tiruvisalur, the daughter of a chief from northern Tamilnadu who had married the Pandya king of the south similarly presented the goddess with a jewel-encrusted gold *tali* and other valuable ornaments (SII 23.46). Later, toward the end of the thirteenth century, we find the wife of a temple Brahmin giving her own *tali* to the goddess of the temple at Tiruvattatturai in South Arcot district (ARE 227 of 1928–1929). The gift of this special ornament, in the case of at least some of these women, would seem to express a particularly feminine concern that the goddess—in all of these cases, the consort of Shiva—be appropriately adorned as a wife. Further, the auspiciousness associated with the *tali* would be greatly enhanced when worn by the goddess (whose husband is immortal), and she who had presented the *tali* would have shared in that heightened auspiciousness, although she would not have received a *tali* in return, as do the *matammas* of Tirupati described by Joyce Flueckiger elsewhere in this volume. On the other hand, the Tamil inscriptions rarely record male gifts to the goddess of jewelry of any kind, and I have come across only one instance where a *tali* was offered by someone other than an individual woman; this is in an inscription of the late tenth century which records the granting of a *tali* to the goddess by the Brahmin assembly at Tiruvallam in North Arcot district (ARE 210 of 1921).

Another dimension of the feminine solidarity expressed through women's adornment of female deities emerges in inscriptions that indicate that a woman's gift to the goddess was a means of linking her with her female kin and of connecting them with the goddess. For example, a gift for the merit of her mother was made by a woman of the Malaiyaman chief's family, who, in 1133, built a shrine and installed an image of the "bedroom goddess" (*tirupalliyarai nacciyar*), the form of the goddess whom the god Shiva would join every evening, at the temple of Siddhalingamadam in South Arcot district (SII 26.422). An inscription of the late twelfth century from Viravanallur in the far south of Tamilnadu (Tirunelveli district) records that a woman serving in the palace of the Pandya kings at Madurai set up an image of the goddess, in the name of her daughter and named after her daughter, to which she presented jewels and other gifts to support worship (ARE 720 of 1916). And a hundred years later, in 1300, a dancing woman (*cantikkutti*) of the temple at Tiruvanaik-kaval built a goddess shrine in the town of Valliyur, again in Tirunelveli district and far to the south of her hometown, where she set up images of the goddess and of her granddaughter (ARE 364 of 1929–1930).[14]

Sometimes the network of female relations and feminine concerns is expressed in terms of a familial relationship between female donors and the goddesses themselves. In two inscriptions of the late tenth century from Tanjavur district, we find women referring to the goddess Uma, whom they

had endowed with land, as their daughter (SII 19.404; *Varalaru* 1, 33–34).[15] But in another inscription of precisely the same period, from a temple farther up the Kaveri River, it is a male donor who claims the goddess Uma as his daughter, provides her with land to support daily worship and offerings, and gives her in marriage to the lord of the temple (ARE 151 of 1936–1937). And several other inscriptions, somewhat later and from farther north, record land grants to goddesses given—by individual men or local assemblies—as *stridhana* (dowry) on the occasion of the goddess's marriage, again expressing a parental role and demonstrating that it was not only women who adopted a highly personal approach to temple patronage.[16]

There are two ways in which this concept of connection with a deity resonates with the Tamil devotional literature of the centuries immediately preceding the time in which the inscriptions were engraved. First, the sense of intimacy is present in both contexts, within the framework of a variety of possible close relationships, including—especially in the cases of the poems of the Alvars dedicated to Vishnu and in the inscriptions at which we have just looked—that of the role of parent to the divine child.[17] Even where a familial connection is not explicitly evoked, the poems and the inscriptions express— each in their own fashion—a familiar personal relationship between the devotee and the divine. Second, the particularity of place is emphasized: the deity being praised by the poet-saints or granted gifts by the worshipper is not represented primarily as an abstract and universal power—although his or her transcendent nature is of course acknowledged—but is recognized as the lord or mistress of a particular locality. The deity's distinctive site-specific personality is far more manifest in the inscriptions than is his or her sectarian or iconographic identity. These qualities of intimacy and local particularity found among worshippers in medieval South India—and the perspective in which the goddess is regarded as a daughter—prompt a comparison with the ritual activities of women in the contemporary celebrations of Durga *puja* in Bengal analyzed by Sandra Robinson. As an example of women's ritual activities that "are separate from but coordinate with brahmanic festivals," Robinson describes what takes place after the priest's conclusion of the formal worship:

> [Women] approach the image of the goddess Durga to place food on her lips as a gesture of farewell before the image is taken away for in a pond or tank. A psychodrama of reluctant departure es this activity, inasmuch as the goddess has come only e again; there are wailing laments which explicitly repli- nticipate the farewells of young brides as they leave their ies to return to their husbands' family homes. (Robinson –198)

In Robinson's analysis of the temple setting of modern Bengal, there is a definite division between the official observances of the male priest, mandated by the Brahminical tradition, and the activities of female worshippers, which are clearly marked as domestic because of their personalized character and which are treated as marginal or supplementary rituals, however essential they seem to the women who perform them. There are two aspects of this dichotomy—the split between formal male ritual and domestic female ritual, and that between the role of the specially qualified ritualist and the role of the "lay" worshipper—and, in each case, the first of the two activities or roles is acknowledged as fundamental, and the second is generally viewed as auxiliary or derivative. In the context of the medieval South Indian temple, on the other hand, at least from the perspective offered to us by the inscriptions, I would argue that there was a recognition of the value of the domestic orientation as expressed through the public religious activities of both women and men, and that lay religious activity—particularly temple patronage—by both women and men had an authority and impact that was not overshadowed by the prestige and expertise of priests and other temple servants.

If we consider the corps of temple personnel as the main actors, and their ritual duties as the crucial functions, we will perceive in the medieval South Indian temple a situation that is more complex but not dissimilar to the picture of the temple in modern Bengal that Robinson has sketched for us, with respect to the recognition of the relative value of male and female roles. While the temple in medieval Tamilnadu presented more possibilities for female ritual participation than is the case today, women's presence and activities in temple ritual were regarded as optional and incidental (Orr 1993, 2000a). Temple women were vastly outnumbered by their male counterparts and were entirely excluded from many of the roles that men fulfilled, including that of priest. The increasing visibility, in the thirteenth century, of temple women as singers and dancers at festivals—displacing, to some extent, the male performers who had earlier had these roles—seems to have been significant more as a manifestation of the privileges accorded to temple women (often in consequence of their gifts to the temple), than as the provision of a necessary service to the temple.[18] But if we shift our gaze from the temple servants to the temple's patrons, we see that women were far from marginal and that the religious activity of gift giving had a profound impact on the shaping of ritual life in the temple, giving form to new services and establishing new deities to be worshipped.

Donors were, of course, not only motivated by the desire to make their mark—both by effecting changes in the temple through their gifts and by documenting their piety and generosity for posterity on the temple walls—but had other objects in view. The expression of purpose that is most commonly encountered in the inscriptions is related to the creation and transfer of the merit that accompanies the making of a religious gift. In the medieval Tamil inscriptions, we do not find the explicit mention of *punya* or other terms denoting "merit," but the transfer of merit is indicated by the statement that a gift was made "for" another or was "connected to" (*cartti*) the recipient of the benefit of the donation. Although both men and women transferred merit at the same rate—in about 5 percent of their gifts—there were clear differences in the identities of the beneficiaries.[19] Merit produced by the gifts of women was almost invariably transferred to relatives, while this was the pattern for men's gifts only about a third of the time; the merit more often went to men unrelated to the donor, including the king or local notables. Of the relatives to whom merit was transferred, by both women and men, male kinsfolk predominated—but the relative most likely to be mentioned by a male donor, his father, was scarcely ever mentioned by women. Here we see women locating themselves through their gift giving within a familial network in a pattern that is familiar from studies of contemporary Hindu women's votive behavior—where vows are undertaken for the benefit of husband and children (and particularly, perhaps, sons)—and it seems that this is more characteristic of medieval women's donative behavior than it is of their male counterparts'. But it cannot be said that men's purposes in making gifts were radically different: they too had domestic motives and used temple patronage as a means of expressing connection with their kinsmen—as well as their mothers, sisters, and wives. That men may, in some ways, have had a *greater* stake than women in domestic goals, at least as these were made public in temple inscriptions, is suggested by the fact that several of the donations by men to temples are said in the inscriptions to be gifts of thanksgiving for having been granted a son (SII 26.516; ARE 366 of 1959–1960). There is nothing equivalent among female donors.

Apart from such donations, made in gratitude, what kinds of future consequences were anticipated as the result of making gifts on behalf of oneself or another? The inscriptions tell us almost nothing about the benefits for the living. But a hint about the goal of gifts made for the merit of those who had left this world appears in an early twelfth-century inscription that records the gift of land for one who was deceased, "praying [that he attain] Shivaloka" (*civalokaprarttam*) (SII 8.460). Other possibilities are suggested by the *pallipatai*, or "sepulcher temple," erected in medieval Tamilnadu over the remains of a prominent person and named after him or her (Srinivasan 1960, 12–13; Sethuraman 1991). Amid the obscurity that surrounds the meaning of these shrines, several authors maintain that their primary function was to legitimate the claim to rule by Chola kings descended from the deceased, who was glorified as a hero and king (Raghotham 1995; Ogura 1999). But the fact that more than half of those interred within the *pallipatais* were women seems to suggest rather different motives.[20] Meanwhile, in religious terms, it is not clear whether gifts for the merit of the departed, or the setting up of *nonpu* stones, hero stones, or *pallipatais*, had to do with fame and the honoring—or even "deifying"—of a person of the past, or whether instead they were a matter of supporting the departed in an ongoing existence in the afterlife, where benefits would flow from the continuing worship carried out in his or her name.

Some further clues come from the inscriptions that record the arrangements made after someone had met a violent death. We have already had occasion to consider the inscription (ARE 162 of 1932–1933) that describes the gift made by Vikrama Kampan in expiation of his murderous attack on a man and the subsequent act of *sati* by that man's wife: in this case, we learn that the two lamps were given for the merit of the two dead and as a means of averting the vengeance of the living. There are a few other such records where violence was purposefully done, either in battle or in rage—there is, for example, the case of the Brahmin who had beaten a man to death and who was required to give a perpetual lamp in expiation of this crime (ARE 528 of 1937–1938). But, according to the inscriptions, most gifts of expiation were made after having inadvertently caused another's death. There were a large number of hunting accidents—described in inscriptions from Chingleput, North Arcot, and South Arcot districts—that prompted such gifts. In one such case, the motive for making the gift seems to have been to placate the spirit of the dead: the local council determined that the man who had accidentally killed another while hunting should donate a perpetual lamp to the temple in order to "remove enmity" (*pakai ara*) (SII 7.85). This is also suggested by the case in which an intruder was stabbed to death by a merchant as the intruder attempted to rape the merchant's concubine; both the merchant and a relative of the deceased were together held responsible for donating gold for a lamp in the temple. Here the resolution does not so much reflect culpability or the need for the merchant to atone for wrongdoing but rather the necessity for there to be a memorial for the deceased (SII 22.77).

Women as well as men figure in these records, both as victims and as perpetrators. We have two inscriptions that order a gift of expiation for having caused the death of a woman—one of whom took poison because her husband was marrying another woman (SII 17.389), and another who killed herself after she had been put through an ordeal to get her to pay taxes she claimed she did not owe (SII 22.80). A chilling inscription of the twelfth century describes an act of violence carried out by a woman: Koccattan Kaman's wife threw a stick at her daughter, which accidentally hit another girl; the girl died twenty days later. It was agreed that a lamp should be donated to the temple by Koccattan Kaman, the husband of the murderous mother (SII 22.148). The inscription provides neither the name of his wife, nor that of the dead girl, who is identified simply as the daughter of Tappi Mintan Kaman. It is unlikely, therefore, that the lamp was being offered for the merit of the nameless girl. In fact, although women are the main actors in this unhappy drama, they seem to be entirely off-stage in the sequel. The gift of expiation was not made by the perpetrator of the violent act, but rather by her husband, who seems to bear responsibility for his wife's action.

If religious activity is regarded as domestic when it is undertaken for personal and individualized motives and for the benefit of family members or other well-loved individuals, it is difficult to make the case that medieval South Indian women's engagement with temple patronage indicates such an orientation to a greater degree than that of their male counterparts. It is true that women were more likely than men to transfer the merit arising from their gift giving to their kinfolk, especially their sons and husbands. But women refrained from making gifts for expiation or thanksgiving, which were the types of gifts that frequently expressed involvement on the part of men in a familial network and that made men the representatives for their family's culpability and its interests. Donations were also the means by which individuals forged links with the divinity enshrined in the temple. On the one hand, women's attention to and special gifts of jewelry for consort goddesses suggest a connection to these deities made more intimate by the sharing of the status of wife. On the other, records of men's gifts to the goddess as daughter express the closeness and tenderness of their relationship with the deity whom they worshipped. And both men and women, through their donations to gods and goddesses alike, participated in a realm of religious activity that was—in terms of its expression (and constitution) of a personal relationship with a deity and its focus on the identity of the particular god of a specific place—highly domestic in character.

Concluding Reflections

The category of the domestic is clearly a useful one in expanding our sense of what can properly and seriously be regarded as a religious context, a religious role, or a religious motive. Religion is not just what yogis and priests do. But the characterization of women's engagement with religion as preeminently domestic—personal, particular, and familial—and distinct from men's frameworks of religious undertaking cannot be maintained in the face of the evidence from medieval Tamilnadu. Women's and men's religious lives were of course dissimilar in many ways. But the spheres of activity in which they found themselves were in large part congruent. If we want to differentiate male and female religious behaviors and purposes, it seems that we can best do this by thinking in terms of different colorings and shadings, rather than different positions or different perspectives on the meanings of their religious activities.

The inscriptions show us that renunciatory and self-sacrificial observances, undertaken by both women and men, had significance both in terms of ultimate, transcendent aims and as expressions of highly specific relationships and this-worldly goals. The devotional activities that were a part of temple life, including making gifts to gods and goddesses, similarly had both feminine and masculine manifestations and simultaneously engaged abstract conceptions of devotion and divinity, on the one hand, and personal connections with the local and particular, on the other. Finally, our exploration of the contexts and roles in which medieval South Indian women functioned suggests that the category of the "religious" itself is in the end less helpful than we might have expected in an analysis of these acts of renunciation and devotion. The inscriptions demonstrate again and again that the religious act has antecedents, meanings, and consequences that spill over into other realms. The records of women's gifts portray them as participants in networks of property transactions, as sponsors of land improvement projects, and as parties to contracts and compacts. The epigraphs, although engraved on the walls of temples, speak to issues of identity, position, and power—and not only mark the special gestures and achievements of individuals but are themselves constitutive of the shifts in status that accompany these acts. The boundary between the religious and the political, or the religious and the economic, is as indistinct as that between women's domestic rituals and men's "high" religion. In other words, what yogis and priests—and women—do is not just religion.

NOTES

I am very grateful to Tracy Pintchman for her patience and perseverance as editor of this volume, to Norma Baumel Joseph for much conversation about and insight into women's ritual lives, to S. Swaminathan for invaluable aid in my work with the inscriptional material, to Padma Kaimal for delightful discussions about kings, queens, goddesses, and temples, to Anne Monius for sound advice on Tamil literary matters, to Katherine Young with whom I first read the *pavai* poems, to Uma Narayan for questions that helped clarify the issues at stake in this chapter, and to Michelle Bakker for her bibliographic assistance.

1. That three of the *nonpu* stones are placed in proximity to a goddess temple, and that one explicitly mentions the observance taking place in a goddess temple also suggests a possible link to contemporary women's votive ritual, which is often dedicated to female deities (Reynolds 1980, 50; McDaniel 2003, 111–112).

2. One of the four *parani* stones records the fact that a pillar (*tari*—evidently the stone itself which bears the inscription) has been erected in recognition of the observance of the *parani*. In general, in inscriptional usage, the term *parani* refers to a division of time (a *nakshatra* or asterism) which occurs every month. That the practice of austerities, or the observance of a vow, should have a specific calendrical referent is not surprising, although I know of no other examples where the *nakshatra parani* has these associations.

3. A temple woman (*tevaratiyal*) was granted the privilege of singing part of the hymn at Tirupampuram's Markali festival in exchange for her gift of several images to the temple, according to an inscription of the early thirteenth century (NK 139). Other references to Markali festivals come from Chidambaram (SII

4.223), from Kudumiyamalai, in Tiruchirappalli district (IPS 291 and 301), and from Tirumogur, in Madurai district, where it was the occasion for the celebration of the marriage of Vishnu to the goddess (ARE 334 of 1918). See Orr 2004 for further discussion of festival observances.

4. Monius (forthcoming) suggests that the *Manimekalai*'s emphasis on *nonpu* indicates that this text is affiliated especially with Hinayana or Theravada Buddhist teachings. Not surprisingly, in *Cilappatikaram*, a Jain text written at around the same time as the *Manimekalai*, we find the word *nonpu* utilized with quite positive connotations, generally with reference to the austerities of Jain renunciants and lay people (10.24, 47; 15.153, 164; 16.18; 26.226), but also applied to the rites of marriage observed by the hero (1.53).

5. We also find *nonpu* referring to the fast to death in *Cilappatikaram* (17.83).

6. The fasts carried out by contemporary Jain women have different aims and different effects from those undertaken by Hindu women as an aspect of the observance of votive rituals. Jain women's austerities bring about a withdrawal from the world and are a means of self-purification; the power generated by fasting (*tapas*) is understood as "cooling" female sexuality (Reynell 1987, 343–351). On the other hand, while the ascetic component of Hindu women's *vratas* equally generates power, this is utilized in the context of engagement with the world, allowing women to influence the welfare of their families; their *tapas*, viewed as "heat," has a beneficent effect because it is channeled toward such ends (Reynolds 1980, 46–50; McDaniel 2003, 108–109; cf. Pearson 1996, 211–217).

7. Three of the eight women whose observance of *nonpu/parani* was commemorated are described only as daughters and not as wives. These may have been very young women carrying out this practice, or it is possible that they were renunciant women, similar to the Jain "religious women" identified in medieval Tamil inscriptions as teachers (Orr 1998a). There are very few inscriptional references to ascetics among women whom we would classify as "Hindu"—terms like *tapasyar* are almost invariably applied to men rather than women—but those few that exist (e.g., SII 8.225; ARE 120 of 1912), as well as the intriguing references to "pilgrim mothers" (*paradeshi ammaimar*—e.g., SII 5.748; ARE 271 of 1927–28), point to the potential for alternative ways of life for women.

8. I am indebted to S. Swaminathan for calling my attention to this inscription, and for providing me with the text, published in the Tamil journal *Avanam*.

9. None of these four records commemorates the death of a royal woman. There is an inscription at the temple of Brahmadesam, in North Arcot district, dating from the middle of the eleventh century, that records the gift of a water shed by the brother of the Chola queen Viramahadeviyar, to quench the thirst of his sister who, having arisen to Shiva's heaven and joined the feet of Brahma, was interred in the *pallipatai* (sepulchre temple) of her deceased husband Rajendra I (ARE 260 of 1915). This inscription has often been considered evidence of the Chola queen's act of *sati*, and it is dated in the same year as Rajendra's death, but, unlike the four inscriptions we have just considered, there is no direct reference to Viramahadeviyar taking her own life. A more explicit indication of such an act by a woman of the Chola royal family—although it is found in a record dating a half century later than the event itself—is found in the lengthy *prashasti* of Rajendra I that prefaces the

Tiruvalangadu copper plate inscription (SII 3.205). Here, in verses 65–66, the queen Vanavanmahadevi is depicted as following her husband Sundara Chola (Rajendra's grandfather) to heaven, jealous of the attentions that the celestial maidens would bestow upon him.

10. Padma Kaimal (1999, 132) points out that the portrait sculptures of donors in early Chola period temples are stylistically similar to the images carved on hero stones, and suggests that this reflects a similarity in the valuation of the worthiness of the acts that are commemorated in the two contexts—both of which involve loyalty, submission, and offering of the self. It is interesting to note that after AD 970, portrait sculptures of female donors virtually disappear (despite the major activities of women as temple patrons), while they were more in evidence in the preceding hundred-year period (Kaimal 2000, 179).

11. On head-offerings to goddesses in South Indian sculpture and literature, see Vogel (1930–32), Srinivasan (1960, 29–30), and Filliozat (1967).

12. These six study areas are—from the northern to the southern part of Tamilnadu—Chingleput taluk in Chingleput district, Cheyyar taluk in North Arcot district, Cuddalore taluk in South Arcot district, Mayavaram taluk in Tanjavur district, Tiruppattur taluk in Ramnad district, and Ambasamudram taluk in Tirunelveli district. For this survey, I relied on the abstracts of the published and unpublished inscriptions (drawn for the most part from the ARE publications) in the volumes of *A Topographical List of the Inscriptions in the Tamil Nadu and Kerala States* (Mahalingam 1985–).

13. Women were much less likely than men to sponsor arrangements for the offering of food to Brahmins, ascetics, and devotees in the temple. This may be because the institutionalization of such feeding eclipsed a sphere of religious activity that had belonged to "the housemistress at the door" (Findly 2002; see also Balbir 1994). The giving of alms to mendicants probably continued to be largely a private, informal, individual, and home-based affair, rather than taking place in the public, permanent, and formal contexts described in the inscriptions, especially the *matha* ("mutt"), which was predominantly a feeding-house in this period. But as feeding came to be a means through which the temple, or the sectarian community, could confer honor and recognition for patronage, service, and leadership, there may have been a diminution of women's importance with respect to this religious activity.

14. Women's gifts to the male deity enshrined in the temple, in support of various offerings and services, could equally serve to create links with female kin—or, for that matter, with the men of their families.

15. Again, I thank S. Swaminathan for alerting me to the existence of the inscription published in the Tamil journal *Varalaru*, and for kindly supplying me with the text.

16. In AD 1037, a gift of land for a garden was given by a Brahmin man as *stridhana* to the goddess Sita who was to be married to Lord Rama, at Vadamadurai in Chingleput district (ARE 262 of 1952–53); in 1160, at the Shiva temple in Brahmadesam in South Arcot district, the Brahmin assembly (*mahasabhaiyar*) provided land as *stridhana* for the goddess who had been established in the temple by a local man (ARE 192 of 1918); and in 1137, the village assembly (*urar*) gave land as

stridhana to the "bedroom goddess" at the Shiva temple of Seyyur, in Chingleput district (SII 8.30). On *stridhana* in medieval Tamilnadu—which meant not only the transfer of property to a daughter, but could involve the transfer from a man to his son-in-law or a woman to her daughter-in-law—see Orr 1998b and Orr 2000a 72–73, 77–78, 226.

17. Despite the theological precedent in Tamil devotional literature, worshippers do not take a parental role in the inscriptions recording their gifts to male deities. The god enshrined in the temple is not addressed as "son"; instead we find the reverse—that records issued in the name of the Lord refer to devotees as "our children." Perhaps this discrepancy can be explained by the fact that the majority of temples providing inscriptions in our period were dedicated to Shiva, a deity who is rarely if ever envisioned as a child—in contrast to his son Murugan, his consort Uma, and various manifestations of Vishnu (see Richman 1997).

18. See note 3 above for an example of a temple woman's "deal," in which her right to participate in ritual resulted from a donation. I have discussed at length temple women's activities—both as temple servants and as temple patrons—in Orr 2000a.

19. This discussion is based on Orr 2000b.

20. In the seven inscriptions where there is an explicit indication of the character of the temple as a *pallipatai*, and a clear identification of the person in whose honor it was built, we find mention of four *pallipatai*s constructed for men (of whom three are Chola kings), and six for women (including five Chola queens). In chronological order, from the ninth to the thirteenth centuries, these inscriptions are: EI, 192ff; SII 8.529; SII 3.15; ARE 271 of 1927; ARE 260 of 1915; EI 41.10B; and ARE 124 of 1936–37. Sethuraman (1991) and Ogura (1999) emphasize the role of Pashupata Shaiva preceptors as officiants at the *pallipatai*s, and Sethuraman considers that those interred in the *pallipatai*s would have been initiated into the Pashupata tradition. The tradition of building royal memorial temples, widespread in the Deccan during this same period, was evidently more deeply-rooted and of a different character from the practice found in the Tamil country, to the south and east (see Wagoner 1996).

REFERENCES

Tamil Inscriptions

Annual Reports on Indian Epigraphy (ARE). 1905–1978. Delhi: Manager of Publications. Transcripts of the inscriptions abstracted in the ARE were graciously made available to me at the Office of the Chief Epigraphist, Archaeological Survey of India, Mysore.

Cenkam Natukarkal (CN). 1972. Ed. Ira Nakacami. Cennai: Tamilnatu Aracu Tolporul Ayvutturai.

Epigraphia Indica (EI). 1892–. Calcutta/Delhi: Director General, Archaeological Survey of India.

Inscriptions (Texts) of the Pudukkottai State Arranged according to Dynasties (IPS). 1929. Pudukkottai.

Nannilam Kalvettukal (NK). 1979–1980. 3 vols. Ed. A. Patmavati. Cennai: Tamilnatu
    Aracu Tolporul Ayvutturai.
South Indian Inscriptions (SII). 1891–1990. Vols. 2–26. Delhi: Director General,
    Archaeological Survey of India.
Travancore Archaeological Series (TAS). 1910–1938. Vols. 1–8. Trivandrum.

Tamil Literature

Cilappatikaram, Ilanko Atikal. Tamil text. Tancavur: Tamilp Palkalaik Kalakam,
    1985.
Cilappatikaram, translation, with an introduction and postscript, by R. Partha-
    sarathy, *The Cilappatikaram of Ilanko Atikal: An Epic of South India*. New York:
    Columbia University Press, 1993.
Manimekalai. Tamil text with commentary by Po. Ve. Comacuntaranar. Tirunelveli:
    South India Saiva Siddhanta Works Publishing Society, 1971.
Manimekhalai (The Dancer with the Magic Bowl) by Merchant-Prince Shattan, transla-
    tion by Alain Daniélou. New York: New Directions, 1989.
Tevaram, Tamil text. Edited by T. V. Gopal Iyer. 3 vols. Pondichéry: Institut français
    de Indologie, 1984–1991.
Tevaram, translations by V. M. Subramanya Aiyar and Jean-Luc Chevillard, in
    Digital Tevaram, courtesy Jean-Luc Chevillard.
Tiruppavai, Tamil text and English translation by Norman Cutler in his *Consider Our
    Vow*. Madurai: Muttu Patippakam, 1979.
Tiruvempavai, Tamil text and English translation by G. U. Pope in *The Tiruvacagam
    or "Sacred Utterances" of the Tamil Poet, Saint, and Sage Manikka-vacagar*,
    103–116. Oxford: Clarendon Press, 1900 (reprinted New Delhi: Asian Education
    Services, 1995).

Secondary Sources

Balbir, Nalini. 1994. "Jainism." In *Religion and Women*, ed. Arvind Sharma, 121–138.
    Albany: State University of New York Press.
Filliozat, J. 1967. "L'Abandon de la vie par le sage et les suicides du criminel et du
    héros dans la tradition indienne." *Arts Asiatiques* 15: 65–88.
Findly, Ellison Banks. 2002. "The Housemistress at the Door: Vedic and Buddhist
    Perspectives on the Mendicant Encounter." In *Jewels of Authority: Women, Text,
    and the Hindu Tradition*, ed. Laurie Patton, 13–31. New York: Oxford University
    Press.
Jayadev, C. J. 1960. "Literary and Ethnographic References to the Tali and the
    Tali Rite." In *Archaeological Society of South India: Transactions for the Year
    1959–60*, 43–71. Madras: Archaeological Society of South India, Madras
    Museum.
Kaimal, Padma. 1999. "The Problem of Portraiture in South India, *circa* 870–970
    A.D." *Artibus Asiae* 59, nos. 1–2: 59–133.
————. 2000. "The Problem of Portraiture in South India, *circa* 970–1000 A.D."
    Artibus Asiae 60, no. 1: 139–179.

Mahalingam, T. V. 1985–. *A Topographical List of the Inscriptions in the Tamil Nadu and Kerala States.* 8 volumes. New Delhi: Indian Council of Historical Research.

McDaniel, June. 2003. *Making Virtuous Daughters and Wives: An Introduction to Women's Brata Rituals in Bengali Folk Religion.* Albany: State University of New York Press.

McGee, Mary. 1991. "Desired Fruits: Motive and Intention in the Votive Rites of Hindu Women." In *Roles and Rituals for Hindu Women,* ed. Julia Leslie, 71–88. Teaneck, NJ: Fairleigh Dickinson University Press.

Monius, Anne. Forthcoming. "The *Manimekalai*'s Buddhist Audience." In *Proceedings of the Eighth International Conference-Seminar on Tamil Studies.* Madras: International Association of Tamil Research.

Ogura, Yasushi. 1999. "The Changing Concept of Kingship in the Cola Period: Royal Temple Constructions, c. A.D. 850–1279." In *Kingship in Indian History,* ed. Noboru Karashima, 119–141. New Delhi: Manohar.

Orr, Leslie C. 1993. "Women of Medieval South India in Hindu Temple Ritual: Text and Practice." *Annual Review of Women in World Religions* 3: 107–141.

———. 1998a. "Jain and Hindu 'Religious Women' in Early Medieval Tamilnadu." In *Open Boundaries: Jain Communities and Cultures in Indian History,* ed. John E. Cort, 187–212. Albany: State University of New York Press.

———. 1998b. "Tracing Women's Lives in Medieval Tamil Inscriptions." Paper presented at the Annual Meeting of the American Academy of Religion, November 21–24, 1998, Orlando, Florida.

———. 1999. "Jain Worship in Medieval Tamilnadu." In *Approaches to Jaina Studies: Philosophy, Logic, Rituals and Symbols,* ed. N. K. Wagle and Olle Qvarnstrom, 250–274. Toronto: Centre for South Asian Studies, University of Toronto.

———. 2000a. *Donors, Devotees and Daughters of God: Temple Women in Medieval Tamilnadu.* New York: Oxford University Press.

———. 2000b. "Women's Wealth and Worship: Female Patronage of Hinduism, Jainism, and Buddhism in Medieval Tamilnadu." In *Faces of the Feminine in Ancient, Medieval, and Modern India,* ed. Mandakranta Bose, 124–147. New York: Oxford University Press.

———. 2004. "Processions in the Medieval South Indian Temple: Sociology, Sovereignty and Soteriology." In *South Indian Horizons: Felicitation Volume for François Gros on the Occasion of His 70th Birthday,* ed. Jean-Luc Chevillard and Eva Wilden, 437–470. Pondichéry: Institut français de Pondichéry/Ecole française d'Extrême-orient.

Pearson, Anne MacKenzie. 1996. *Because It Gives Me Peace of Mind: Ritual Fasts in the Religious Lives of Hindu Women.* Albany: State University of New York Press.

Peterson, I. V. 1988. "The Tie That Binds: Brothers and Sisters in North and South India." *South Asian Social Scientist* 4, no. 1: 25–52.

Raghotham, Venkata. 1995. "Kinship, Politics and Memory in Early Medieval Tamil Country: A Study of the Funerary Shrines of the Cholas." In *Sri Nagabhinandanam: Dr. M. S. Nagaraja Rao Festschrift,* ed. L. K. Srinivasan and S. Nagaraju, 593–608. Bangalore: Dr. M. S. Nagaraja Rao Felicitation Committee.

Rajasekhara, S. 1982. "Rastrakuta Hero-stones: A Study." In *Memorial Stones: A Study of Their Origin, Significance and Variety*, ed. S. Settar and Günther D. Sontheimer, 227–230. Dharwar: Karnatak University.

Reynell, Josephine. 1987. "Prestige, Honour and the Family: Laywomen's Religiosity amongst the Svatambar Murtipujak Jains in Jaipur." *Bulletin d'Etudes Indiennes* 5: 313–359.

Reynolds, Holly Baker. 1980. "The Auspicious Married Woman." In *The Powers of Tamil Women*, ed. Susan S. Wadley, 35–60. Syracuse, NY: Maxwell School of Citizenship and Public Affairs, Syracuse University.

Richman, Paula. 1997. *Extraordinary Child: Poems from a South Indian Devotional Genre*. Honolulu: University of Hawai'i Press.

Robinson, Sandra P. 1985. "Hindu Paradigms of Women: Images and Values." In *Women, Religion, and Social Change*, ed. Y. Y. Haddad and E. B. Findly, 181–215. Albany: State University of New York Press.

Sered, Susan Starr. 1992. *Women as Ritual Experts: The Religious Lives of Elderly Jewish Women in Jerusalem*. New York: Oxford University Press.

Sethuraman, N. 1991. "Crusade against Guhai (Monastery)." *Journal of the Epigraphical Society of India (Purabhilekha Patrika)* 17: 29–37.

Settar, S. 1982. "Memorial Stones in South India." In *Memorial Stones: A Study of Their Origin, Significance and Variety*, ed. S. Settar and Günther D. Sontheimer, 183–197. Dharwar: Karnatak University.

Settar, S., and Ravi K. Korisettar. 1982. "Nisidhis in Karnataka: A Survey." In *Memorial Stones: A Study of Their Origin, Significance and Variety*, ed. S. Settar and Günther D. Sontheimer, 283–293. Dharwar: Karnatak University.

Sontheimer, Günther D. 1982. "Hero and Sati-stones of Maharashtra." In *Memorial Stones: A Study of Their Origin, Significance and Variety*, ed. S. Settar and Günther D. Sontheimer, 261–281. Dharwar: Karnatak University.

Soundara Rajan, K. V. 1982. "Origin and Spread of Memorial Stones in Tamil Nadu." In *Memorial Stones: A Study of Their Origin, Significance and Variety*, ed. S. Settar and Günther D. Sontheimer, 59–76. Dharwar: Karnatak University.

Srinivasan, K. R. 1960. *Some Aspects of Religion as Revealed by Early Monuments and Literature of the South*. Madras: University of Madras.

Tewari, Laxmi G. 1991. *A Splendor of Worship: Women's Fasts, Rituals, Stories and Art*. New Delhi: Manohar.

Venkataraman, B. 1976. *Temple Art under the Chola Queens*. Faridabad: Thomson.

Vogel, J. P. 1930–1932. "The Head-offering to the Goddess in Pallava Sculpture." *Bulletin of the School of Oriental and African Studies* 6: 539–543.

Wagoner, Phillip B. 1996. "From 'Pampa's Crossing' to 'The Place of Lord Virupaksha': Architecture, Cult and Patronage at Hampi before the Founding of Vijayanagara." In *Vijayanagara: Progress of Research 1988–91*, ed. D. V. Devaraj and C. S. Patil, 141–174. Mysore: Directorate of Archaeology and Museums.

7

The Anatomy of Devotion: The Life and Poetry of Karaikkal Ammaiyar

Elaine Craddock

In the southernmost Indian state of Tamilnadu, Shaiva Siddhanta developed over many centuries to become the dominant philosophical, theological, and ritual system associated with the god Shiva. The tradition was systematized between the twelfth and fourteenth centuries but draws its devotional perspectives from the stories and hymns of the Nayanars, or "Leaders," the sixty-three devotees of Shiva who were canonized as saints in Cekkilar's twelfth-century hagiography, the *Periya Puranam*. Seven of these saints wrote poems to Shiva between the sixth and ninth centuries. Along with the Alvars, who sang to Vishnu, these poets were part of the *bhakti*, or devotional, movements that began in South India and spread the emotional worship of a personal god throughout the Indian subcontinent.

Karaikkal Ammaiyar, the "Mother from Karaikkal," was the first poet to write hymns to the god Shiva in Tamil, in the mid-sixth century, when the boundaries between Shiva's devotees and competing groups were just starting to be articulated in a self-conscious way. Speaking to God in one's mother tongue, rather than Sanskrit, was pivotal to the triumph of Hindu devotionalism over the religions of Jainism and Buddhism, which reached the apex of their popularity in South India during the fifth and sixth centuries.[1] Her powerful poetry is what Indira Peterson calls a "rhetoric of immediacy," as it speaks to a particular community defining itself in a context of competing religious allegiances (1999, 165). Along with the hymns of the later saints, Karaikkal Ammaiyar's 143 poems envision a world where devotees can dwell in perpetual bliss with Shiva, ridicule those who cannot see that Shiva is the only Truth, and include elements of the sophisticated philosophy that would be systematized as Shaiva Siddhanta centuries later.[2]

Her story remains popular in Tamilnadu,[3] and it vividly encapsulates notions of gender and devotion that are embedded in Tamil culture while problematizing the connection between women's ritual activity and the domestic realm. Before Karaikkal Ammaiyar became a poet, she was the model of a dutiful Hindu wife; her devotion to Shiva forms part of the continuum of her domestic life, in which she faithfully serves both her husband and her god. Yet it is her unswerving devotion to Shiva that ultimately ruptures her orderly domestic world and drives her to restructure her life outside the or-

FIGURE 7.1. Drawing of Karaikkal Ammaiyar by Haeli Colina.

dinary domestic realm. The ascetic path she embodies and praises forms a critique of her previous life as a devoted wife. Karaikkal Ammaiyar's story and poetry portray a life lived as a ritual offering to Shiva as the only true life, wherein rituals are not performed to achieve specific goals, as in the domestic sphere, but where goal and ritual merge in perpetual devotion to Shiva alone: text is practice, and practice is text. Her praise poems are the central ritual activity of her life pursuing personal salvation, but they are also a record that transcends her individual path and communicates her knowledge of Shiva to the members of a newly emerging devotional community.

The devotional movements contained elements of social as well as religious reform, protesting Brahminical orthodoxy along with the heterodox faiths of Buddhism and Jainism. But this revivalist Hinduism was rooted in the temple, which depended on royal patronage and the evolving sociopolitical alliance between Brahmins and agriculturalists.[4] So, although the devotional ideology undercut caste and gender hierarchies in principle, in practical terms the patriarchal boundaries remained. Statistically, women are not very visible among the Tamil devotional movements: Andal is the only woman Vaishnava saint, and out of the sixty-three Shaiva Nayanars, only three are women (Ramaswamy 1997, 120–121). However, the life and poetry of Karaikkal Ammaiyar, the only woman poet among the Nayanars, reveals a fascinating portrait of the localization of a pan-Indian god and the potential space for women in this emerging tradition.

Her Story

Karaikkal Ammaiyar was born in the sixth century into a well-to-do trading family in the coastal town of Karaikkal; she was originally named Punitavati.[5] In the well-known story about her, she was a beautiful girl who was married to the rich merchant Paramatattan, to whom she was a faithful wife, although this role proved to be at odds with her ardent devotion to Shiva. One day, Paramatattan's customer gave him two mangoes, which he told his wife to serve him later for his midday meal. But before he returned home for lunch, a Shaiva holy man came to the door for alms, so Punitavati gave him one of the mangoes and some rice. When her husband came home, she gave him his meal along with the remaining mango. He thought the mango was delicious and asked for the other one. Punitavati went to the kitchen to pray to Shiva for help; another mango appeared, which she served to her husband. This one was so much more delicious than the first that her husband was suspicious and asked his wife where she'd gotten it. She reluctantly told him, but he doubted her story and asked her to repeat the miracle in his presence. Again, Punitavati prayed to Shiva, and another mango appeared; her husband was terrified of her power and fled without releasing her from her wifely duties.

He set up another household in another city, while Punitavati continued to keep up his house and her appearance in anticipation of his return. Eventually, her parents found out where he was and took their daughter to him. He and his second wife and daughter, named Punitavati, fell at her feet in worship, calling her a goddess. When Punitavati learned that her husband didn't want her as a wife any more, she begged Shiva to take away the beauty she no longer needed and to give her a demon form. He granted her wish; she then made a pilgrimage to the Himalayas, walking on her hands so as not to defile god's heavenly abode with her feet. Shiva was so moved by her devotion he called her "Ammai," or mother, and allowed her to join his troupe of ghouls, his *ganas*, and to perpetually witness his dance at Tiruvalankatu, where she lived as his adoring slave.[6]

This story upholds the traditional notion that a woman's religious duty is to be devoted to her husband and her home: Punitavati does not forsake her wifely role until her husband has officially renounced her.[7] Punitavati's husband acknowledges her as a goddess, but cannot accept her as a wife; Punitavati's dramatic role reversal begins with her husband falling at her feet. Punitavati's gift for sincere devotion is, paradoxically, what disrupts the household's harmony; the boundaries of the domestic realm prove to be porous. Punitavati can finally indulge the true focus of her unswerving devotion: the god Shiva.

Ritualization and Asceticism

The story and the sculptures of Punitavati before her transformation stress that she is beautiful (Dehejia 1988, 135–137), but as soon as her husband releases her from her wifely role, she asks Shiva to take away her beauty, her femininity and sexuality, and give her the demonic form she considers worthy for worshipping him.[8] Ammaiyar is also called "Pey," or Demon; she identifies herself as the demon or ghoul from Karaikkal in several stanzas among her four works.[9]

> A female ghoul with withered breasts, bulging veins, hollow eyes,
>   white teeth and two fangs,
> shriveled stomach, red hair, bony ankles, and elongated shins,
> Stays in this cemetery, howling angrily.
>
> This place where my Lord dances in the fire with a cool body,
>   His streaming hair flying in the eight directions,
>   is Tiruvalankatu. (*Tiruvalankattu Mutta Tirupatikam*, 1.1)[10]

In another poem she says:

The One who has kept another eye on His forehead,
Has made me understand a little of Him.
I am one of the ghouls among His good *ganas*.
Whether or not this grace lasts,
I don't want anything else. (*Arputattiruvantati*, 86)

And in the last stanza of her longest work, she says:

By speaking this garland of *antati venpa* verses,
The words uttered by the Demon of Karaikkal, melting
    with love,
Those who worship with unending love will reach Shiva,
And worship Him with great love. (*Arputattiruvantati*, 101)[11]

Many of the Nayanars performed dramatic feats of self-sacrifice out of devotion to Shiva, but Karaikkal Ammaiyar's transformation from ideal wife to ideal demon devotee is particularly transgressive and serves to highlight the rupture between the domestic world of ordinary rituals and a life lived entirely as a ritual offering to Shiva. Karaikkal Ammaiyar's renunciation of domestic life to live in the cremation ground, praising Shiva, is an example of "ritualization," a term used by several theorists and defined by Catherine Bell as ritual as lived practice, as a way of acting that uses diverse strategies to differentiate meaningful, powerful, or sacred action from ordinary behavior (Bell 1992, 88–93). Ritualization creates a spatial/temporal environment in which an individual embodies and enacts structures of personal and social meaning within a perceived field of possibilities. Bell writes:

Ritualization always aligns one within a series of relationship[s]
linked to the ultimate sources of power. Whether ritual empowers or
disempowers one in some political sense, it always suggests the
ultimate coherence of a cosmos in which one takes a particular place.
This cosmos is experienced as a chain of states or an order of existence that places one securely in a field of action and in align-
ment with the ultimate goals of all action. (Bell 1992, 141)

Through her poetry, Karaikkal Ammaiyar delineates the only realm of ac-
tion that has ultimate meaning: sublimating herself as one of Shiva's adoring, ghoulish attendants. Her poetry expresses in literary Tamil a life of perpetual, spontaneous worship of Shiva in which all thought and action fuse in a ritual offering of pure awareness of God. Unlike female devotional poets who relate to God as their beloved, such as Andal relates to Krishna, Karaikkal Ammaiyar does not violate rules regarding chastity. In one sense, her life has moved along a continuum of devotion to others, with the others simply changing in importance.[12] But ultimately, Karaikkal Ammaiyar rejects the entire social and

domestic world of rules and obligations to pursue personal salvation, relocating her sphere of activity on the periphery of the social world (Mahalakshmi 2000, 33). This is not the classic renunciation called *sannyasa* that is typically undertaken at the end of life after fulfilling one's obligation to a family; the severe asceticism she undertakes in the prime of her life implicitly critiques the location of women in a domestic space of family relationships.[13] Karaikkal Ammaiyar's poetry dismantles the paradigm of human order and duty rooted in the household not by focusing on gender roles, but by extolling devotion to Shiva in a community of devotees in which gender is irrelevant.

Localizing God

Karaikkal Ammaiyar descends from her vision of Shiva and Parvati on Mt. Kailash to spend the rest of her life singing to Shiva as he dances in the cremation ground at Tiruvalankatu, or "Sacred Banyan Tree Forest," where he performs his fierce dance called *kalikatandava* or *urdhvatandava*, in which he defeats Kali by lifting his leg up to the sky (in this case, his left leg).[14] The Tiruvalankatu temple, north of Chennai, must have originally been at the base of a banyan tree (Dorai Rangaswamy 1990, 825). But now, in the Tiruvalankatu temple, Shiva dances in the Ratnasabhai, one of the five *sabhais*, or temple halls, in Tamilnadu associated with Shiva Nataraj, Shiva as Lord of the Dance.[15] Karaikkal Ammaiyar is shown at the feet of Shiva, playing cymbals and singing her praises to him. Her closed *samadhi* or shrine is behind this main image, not far from the giant banyan that is the temple tree (*sthala vriksham*); some of her verses are inscribed inside the temple. There is a separate shrine where Kali is seen dancing.

> In the cemetery where you hear crackling noises
> and the white pearls fall out of the tall bamboo,
> The ghouls with frizzy hair and drooping bodies,
> shouting with wide-open mouths,
> Come together and feast on the corpses.
> In the big, threatening cremation ground,
> When The Lord dances,
> The Daughter of the Mountain watches Him,
> In astonishment. (*Tiruvalankattu Mutta*
> *Tirupatikam*, 2.8)

Karaikkal Ammaiyar's poetry reveals an early stage in the process of the transcendent, pan-Indian deity Shiva taking up residence in a landscape dense with local, and sometimes competing, religious and cultural meaning. The poetry is filled with vivid images of Shiva as the heroic god whose grace rescues his devotees from the sorrows of the world, sometimes conveyed through detailed descriptions and at other times through metonymic references that imply that Karaikkal Ammaiyar's audience was at least minimally acquainted with Shiva's stories. These rhetorical strategies help to create and define a nascent community dedicated to the worship of Shiva.[16]

> I thought of only One.
> I was focused on only One.
> I kept only One inside my heart.
> > Look at this One!
> > It is He who has Ganga on His head,
> > A moonbeam in His hair,
> > A radiant flame in His beautiful hand.
> > I have become His slave. (*Arputattiruvantati*, 11)

Her poetry conveys to her audience a conception of Shiva drawn from the Sanskritic culture that began to permeate South India in the early centuries of the common era. She refers to several of Shiva's most famous deeds and manifestations: his heroic destruction of the Three Cities of the Demons; his burning of Kama; his crushing Ravana with his big toe when Ravana tries to lift Mt. Kailash; his swallowing the poison during the churning of the ocean so that his throat is blue; his rescuing of Markandeya from death; his killing of the elephant demon; his manifestation as the fiery *linga*; his terrifying Bhairava form, forced to wander as a beggar in penance for Brahmanicide; and most centrally for Karaikkal Ammaiyar, dancing with Kali in the cremation ground. She refers to Shiva as the Knower of the Vedas, indeed as the Vedas.[17] She thus builds a detailed iconography that unites the emerging Shaiva community and links it to the broader Indian traditions surrounding Shiva. It seems clear that even at this early date Karaikkal Ammaiyar and the emerging community of worshippers were seeing iconographic images of Shiva in temples, whether those temples were actual structures or open-air shrines.[18] However, unlike the later poets, she does not talk about temple worship and in one verse even criticizes those who expect to see Shiva through empty ritual.[19] Karaikkal Ammaiyar does not praise the Tamil landscape nor the Tamil language as the later poets do. Karaikkal Ammaiyar praises Shiva in the cremation ground at Tiruvalankatu. Through her powerful poetry, Karaikkal Ammaiyar reveals that the horrific cremation ground is really the cosmos, and the terrifying form of Shiva performing his dance of destruction is really the most sublime and blissful experience of the lord. She makes the terrible beautiful (Dorai Rangaswamy 1990, 441, 387) and leads the devotee beyond the limits of ordinary awareness into a transcendent knowledge of Shiva as Truth, as the dancer who dances the world and into the heart of his adoring devotee.[20]

The Tamil word *katu* means forest, jungle, or desert, but it also means cremation or burial ground, as well as boundary or limit.[21] In the life and poetry of Karaikkal Ammaiyar, the cremation ground encompasses the notion of the forest as the opposite of civilization (Tamil *natu*, city), in addition to the pollution, fear of death, and ghoulish forces traditionally associated with a burning ground. Her poetry is connected to the Shaiva tradition that develops after her, but it also resonates with the earlier Cankam *puram* poetry that praises heroes in war and provides detailed descriptions of the battlefield, gruesome places of death and sacrifice, where demons feast on the corpses lying on the field and dance, garlanded with intestines. Korravai, the Tamil goddess of victory, is described in Cankam poetry as surrounded by demonesses, eating flesh and dancing with dead bodies on the battlefield (Hart 1975, 31–41; Ramaswamy 1997, 129–130; Mahalakshmi 2000, 24–27). Indeed, Karaikkal Ammaiyar uses a trope of the heroic warrior to describe Shiva as the conqueror of death for the devotee and as the ultimate sovereign of the universe:

> Ghouls with flaming mouths and rolling, fiery eyes,
> Going around, doing the *tunankai* dance,
> Running and dancing in the terrifying forest,
> Draw out a burning corpse from the fire and eat the flesh.

> The place where our Lord raises His leg in the *vattanai* posture
>   with the *kalal* jangling and the anklets tinkling,
> Dancing so that the fire in His hand spreads everywhere and
>   His hair whips around,
> Is Tiruvalankatu. (*Tiruvalankattu Mutta Tirupatikam*, 1.7)

Here, Shiva is dancing with Kali and takes the *vattanai* posture with his leg in the air—his special posture at Tiruvalankatu—to defeat her. The poem uses two sets of ankle bracelets to signify the divine competition: Kali's anklets jingle as she dances, and Shiva's *kalal*, or hero's victory anklets, jangle as he dances so dynamically that his hair whips around in his frenzy, dancing as the god of destruction, but also as the conqueror of death (Shulman 1980, 213–221). The *tunankai* dance is associated with Korravai; it was also danced at festivals,[22] and in fact can mean "festival." It is a type of village dance in which the arms are bent and struck against the sides of the body. *Tunankai* is also a kind of *pey*, or demon.[23] The Tamil imagery that Karaikkal Ammaiyar uses in her poetry serves to localize the god in a familiar landscape and to connect local sacred forces to the Shaiva pantheon. During the post-Cankam period (approximately 300–600 C.E.), Korravai is increasingly associated with Durga and Kali, and therefore with Shiva. It seems that Karaikkal Ammaiyar is consciously associating the powerful forces of the demons occupying Tiruvalankatu with the transcendent god dancing in the cremation ground. By becoming one of Shiva's *ganas*, or ghouls, she assumes a kind of power familiar in the early Tamil world and connects the indigenous demon tradition with one of the central myths of Shiva (Mahalakshmi 2000, 29). Karaikkal Ammaiyar is also linked closely to Tiruvalankatu because of Nili, the ancient and fierce goddess located in the nearby town of Palaiyanur.[24] Despite the strong goddess tradition in the area, however, Karaikkal Ammaiyar remains focused on Shiva; Parvati appears in several of her verses, but Ammaiyar's single-minded devotion never wavers from the lord.[25]

Defining a Path

The cremation ground is the stage for Shiva's dance of life and death and salvation. It is also the space in the heart of the devotee where the ego is burned up as she surrenders to him.[26] Through vivid and jarring imagery, Karaikkal Ammaiyar reveals that the terrifying place of death is really the beautiful and blissful abode of the lord and the sacred grove of liberation from this world.

> The *picacu*, wearing a white skull garland tied tightly,
>   Swallowed up the congealed fat.
> Having named its child Kali,
>   Bringing her up with comfort,
>   She wiped the dust off the child, suckled it, then went away.
> The child, not seeing the mother returning, cried itself to sleep.
> The place where our Lord dances in the cemetery is
>   Tiruvalankatu. (*Tiruvalankattu Mutta Tirupatikam*, 1.5)

Karaikkal Ammaiyar's close attention to mundane activities confronts the devotee's habitual understanding of the cremation ground as a threatening, marginal, "other" place. Here, the *picacu* ghoul is a gentle mother, caring for a child. The intimate scene plays out in the same space as Shiva's dance, breaking down the barrier between domestic space and the place of death. Karaikkal Ammaiyar attempts to shatter the illusions of ordinary awareness and show that ultimately, the cremation ground is a state of mind, where the true devotees who meditate on Shiva overcome their fear of death and experience him as the beautiful lord, with his upraised dancing foot pointing to liberation through him.

> If, with wisdom,
> And without ridiculing His body that is garlanded with bones,
> They praise the One who wears a moon on His long matted
>   hair, and
> Who conquered the three great cities of the powerful *asuras*
>   who did not respect Him;
> They will not be born here in this world in a body with bones.
>   (*Arputattiruvantati*, 37)

As we see in this poem, bones are a central liberation motif in Karaikkal Ammaiyar's poetry. Shiva ornaments himself with a garland of bones he finds in the cremation ground, the bones of everyone and anyone; he does not discriminate, just as he responds to all devotees.[27] But devotees must get beyond terror and revulsion at his horrific form to see that he is the conqueror of death. If they are able to reach this point, Shiva will liberate them from life in this world "in a body with bones." Karaikkal Ammaiyar is an emaciated skeleton of a figure, an assemblage of bones at home in the cremation ground but liberated by it.

The other major symbol of liberation is fire. The cremation ground burns with funeral fires, signifying the end for all those whose ignorance clouds their vision of the lord. Shiva's terrifying dance takes place in fire, and he holds fire in his hand. Whether that fire is terrifying, signaling death and destruc-tion, or illuminating depends on the devotee's consciousness. The center of this crowded, gruesome scene is Shiva dancing in the fire of destruction, yet his yogi body is cool, not affected by the fire he creates. Karaikkal Ammaiyar promotes a vision of Shiva as the beautiful embodiment of the rhythm of life, burning away our illusions with the fire in his hand.

> If you consider the One who has the complexion of the red
>   rays of the setting sun, and of a smoldering fire,
>   And whose matted hair hangs down,
> You would say that to those who have surrendered to Him,
> He shines like a golden flame;
> But to those who move away without taking refuge in Him,
> He has the nature of leaping fire. (*Arputattiruvantati*, 82)

Creating Community

The devotional movement denies caste or gender privileges, but ultimately the only real egalitarianism is the spiritual equality of the worshippers of Shiva, in contrast to other religious groups, including devotees who follow a different path to Shiva (Zvelebil 1973, 194). Karaikkal Ammaiyar is pursuing her own path to salvation, but at the same time she is working to create a community of devotees who also understand that Shiva is the ultimate Truth. In addition to sharing a Vedic, mythic understanding of Shiva, the Tamil Shaiva community was forged partly by the harsh rhetoric of the Tamil Shaiva saints against the Buddhists and Jains in particular. Peterson argues that "the negative represen-tation of Jains was an important part of a process of self-definition and consoli-dation of power for the Tamil Shaiva sect.... Jains were not only a threatening rival group, but a very useful foil against which to establish the superiority of the Shaiva religion" (1999, 164). Karaikkal Ammaiyar does not refer to any group by name, lumping together as "others" the people against whom she is defining her spiritual path.[28] But it is clear that she is referring to non-Vedic groups. She says:

> Look!
> Having become a slave to the beautiful feet of the
> One whose red matted hair has the waves of Ganga,

We have realized Him through scriptures,
We have become suitable for this life and for the other world.
Why do others gossip about us behind our backs?
Understand us. (*Arputattiruvantati*, 91)

In other poems, she is even more scathing:

Ignorant mind,
Worship the feet of the devotees, again and again
Focusing on them, and praising them with words.
Leave that group of people who do not think about
The One who wears a moon as a small garland,
Which no one else wears. (*Arputattiruvantati*, 40)

Oh! You pitiable people
Who are without wisdom.
It is an easy way to live,
Thinking of our Lord all the time,
Our Father with the gleaming throat,
Who wanders around,
Wearing a snake. (*Arputattiruvantati*, 46)

His greatness is such that it is not known by others.
[But] [o]thers know he is the great consciousness.
Our Lord, wearing the bones of others,
Happily dances along with the strong ghouls
In the fire at night. (*Arputattiruvantati*, 30)

In this poem, the first "others" refers again to the usual suspects who do not understand him. The second "others" refers to his devotees, who do realize who he is. The third, "the bones of others," refers to "just anyone," conveying that Shiva does not discriminate against anyone concerning whose bones he wears; he treats all equally, is God to all equally, and is open to all devotees. The many references to these "others" who do not understand Shiva reveal how influential these heterodox communities were. The lumping together of all these groups probably reveals that the Jains were not the only powerful voice that the Shaivas had to resist. But, perhaps most important at this early period, Karaikkal Ammaiyar's refusal to specify any one community conveys the key point: everyone who doesn't follow the right path to Shiva is equally ignorant. She urges followers to "worship the feet of the devotees," requiring that worthy individuals be identified as belonging to the emerging community. Serving Shiva by serving his devotees remains an important part of the tradition (Peterson 1989, 41–47).

All those other people who do not understand that He
   is the real truth, Have seen only His ghoul form:

> His lotus-like body smeared with ash and garlanded with bones.
> See that they ridicule Him? (*Arputattiruvantati*, 29)

Although Karaikkal Ammaiyar doesn't transgress the boundaries of chastity for a woman, she does transgress other boundaries, evoking a tantric orientation to the world.[29] Karaikkal Ammaiyar's transgressive behavior does not go to the extremes of some Shaiva worshippers of her milieu, but she engages in behavior that turns ordinary categories of personal and social perception upside down in order to force a transcendent spiritual awareness, including an understanding of the self as rooted in divine power. This perspective is intensified by the Tamil view of the world as pervaded by powers, including the forces present in places of death, such as the cremation ground. Karaikkal Ammaiyar's extreme ascetic emphasis reveals the early, broad roots of the Tamil Shaiva tradition before it is systematized into a temple-based orthodoxy. This asceticism is rooted in a milieu of multiple traditions, drawing particularly from the earliest Shaiva sects, often grouped together as the Pashupatas, whose followers imitated Shiva in his terrible Bhairava form, often in the cremation ground. These devotees enacted Shiva's penance for Brahmanicide, which he incurred by cutting off Brahma's fifth head when he tried to sleep with his own daughter, and because of which Shiva is known as the beggar Bhiksayatana and as Kapalin the skull-bearer.[30] Later poets refer to Pashupata ascetics worshipping at Shiva's shrines, but the emerging orthodox tradition rejected their devotional mode. This is probably one major reason that Karaikkal Ammaiyar's poetry is not regularly sung in Shiva temples today, in contrast to the Tevaram poets, whose hymns are regularly sung. Perhaps because the nearby town of Tiruvorriyur is known to have had a significant Pashupata presence at this time, Karaikkal Ammaiyar was drawn to a more extreme asceticism than the later Nayanars embodied (Krishna Murthy 1985). In one poem, she takes the point of view of a male ascetic:

> My heart!
> Give up your bondage, your wife and children.
> Saying that you take refuge here at His feet,
> Think of Him and worship. (*Tiruvirattai Manimalai*, 13)

And elsewhere she says:

> Not following a false path ruled by the five senses,
> We have achieved merits,
> > Because of the Lord's love for His slaves. (*Tiruvirattai
> > Manimalai*, 16)

> Now we have been elevated;
> > We have reached God's feet.
> > Now we do not have any troubles.
> > O my heart!

You will see that we have now crossed over the turbulent
   sea of inescapable births
That causes an ocean of karma. (*Arputattiruvantati*, 16)

The intimacy of Ammaiyar's relationship to Shiva combines with her living beyond social norms to create a powerful model of the devotional path. A wife is expected to serve her husband and sacrifice herself for his welfare; Karaikkal Ammaiyar relocates this behavior in the cremation ground, where she serves Shiva as her lord. Through Karaikkal Ammaiyar's life and poetry, a new form of Shiva takes shape (Ramaswamy 1997, 129). Karaikkal Ammaiyar's poetry does not describe the ecstatic fusing with the divine seen in other devotional poetry (Hardy 1983, 306–307). The goal of Shaivism is to become liberated from the cycle of rebirth by becoming like Shiva or, at least, more like him.[31] Karaikkal Ammaiyar exhorts devotees to focus all of their energies in constant meditation on Shiva as the discipline that leads to salvation. Her poetry is intellectual, focusing on the experiential understanding of Shiva as knowledge and the ultimate truth gained through meditation, an important perspective in the development of the orthodox Shaiva Siddhanta tradition.

He is the one who knows.
He is the one who makes us know.
He is the one who knows because He is knowledge itself.
He is the truth that is to be known.
He is the sun and moon, the earth, sky,
   and all the other elements. (*Arputatiruvantati*, 20)

In the ritualization of her life, Karaikkal Ammaiyar renounces her life in the domestic sphere, becomes one of Shiva's ghoul attendants, and dwells in perpetual bliss with him. Her radical transformation from a lovely, dutiful wife into an emaciated, frightening demon reveals that knowing Shiva requires the devotee to transcend ordinary human awareness and to see that the terrifying cremation ground is really the beautiful place of liberation. Her poetry urges people to give up a life rooted in family relationships and bounded by conventional rituals and goals, and instead to live their lives as ritual offerings to Shiva. Through vivid descriptions of the beautiful lord Shiva, multiple mythic references to his deeds, and regular references to a host of ignorant "others," Karaikkal Ammaiyar delineates a spiritual path and creates a community that centers on a self-conscious understanding of Shiva as the ultimate Truth and the only path to liberation.

NOTES

   1. On the interplay of multiple religions in medieval South India, see in addition, Sastri 1975, 3, 130, 135, 137; Davis 1999; Peterson 1999; and Monius 2001.

The great Tamil Jain epic *Cilappatikaram* and the Tamil Buddhist epic *Manimekalai* were composed during this period.

2. See Monius 2001, especially ch. 1, for a discussion of imagined and imaginary community.

3. In addition to written versions, her story is told in a Tamil film, *Karaikkal Ammaiyar*.

4. See Stein 1980; Davis 1999; Peterson 1999; Mahalakshmi 2000, 17–19; Ramaswamy 1997, 118–121. On the development of the Shaiva Siddhanta tradition, which is beyond the scope of this chapter, see Davis 2000 and Prentiss 1999. Shaiva Siddhanta was originally a pan-Indian tradition that for a number of reasons survived and thrived in Tamilnadu. On the *bhakti* movements in South India, see Peterson 1989, Hardy 1983, and Champakalakshmi 2004.

5. The story was originally told in Cekkilar's *Periya Puranam*, which is retold in many versions. I am also drawing here on the *Tiruvalankattu Talavaralarum*, the temple history book sold at Tiruvalankatu.

6. Shiva at Tiruvalankatu is called Vatanaroshvara, and the temple is called Vatanaroshvara Swamy Tirukoyil. On the back cover of the temple's official history is an upside-down picture of Mt. Kailash, which is the view Karaikkal Ammaiyar had as she walked down from Mt. Kailash to Tiruvalankatu on her hands. The last part of the temple book contains the story of her life from Cekkilar's hagiography and a few verses of her poetry. There is a sculpture in the temple of Karaikkal Ammaiyar climbing on her hands to see Shiva and Parvati. This is the only instance when Shiva called anyone "mother" (*Periya Puranam*, 539).

Karaikkal Ammaiyar is most closely associated with Tiruvalankatu, but there is a yearly mango festival in her honor during the month of Ani (June–July) in her hometown of Karaikkal; see Ramaswamy 1997, 132.

7. There is a large literature on women's roles in Hindu life; see, for instance, Harlan and Courtright 1995.

8. Mahalakshmi (2000) discusses the notion, raised by other scholars, that Karaikkal Ammaiyar renounced her body as a reaction to her husband abandoning her. She maintains that Karaikkal Ammaiyar's evocation of the demonic figure "suggests a deliberate evocation of certain symbols, and the denial of still others" (33).

9. These four works are *Arputattiruvantati* with 101 *venpa* verses; *Tiruvirattai Manimalai* with 20 stanzas in *venpa* and *kattalaik kalitturai*; and the two *patikams* called *Tiruvalankattu Mutta Tirupatikankal* with 11 verses each. She probably wrote the first *prabandha* literature, and invented the *antati* form. See especially Zvelebil 1975, 136–137. Zvelebil states that Karaikkal Ammaiyar likely introduced the *kattalaik kalitturai* form. Accounts of her life suggest she wrote the first two works before going to Mt. Kailash, then she wrote the Tiruvalankatu poems when she arrived there; see Dorai Rangaswamy 1990, 972–973.

10. All translations are my own, which I made in partnership with Dr. R. Vijayalakshmy, professor emeritus at the International Institute of Tamil Studies. This text is from *Tiruvalankattu Talavaralarum Tiruppatikankalum*.

11. The *antati* is a poetic structure in which the last syllable or word of a verse is repeated as the first syllable or word of the next verse, forming a kind of chain.

Venpa is a poetic meter that consists of two, three, or four lines per verse. The last line of the verse contains three feet (Tamil *cir*); the other lines contain four feet. See Zvelebil 1975, 135–137, 278–280; and Hart 1975, 197–199.

12. Caroline Walker Bynum's works on medieval European Christianity have addressed women's spiritual lives as continuous with their domestic lives and their explorations of the connections between femaleness and physicality. See, for example, Bynum 1987.

13. See Denton 1992 on women's asceticism.

14. For a discussion of whether the *urdhvatandava* pose requires the right leg, see Dorai Rangaswamy 1990, 456.

15. The others, represented and labeled at the Tiruvalankatu temple, are Chidambaram, Madurai, Tirunelveli, and Kutralam. Dorai Rangaswamy lists them as Kanchipuram, Tiruceenkattangudi, Tenkasi, and Taramangala (1990, 452).

16. Several scholars have written about how a text can construct community. For South India in particular, see Monius 2001; Richman 1988.

17. Such as in *Arputattiruvantati*, 15.

18. Dorai Rangaswamy 1990, 3–18; Hardy 1983, 202–213; Prentiss 1999, 51; Ayyar 1974, 211; Krishna Murthy 1985, 6–14, 42–47; Peterson 1982, 72.

19. See *Arputattiruvantati*, 17.

20. See Narayanan 2003, especially 500–501.

21. *Tamil Lexicon* 1982, 855. See also Hart and Heifetz 1999, 362–363.

22. Hart 1975, 23, 45, 142; Hart and Heifetz 1999, 166.

23. *Tamil Lexicon* 1982, 1963.

24. The story of Nili is told in the epic *Cilappatikaram*, Canto 23. Nili's story is included in the temple's history, the *Tiruvalankatu Talavaralaru*, 178–196; her story continues to be important in the area. See Mahalakshmi 2000, 33–40; Shulman 1980, 194–197, 213–221; and Peterson 1989, 203.

25. This pure focus on Shiva is contrasted in the film about Karaikkal Ammaiyar in which Parvati tells her she must first worship the goddess in order to get to Shiva.

26. See Coomaraswamy 1999, 89.

27. See also *Arputattiruvantati*, 30.

28. In Shaiva poetry, "others" are sometimes referred to as "the six faiths" (*akacamayam*), which can refer to six sects of Shaiva Siddhanta, or six sectarian groups with different cultic deities. *Tamil Lexicon* 1982, 8; Peterson 1989, 132–133, n.52.

29. Tantra is a vast subject that cannot be taken up in detail here. There are many perspectives on and definitions of tantra, as the scholarship shows, including elements of yoga and meditation. See Denton 1992, 225–227; Brooks 1990, 3–6; Padoux 2002. Among other things, Padoux addresses the porous boundary between tantra and *bhakti*. The later Shaiva Siddhanta tradition uses the tantric texts called Agamas as the ritual manuals in temple worship; see Davis 2000; Prentiss 1999; Filliozat 1983.

30. Flood 1996, 154–173; Bhandarkar 1983, 145ff.; Dorai Rangaswamy 1990, 392–393, 400, 1265.

31. Davis 1999, 221.

REFERENCES

Ayyar, C. V. Narayana. 1974. *Origin and Early History of Saivism in South India*. Madras: University of Madras.

Bell, Catherine. 1992. *Ritual Theory, Ritual Practice*. New York: Oxford University Press.

Bhandarkar, Ramkrishna Gopal. 1983. *Vaisnavism, Saivism and Minor Religious Systems*. New Delhi: Asian Educational Services.

Brooks, Douglas Renfrew. 1990. *The Secret of the Three Cities: An Introduction to Hindu Sakta Tantrism*. Chicago: University of Chicago Press.

Bynum, Caroline Walker. 1987. *Holy Feast, Holy Fast: The Religious Significance of Food to Medieval Women*. Berkeley: University of California Press.

Champakalashmi, R. 2004. "From Devotion and Dissent to Dominance: The Bhakti of the Tamil Alvars and Nayanars." In *Religious Movements in South Asia 600–1800*, ed. David N. Lorenzen, 47–80. New Delhi: Oxford University Press.

Cilappatikaram. 1997. Trans. V. R. Ramachandra Dikshitar. Chennai: International Institute of Tamil Studies.

Coomaraswamy, Ananda. 1999 [1918]. *The Dance of Shiva*. New Delhi: Munshiram Manoharlal.

Davis, Richard H. 1999. "The Story of the Disappearing Jains." In *Open Boundaries: Jain Communities and Cultures in Indian History*, ed. John E. Cort, 213–224. Delhi: Sri Satguru.

———. 2000. *Worshiping Siva in Medieval India: Ritual in an Oscillating Universe*. Delhi: Motilal Banarsidass.

Dehejia, Vidya. 1988. *Slaves of the Lord: The Path of the Tamil Saints*. New Delhi: Munshiram Manoharlal.

Denton, Lynn Teskey. 1992. "Varieties of Hindu Female Asceticism." In *Roles and Rituals for Hindu Women*, ed. Julia Leslie, 211–231. Delhi: Motilal Banarsidass.

Dorai Rangaswamy, M. A. 1990 [1958–1959]. *The Religion and Philosophy of Tevaram*. Madras: University of Madras.

Filliozat, Jean. 1983. "The Role of the Saivagamas in the Saiva Ritual System." In *Experiencing Siva: Encounters with a Hindu Deity*, ed. Fred W. Clothey and J. Bruce Long, 81–101. Columbia, MO: South Asia Books.

Flood, Gavin. 1996. *An Introduction to Hinduism*. Cambridge: Cambridge University Press.

Hardy, Friedhelm. 1983. *Viraha-Bhakti: The Early History of Krsna Devotion in South India*. New Delhi: Oxford University Press.

Harlan, Lindsey, and Paul B. Courtright. 1995. "Introduction: On Hindu Marriage and Its Margins." In *From the Margins of Hindu Marriage*, ed. Lindsey Harlan and Paul B. Courtright, 3–18. New York: Oxford University Press.

Hart, George L. 1975. *The Poems of Ancient Tamil*. Berkeley: University of California Press.

Hart, George L., and Hank Heifetz, trans. and eds. 1999. *The Four Hundred Songs of War and Wisdom*. New York: Columbia University Press.

Karaikkal Ammaiyar. 1973. Directed by A. P. Nagarajan. EVR Films.

Karaikkalammaiyar Pirapantankal. 1961. Commentary by Shri Arumukattampiran. Tiruvavatuturai: Tiruvavatuturai Math.

Krishna Murthy, C. 1985. *Saiva Art and Architecture in South India*. Delhi: Sundeep Prakashan.

Lorenzen, David N. 1972. *The Kapalikas and Kalamukhas: Two Lost Saivite Sects*. Delhi: Motilal Banarsidass.

———. 2002. "Early Evidence for Tantric Religion." In *The Roots of Tantra*, ed. Katherine Anne Harper and Robert L. Brown, 25–36. Albany: State University of New York Press.

Mahalakshmi, R. 2000. "Outside the Norm, within the Tradition: Karaikkal Ammaiyar and the Ideology of Tamil Bhakti." *Studies in History* 16, no. 1, n.s.: 17–40. New Delhi: Sage.

Monius, Anne E. 2001. *Imagining a Place for Buddhism*. Oxford: Oxford University Press.

Narayanan, Vasudha. 2003. "Embodied Cosmologies: Sights of Piety, Sites of Power." *Journal of the American Academy of Religion* 71, no. 3 (September): 495–520.

Padoux, Andre. 2002. "What Do We Mean by Tantrism?" In *The Roots of Tantra*, ed. Katherine Anne Harper and Robert L. Brown, 17–24. Albany: State University of New York Press.

Periya Puranam: A Tamil Classic on the Great Saiva Saints of South India, by Sekkizhaar. 1985. Trans. G. Vanmikathan. Madras: Sri Ramakrishna Math.

Peterson, Indira V. 1982. "Singing of a Place: Pilgrimage as Metaphor and Motif in the Tevaram Songs of the Tamil Saivite Saints." *Journal of the American Oriental Society* 102, no. 1: 69–90.

———. 1989. *Poems to Siva*. Princeton, NJ: Princeton University Press.

———. 1999. "Sramanas against the Tamil Way." In *Open Boundaries: Jain Communities and Cultures in Indian History*, ed. John E. Cort, 163–185. Delhi: Sri Satguru.

Prentiss, Karen Pechilis. 1999. *The Embodiment of Bhakti*. New York: Oxford University Press.

Ramaswamy, Vijaya. 1997. *Walking Naked: Women, Society, Spirituality in South India*. Shimla: Indian Institute of Advanced Study.

Richman, Paula. 1988. *Women, Branch Stories, and Religious Rhetoric in a Tamil Buddhist Text*. Syracuse, NY: Maxwell School of Citizenship and Public Affairs, Syracuse University.

Sastri, K. A. Nilakanta. 1975. *A History of South India*. New Delhi: Oxford University Press.

Shulman, David Dean. 1980. *Tamil Temple Myths: Sacrifice and Divine Marriage in the South Indian Saiva Tradition*. Princeton, NJ: Princeton University Press.

Stein, Burton. 1980. *Peasant State and Society in Medieval South India*. New Delhi: Oxford University Press.

Tamil Lexicon. 1982. Madras: University of Madras.

Tiruvalankattu Talavaralarum Tiruppatikankalum. 1998. Tiruttani: Cuppiramaniya Swamy Tirukoyil.

Tiruvalankatu Talavaralaru: Alankattil Antamura Nimirntatum Maniyampalakkuttan. n.d. Chennai: Kavuniyan.

Zvelebil, Kamil. 1973. *The Smile of Murugan: On Tamil Literature in South India*. Leiden: Brill.

———. 1975. *Tamil Literature*. Leiden: Brill.

8

The Play of the Mother: Possession and Power in Hindu Women's Goddess Rituals

Kathleen M. Erndl

Context: *Shakti* "Plays"

This chapter explores Hindu women's religious empowerment in connection with goddess possession rituals in the Kangra Valley area of Himachal Pradesh. In Kangra, as in many other regions of India, it is not uncommon for a goddess to "play" in the body of a woman, or as it is also stated idiomatically, for a woman to "play," that is, to embody the *shakti* (power, creative energy, consciousness) of a goddess, to speak with her voice, and to heal and prophesy in her community. Those women who experience this *shakti* deeply and on a continuous and sustained basis may attain the status of a *mataji*, that is, a respected mother, a religious leader, a holy woman, a goddess herself. Divine possession as a form of religious expression is interconnected with such practices as pilgrimage to temples, *puja* (image worship), recitation of sacred texts, fasting, and meditation, which comprise the *bhakti-* (devotion) and *tantra-* (esotericism) oriented religious complex of Shaktism or goddess worship in the region. In the Kangra area, there are several famous goddess temples, such as Jvala Mukhi and Camunda Devi (Erndl 1993), and hundreds of smaller, more localized goddess shrines. Although the worship of male deities such as Krishna, Shiva, and Baba Balak Nath is also prevalent, the worship of goddesses is so pervasive that in the Kangra context, Shaktism can be considered practically congruent with general popular Hinduism rather than a sectarian designation.

The material in this chapter is taken from a larger study, based on fieldwork conducted in Kangra with holy women, known as *matajis*, who become possessed, and their devotees, both female and male.

In the Hindi, Panjabi, and Kangri languages in which this research was conducted, "playing" (*khelna, khedna*) refers to the creative, dynamic, and awesome activity of both the goddess and the woman who is possessed by her. Similarly, words meaning "mother" (*ma, mata, mataji*) refer not only to ordinary mothers but also both to the goddess and to the woman she possesses. In other words, the woman both plays and the goddess plays in her; the woman is both the agent and instrument of the playing. Thus, the title of this chapter, "The Play of the Mother," is a play on words suggestive of the ambiguous fluidity between human and divine identities and powers in the phenomenon of Hindu goddess possession.

The questions informing my inquiry into this phenomenon include the following: to what extent do women's ritual activities, especially those connected with goddess possession, articulate a discourse that reproduces, legitimates, and validates the social order (i.e., the elite Brahminical ideology of women's subordination), and to what extent do they articulate a discourse that challenges, alters, and transforms the social order? To what extent do these rituals reflect women's roles in the domestic sphere, and to what extent do they transgress these boundaries? How does goddess possession transform women's identities and socioreligious roles? In what sense are *matajis* and their devotees powerful? In this brief chapter, I will not address all of these issues explicitly or in detail, but they do form the background of my inquiry. Here, I present women's goddess possession rituals as traditional cultural resources which create an arena for women's empowerment in the varied and rapidly changing context of contemporary India.

I wish to state at the outset that I do not see possession as a pathological condition either of the individual person or of the society, nor do I see it as an exotic remnant of the distant past, an anachronism which will (or should) soon disappear as people give up "superstition" or adopt a more "rational" outlook. I would like to think that such notions are outdated, if not in popular understanding, then in scholarly discourse, but such is not the case. Such views are ethnocentric in that they privilege the culturally constructed post-Enlightenment European notion of a separate, individual, impenetrable, and inviolable self, what Alan Watts called the "skin-encapsulated ego" and Gregory Bateson decried as "the epistemological error of Occidental civilization" (Macy 1990, 53). Nor do I see goddess possession as a less important or inferior form of religious expression, as compared with the more male-dominated, textual, and elite Sanskritic rituals. In general, I am in agreement with such feminist scholars as Janice Boddy (1989) and Susan Starr Sered (1994), who view possession trance as part of the normal range of human experience, even a talent, which tends to appear more often among women, not because of any essential quality of women, but because their life experiences and culturally constructed roles and identities predispose them to it. Considering spirit possession cross-culturally and seeing it as a prime example of the this-worldly orientation and immanence of the divine characteristics of female-dominated religions, Susan Sered has eloquently written:

> If we take stock of . . . explanations of women and spirit possession, an interesting pattern becomes evident. All the theories . . . (social deprivation, sexual deprivation, calcium deprivation, and over-determination of gender) start from the assumption that possession trance is an abnormal phenomenon. Therefore, the explanation for women's involvement in spirit possession necessarily lies in some form of divergence from normal, healthy human experience. I would like to raise a different possibility. Is it possible that possession trance is one of a range of normal human abilities or talents, in much the same way that musical ability or athletic ability is? Could it be that in many cultures male socialization prevents most men from developing the ability to embrace the enriching, exciting, *normal* experience of spirit possession? Is it perhaps the case that the vast majority of men, for a variety of psychosocial reasons, are so preoccupied with guarding their ego boundaries from the threat of "invasion" that they reject, or refuse to recognize, a religious experience that involves melding one's being with another entity? As Janice Boddy writes, "It is imperative to ask why so many Western scholars . . . are committed to viewing possession as a consequence of women's deprivation rather than their privilege, or perhaps their inclination" (1989, 140). The answer to her question, it seems to me, lies in the double-barreled intellectual weakness of ethnocentrism and androcentrism. (Sered 1994, 190–191)

I have come to understand the possession experience, both for the woman possessed and for her devotees who may be observing her, as continuous with ordinary lived experience, so that women's experiences in possession rituals both influence and are influenced by their everyday lives. Moreover, I largely reject the so-called deprivation theory, proposed by anthropologist I. M. Lewis (2003) and other scholars, which holds that women and other low-status people resort to possession and ecstatic religious expressions in order to compensate for their relative lack of power in secular life. Besides noting the fact that many high-status women, as well as some men, are involved in ecstatic religious practices, I suggest not only that such religious or spiritual power is valid in its own right, not inferior to, derivative of, or a substitute for economic or social power, but also that "religious" and "secular" power are simply convenient analytical categories that often obscure more than they illuminate. Furthermore, goddess possession should not be viewed as an isolated phenomenon but in the Hindu context must be viewed as a religious expression coexisting and intertwined with many other ritual, devotional, yogic, and contemplative practices associated with Shakta traditions.

Matajis: Shakti-filled Women

Possession by many types of deities and spirits, benevolent and malevolent, is widespread, particularly among women throughout South Asia (Schoembucher 1993). Divine possession by goddesses, again primarily among women, is prevalent in the northwest part of India, which includes Kangra, and in other areas of India, such as Bengal (McDaniel 2004).[1] The goddess—in Kangra worshipped by such names as Vaishno Devi, Jvala Mukhi, Durga, and Kali—manifests herself in many different personalities and modes, including icons (murti), stone pillars (pindi), and flame (jot or jyoti), but possession is the most dramatic of these manifestations, for it brings the goddess in face-to-face and voice-to-voice contact with her devotees. The shakti, or divine power, of the goddess enters into, or plays with, the body and temporarily blots out the consciousness of the human medium. While in this possession trance, the medium speaks with the voice of the goddess. Afterward, she returns to her "normal" state of consciousness and may or may not remember what was said in trance. By word of mouth, such women typically begin to attract followers who come to them for help with problems and address them as mataji, a term which not only means mother in the ordinary sense, but also a respected holy woman or even a goddess herself. A transformation takes place through repeated possession, so that the woman becomes more and more "goddess-like," more and more divinized, even in her nonpossessed state. Matajis may be married or single, householders or renunciants, high caste or low caste, and locally, regionally, or even nationally known. I give brief snapshots here of three matajis to give a sense of the spectrum of women who play.

One such woman was Tara Devi, a barely literate housewife with several children who lived in a village near Baijnath. She was transformed through a process of repeated possession and "negotiation" with the goddess Jvala Mukhi into a respected healer with a home temple and a large clientele. In an earlier publication (Erndl 1997), I focused on her life and activities, suggesting that Tara Devi's identification with the goddess was empowering for her and for other women in her family and village. I also suggested that because of the prominence of goddess worship in Kangra and the cultural acceptance of women as her legitimate vehicle, Tara Devi had tapped into (or was led into, depending on where one places the agency) a traditional source of power for women.

Tara Devi had to work within the constraints of her marriage and motherly duties to live her life dedicated to serving the goddess, but other matajis operate more independently, rejecting marriage, often at the behest of the goddess herself. Such women are self-supporting through their healing and ritual activities and are often well respected and sought after in their communities (Erndl 1993, 113–134). Divine possession by the goddess is one of the few culturally accepted forms of avoiding marriage in traditional Indian society, which allows few avenues of self-expression or economic support for women outside marriage. However, while such unmarried *matajis* are viewed in their communities as extraordinary women to whom the normal rules do not apply, they do exercise influence concerning women's roles.

An example is Passu Mataji, an unmarried healer with her own Vaishno Devi temple in a village near Dharamsala in Kangra district. Interestingly, I first heard of Passu Mataji some years before meeting her through a Dharamsala psychiatrist, who told me that he sometimes referred clients to her. This psychiatrist explained his views on possession to me in terms of classical Freudian psychoanalytic theory, but it was clear that he respected the traditional healers and mediums and considered that their practices could help at least some patients. He also told me some tantalizing details of Passu Mataji's life, which she confirmed and expanded upon when I later spent several months visiting her and her devotees. She was born around the time of Indian independence (1947), the youngest of six children to an impoverished family of the Giraths, a low-caste cultivating community of Kangra. She had no formal education and never learned to read or write. As a child, she never played with the other village children but only with another little girl who was always with her, but whom only she could see. When she told her mother about this little girl, her mother became concerned and brought her to a healer, a Harijan (Untouchable caste) who made "tantra-mantra" (a type of magical incantation or sorcery) on her and gave her holy water and cardamom. After that, she "went crazy," and a wandering holy man came by her house, saying that the goddess wanted to come there, but that it was contaminated. Her parents arranged a marriage for her when she was very young and tried to send her off to her husband's home at about age twelve. When she was placed in the palanquin, the goddess entered into her and said, "Don't go there; stay here and build a temple for me." She followed the goddess's order, though it is unclear how much family resistance she faced. Nevertheless, she did build a temple at her parents' home, and some years later, again ordered by the goddess, moved her temple and residence to its present location in another village. She never married again and characterizes herself as "not a householder," though she does maintain a household and has brought up several relatives' children. She is very active in the local Mahila Mandal (Women's Organization), has been appointed to the board of a nearby free medical clinic, and supports educational, social, and economic opportunities for women. More radically, while respecting the status of the householder and stressing interdependence and an ethic of caring among men, women, and children in the family, she believes that marriage is not necessarily a sacred duty for women. She told me that women should think long and hard before agreeing to marriage and that no one should be forced into marriage against her will. Interestingly, this attitude assumes that women have some agency over the events of their lives and are not merely passive recipients of others' decisions or of a social system beyond their control. In response to a question of mine, she also said that some men worship the goddess but mistreat their wives and other women, because they have a problem with inflated egos ("they think they are big"). Such ideas she attributes to the influence of the goddess in her life, for she is illiterate and has had virtually no exposure to Western ideas.

Some *mataji*s have taken on a renunciant lifestyle and have become gurus in a broader sense, teaching meditation to their devotees, building ashrams and in some cases free clinics and schools, and giving discourses on *bhakti* (devotion) and other spiritual paths. An example is Usha Mataji, about whom I have previously written as Usha Bahn or Sister Usha (Erndl 1993). When I first met her in 1982, Usha, a West Panjab émigré based in Agra, had a growing following due to her personal charisma and her standing as a vehicle of Vaishno Devi and Kali. In the intervening years, she has expanded her movement to include a large temple and ashram in Delhi and an ashram in Nurpur, Himachal Pradesh, adjacent to Kangra, as well as hospitals and clinics. While still experiencing possession trance, she also practices and teaches meditation techniques and mantras to her disciples. She now identifies herself as a renunciant (*sannyasini*) and initiates women and men as both lay disciples and renunciants. By her own account, some years ago, she was granted the title Mahamandaleshwar, the highest renunciant designation, by an assembly of *sannyasi*s in Hardwar. She leads mass pilgrimages every year to Vaishno Devi and other goddess temples, travels around India, and has even visited her devotees in the United States. Some of the women I met who are devotees of local *mataji*s in Kangra have also taken initiation from Usha Mataji, thus showing continuity between village-style healer *mataji*s and international tantric-style gurus. I met Usha Mataji again in 1997 in Nurpur and at her ashram in Delhi, where she answered my questions about her experience of *shakti*, her religious teachings, and her understanding of renunciation. In contrast to some renunciants who have become involved in Hindu nationalist activities, she emphasized to me that she was totally opposed to their activities and had absolutely nothing to do with them.

Possession Rituals

What happens during a possession ritual? There is considerable variation.[2] The possession may take place at a temple, in a woman's home, in an outdoor area, or in a small shrine which a woman has built in her home compound. The possession may be unpredictable and spontaneous, or it may be a more regular, predictable occurrence. Most of the *matajis* I have encountered set aside particular times and days of the week for devotees to come and consult them about their problems. They typically will sit in front of a small shrine with goddess images, such as those of Durga, Vaishno Devi, Jvala Mukhi, or Kali. At the beginning of the session, before the *mataji* goes into trance, devotees begin to gather outside, and after removing their shoes and washing their hands, they enter and bow to the *mataji* and to the goddess image. They may make offerings of food, flowers, incense, or cash and may also exchange a few words of greeting with the *mataji*. If they plan to ask a question, they will place a personal item such as a watch, ring, article of clothing, or clay from their house in front of her. Then they will seat themselves and join the singing of devotional songs to the goddess.

After some time, the goddess will enter into, or play, in the *mataji*. The *mataji* begins to sway, her eyes glaze over, and her head may begin to rotate in a circular fashion, causing her hair to loosen and fly about. While the *mataji* is in this trance, a voice speaks, identifying herself as a particular goddess or signaling her presence by a phrase like *Jay Mata di* (Victory to the Mother). She picks up each object in turn, asking whose it is. She talks to the devotee, asking questions, stating the problem, giving a diagnosis, and prescribing a remedy. Sometimes, the devotee asks questions and engages in a conversation with the goddess. In this way, the *mataji* moves from one item to the next. Usually, she will pick up all the items and answer all of the questions before departing, but sometimes the goddess will depart abruptly. After the trance is over, devotees will line up to receive *prasad* (usually sweets or fruits that have been previously offered to the goddess), the blessings of the *mataji*, and any blessed items such as holy water, cardamom, or colored threads which have been prescribed during the trance.

The questions that devotees present to the goddess concern the entire array of personal problems, including infertility, illness of a family member or domestic animal, possession by a harmful spirit, family or marital disharmony, depression, legal cases, employment troubles, or an upcoming examination. Highly personal and painful tragedies are discussed openly within earshot of all participants. The personal objects that the devotees place before her often have some direct connection with the problem: job application papers, a sick child's shirt, a family photograph. Once, I even saw the owner's manual for a motorcycle. In some cases, the *mataji* tells them that the outcome will be good and that they shouldn't worry. In others, she gives a more specific diagnosis which may fall into one or more of the following categories: (1) sorcery, in which some evil wisher has brought harm by feeding the devotee something unwholesome or burying it in her house, (2) an inauspicious astrological influence, such as Saturn or the sun, or (3) some action or omission on the part of the devotee or the devotee's family member, such as quarrelsome behavior or failure to perform a prescribed ritual. Remedies prescribed include sacred ash, holy water, and cardamom; wearing a multicolored thread; performance of a ritual such as a *havan* (fire sacrifice); making an offering to a deity; and adhering to certain dietary restrictions. Devotees who have been helped or cured return later to give a thanks offering, and many of them become regular visitors, participating in devotional singing, helping out with ritual chores such as distributing holy water, and just hanging around to talk with the *mataji* or other devotees. Healing takes place within a context of religious devotion to the goddess and a shared community, albeit a temporary one, of devotees who have joined together to consult the *mataji*.

Women's Space

The importance of the "hanging out" time before and after the actual trance session should not be minimized, as it creates a space and opportunity for women of different castes and backgrounds to come together in ways that they might not otherwise and to form a community. In rural Kangra, there are few such legitimate public spaces for women. Women may visit the bazaar and move about publicly, but only for some specific errand. Men may chat and smoke in the bazaars with their friends and wile away the hours gossiping in tea stalls, but women seldom do. They are expected to conduct their business and leave, not to linger and socialize. In contrast, the courtyard or temple of a *mataji* is a place where women can legitimately and safely spend leisure time and where they can also turn to other women for solace and even practical assistance.

For example, on one occasion, I was sitting with a group of about ten women on Passu Mataji's veranda, waiting for her to return from a doctor's appointment. Most of the women were from relatively high-status, prosperous, peasant families, and a few were office workers or teachers. Among us that day was a low-caste teenage woman with a young daughter from a neighboring village. Most of us knew her slightly, as she had come to see the *mataji* a few times before. I remembered her especially well, because unlike the other women and girls I had met, she knew no Hindi or Panjabi and could speak only the local Kangri dialect. That day, she was crying and despondent, telling us that her mother-in-law beat her and that her husband wanted to divorce her. Her husband had offered her a rather large sum of money if she would take her daughter and leave. She was reluctant to do this, as she felt it was her duty to stay in her husband's home and accept her fate. Also, she was afraid about what would become of her, as her natal family was of no help. The other women rallied around and provided support. No one blamed her for her plight or encouraged her to stay with her husband. In fact, the general consensus was that she should take the money, put it into a fixed deposit for her daughter's future, and get a job. One of the women said that she would help her at the bank, and another said that she would get her a job as a maintenance worker in an office. This story illustrates the fact that, while oppression of women is very real, there are ways to deal with it, both spiritual and practical. Not all of the cards were stacked against this young woman since she had the support of this multicaste group of women from outside her family. While the *mataji* was not even present during this exchange, she provided the space for it to take place. It was their devotion to the *mataji* and their desire to take part in her rituals that brought these women together. Such spaces may be seen as "cracks" in a patriarchal system, that is, spaces that exist at least in part because of patriarchy but which provide sites for women's creativity and interconnection, sites for thoughts and activities that can never be completely controlled by patriarchal norms and which furthermore have the potential to resist, transcend, or transgress patriarchy.[3] A cross-cultural example comes to mind. When the Taliban took control of Afghanistan, hard-won women's rights were eroded one by one, as women were deprived of jobs, education, freedom of movement, and civil liberties. But the fatal blow came when the Taliban closed down the *hamam*, the traditional bath houses for women, the one place where women could congregate and communicate away from the watchful eyes of men. Perhaps the Taliban saw the *hamam* as not only a place where women could experience (hitherto legitimately) bodily sensual pleasure, but also as a site of potential rebellion against the regime.

Possession rituals are a traditional cultural resource that can be a source of empowerment for women. In no way am I suggesting that possession rituals are necessarily liberating nor that they are "the answer" to women's problems. But I do believe that women's lives are enriched—spiritually, socially, and emotionally—in ways they would not be if they did not have these practices and that possession rituals give them a sense of confidence that there is something they can do about their problems and that they are not helpless victims. Possession is an embodied phenomenon in which women experience the divine either within their own bodies, as in the case of the *matajis* themselves, or as part of a collective, participatory process, as in the case of the *matajis'* clients and devotees. In either case, women gain access to power, many kinds of power, including the power to improve their lives, mitigate suffering, help others, and achieve spiritual insight.

NOTES

1. I do not want to give the impression that either possession in general or even possession by goddesses is an exclusively female activity. In Kangra, for example, men are occasionally possessed by goddesses, though it is generally a female-dominated activity. See Erndl 2001 for my discussion of a male *mataji* who takes on the guise of a woman while possessed by his goddess. Also, in some regions of India in some ritual contexts, possession is primarily a male activity as, for example, in the

Bhadrakali performance traditions of Kerala. Sarah Caldwell (2001) explains why this is so in Kerala, while hypothesizing that tribal hill women were the original mediums for the goddess Bhadrakali.

2. See Erndl 2000 for the transcript of a particular session at Passu Mataji's temple.

3. Janet Chawla (2002, 165) points out that childbirth, like possession, is also a liminal embodied phenomenon and thus can never be completely controlled by patriarchy.

REFERENCES

Boddy, Janice. 1989. *Wombs and Alien Spirits: Women, Men, and the Zar Cult in Northern Sudan*. Madison: University of Wisconsin Press.

Caldwell, Sarah. 2001. *Oh Terrifying Mother: Sexuality, Violence, and Worship of the Goddess Kali*. New York: Oxford University Press.

Chawla, Janet. 2002. "Negotiating Narak and Writing Destiny: The Theology of Bemata in Dais' Handling of Birth." In *Invoking Goddesses: Gender Politics in Indian Religion*, ed. Nilima Chitkopekar, 165–199. New Delhi: Shakti.

Erndl, Kathleen M. 1993. *Victory to the Mother: The Hindu Goddess of Northwest India in Myth, Ritual and Symbol*. Oxford and New York: Oxford University Press.

———. 1997. "The Goddess and Women's Power: A Hindu Case Study." In *Women and Goddess Traditions in Antiquity and Today*, ed. Karen L. King, 17–38. Minneapolis, MN: Fortress.

———. 2000. "A Trance Healing Session with Mataji." In *Tantra in Practice*, ed. David G. White, 97–115. Princeton, NJ: Princeton University Press.

———. 2001. "Goddesses and the Goddess in Hindu Religious Experience: Constructing the Goddess through Personal Experience." In *In Search of Mahadevi: Constructing the Identities of the Hindu Great Goddess*, ed. Tracy Pintchman, 199–212. Albany: State University of New York Press.

Lewis, I. M. 2003 [1971]. *Ecstatic Religion: A Study of Spirit Possession and Shamanism* (3d ed.). London: Routledge.

Macy, Joanna. 1990. "The Greening of the Self." In *Dharma Gaia: A Harvest of Essays in Buddhism and Ecology*, ed. Alan Hunt Badiner, 53–63. Berkeley, CA: Parallax.

McDaniel, June. 2004. *Offering Flowers, Feeding Skulls: Popular Goddess Worship in West Bengal*. Oxford and New York: Oxford University Press.

Ram, Kalpana. 2001. "The Female Body of Possession." In *Mental Health from a Gender Perspective*, ed. Bhargavi V. Davar, 181–216. New Delhi: Sage.

Schoembucher, Elisabeth. 1993. "Gods, Ghosts, and Demons: Possession in South Asia." In *Flags of Fame: Studies in South Asian Folk Culture*, ed. Heidrun Brüchner, Lothar Lutze, and Aditya Malik, 239–267. New Delhi: Manohar.

Sered, Susan Starr. 1994. *Priestess, Mother, Sacred Sister: Religions Dominated by Women*. New York: Oxford University Press.

9

Does Tantric Ritual Empower Women? Renunciation and Domesticity among Female Bengali Tantrikas

June McDaniel

There is a variety of roles for women in Indian religion, ranging from the female ascetic who renounces the world to the wife and mother who practices religious ritual as part of her household obligations. In this chapter, we shall explore Hindu understandings about female Shakta tantric practitioners in West Bengal. Tantra allows women a broad range of responses to domestic norms, from conformity to rejection of domesticity as an important arena of female religious expression. But women who are tantric celibates tend to have higher social status in Bengali culture, while women who perform tantric sexual rituals tend to have lower status, suggesting a larger religious valorization of asceticism and renunciation over domesticity and householdership.

This chapter will contrast the roles for women as written in tantric texts and as lived out in women's practice. These are in many ways quite different. Tantric texts describe three major roles for women: they can be incarnations of the goddess, or consorts for sexual ritual, or female gurus. These are the roles most often mentioned in the texts, though other roles are occasionally noted. However, women's lived roles in tantric practice are much broader than these three roles. We see female tantrikas who are renunciant practitioners, holy women of various types: the woman who has renounced worldly life (*sannyasini*); the woman who is dedicated to celibacy, service, and obedience to a tradition (*brahmacarini*); the woman who practices yoga, especially kundalini yoga (*yogini*); the woman who is married but has left her husband to pursue a spiritual life (*grihi sadhika*). A woman may be a devotee of a tantric deity and worship with tantric mantras, or she may get possessed as a vocation (thus becoming a *"bhar lady"*). The female tantrika may also be a wife who practices tantric sexual rituals as part of her marriage, or a professional ritual partner in tantric sexual practices outside of marriage. She may be a female teacher (*stri-guru*), usually celibate and head of a group of devotees or an ashram. She may also be a widow or celibate wife, whose practice involves ritual tantric worship (*puja*), a mixture of devotional love of a deity, service to that deity, and tantric ritual meditation.

Woman and Text

The descriptions of women in the tantric texts tend to follow an exaggerated style—they are strongly sexual, or attractive at a distance, or both. One does not often get the sense of the physical women used as models for them. Rather, these women are "perfect" in various senses (beautiful, graceful, happy, quiet, obedient), or they are imaginary women, also beautiful and graceful but dwelling on lotuses wearing silk and jewels, sometimes having a frightening demeanor. Women in tantric texts are described primarily in terms of their looks and actions: the male tantrika should find a suitable woman (according to a long list of qualifications) and then perform rituals with her. The *Kularnava Tantra* states that the woman must be beautiful, young, pious, devoted to her guru and god, always smiling, pleasing, and without jealousy, among other qualities.[1] The female tantrika cannot be unattractive or old or sleepy, and she cannot feel desire or argue with her partner—these disqualify her from tantric practice, even if she has been initiated.[2]

Ritual Incarnations of the Goddess

The attitude toward women in tantric texts is generally positive. Many texts say that women can be tantric gurus, and a male practitioner's mother is the best guru possible. A woman may be knowledgeable as a tantric consort without regard to her social status: she may be a courtesan or laundrywoman or dancer or fisherwoman, a woman who sells meat or one who works with leather. Some tantras encourage the worship of goddesses within living women and girls, for women may incarnate Shakti. Some tantras say that one must never harm a woman nor look down upon her nor even hit her with a flower. In the *Kali Tantra*, women are respected, especially the *kula* woman (a female tantric practitioner of the *kula marga*):

5. [The practitioner] should imagine the whole world as female, and he should also think of himself as female.

6. A wise person should consider drink, food to be chewed or sucked, all edible things, the household, himself and everything else, as a young woman. When he sees a *kula* woman, he should bow [to her] with reverence.

7. If by good fortune he should encounter a *kula* woman, he should mentally worship her.

8. He should bow respectfully before a young girl, a teenaged girl, an old woman or a young woman, even if she is nasty, ugly or bad.

9. Women should never be beaten, insulted, or cheated, and should never be treated badly. If a person does treat a woman badly, he will be unable to attain success [in his practice].

10. Women are deities, women are life [*prana*], women are beauty.[3]

In texts that speak of the woman as a ritual incarnation of the goddess, a suitable woman is found and offered worship. Sometimes a young girl is worshipped (*kumari puja*), and sometimes a mature woman is the object of worship (*stri puja* or *shakti puja*). *Kumari puja* is often performed during the nine-day festival of Durga Puja, and it is believed to bring great blessings. The *Kubjika Tantra* details the worship of young virgins in *kumari puja* (primarily for girls ranging in age from five to twelve years, though the Mahacina mode includes worshipping girls ranging from one to sixteen years), and girls from the ages of six to nine years old are especially to be desired, as such worship grants the devotee all wishes. This tantra also includes worshipping both one's own wife and the wives of others as goddesses, repeating mantras 108 times and seeing the woman as the symbolic form in which the goddess dwells.[4] As well as being within the woman, the goddess may be located in food, wine, fish, red cloth, red flowers, and a red sun. The *Guptasadhana Tantra* speaks of the nine types of virgin girls who may incarnate the goddess, including the actress, prostitute, Brahmin woman, low-caste woman, wives of washermen and barbers, and daughters of a *kapalika* (skull-carrying) ascetic, cowherd, or garland maker.[5]

In the *Kulacudamani Tantra*, the goddess describes the worship of eight women, who represent the eight *shakti*s, or mothers. They are sometimes called the consorts or powers of the Vedic gods (as one may deduce from their names, such as Brahmani, Maheshvari, and Indrani). However, they are usually worshipped independently of the gods, and they are said to grant supernatural powers, good karma, and the removal of obstacles to the desires of the tantrika. The text gives directions, suggesting that the tantrika bring the women to a deserted place, such as a river bank, a crossroads, a burning ground, or the foot of a *bilva* tree. He brings the women sanctified water and looks closely at them.

28. By observing the differences in the appearance, mood and behaviour of the women, they are given the names of the eight *shaktis* beginning with Brahmani, etcetera.

29. First offering them a seat and welcoming them with a mantra, [he should present] blessed water for drinking, water for the feet, plain water and an offering of milk and honey.

30. He should bathe and dress the hair with scents and flowers and after censing the hair, he should offer silken garments [to the *shaktis*].

31. Then spreading out a seat in a different place and having led the *shaktis* there, when he has given [them] a pair of sandals [and] adorned [them] with jewels and ornaments,

32. He should offer ointments, scents, and garlands. And having invoked the *shakti* of each of them, he should place [the designated *shakti*] on the head of each of the women.[6]

The practitioner gives each woman the name of one of the mothers, and he chants a brief hymn to each woman. The goddess explains that without these hymns, the *tantrika* will lose the fruits of his worship. He should also give them betel nuts and sweet seeds, as well as a garland with sandalwood paste and perfume. In the interests of inclusiveness, the goddess adds:

52. . . . Oh Bhairava! If there is a man there who knows the *kula* teachings, he [too] is deserving of worship!

The worship of the human woman as the goddess is generally a temporary phenomenon; the goddess does not remain in her body after the ritual is over. The human woman is much like a statue in this ritual, used as a temporary home for the goddess who comes to visit. Goddesses may ritually dwell almost anywhere—from trees to corpses. However, because the human female has her own feminine power, or *shakti*, she is an especially appropriate place for a goddess to dwell.

Female Ritual Consorts

The second and most publicized role for a woman in the tantric texts is the role of consort in sexual rituals. The *Niruttara Tantra* suggests worship of the *vesya* (the term traditionally means prostitute), including those who come from a tantric family, those who are independent of family, those who join (the profession) voluntarily, those who are married to male *tantrikas*, and those who have been ritually united with the deity.[7] In this usage, the term *vesya* does not refer specifically to a prostitute, but rather to a woman who roams about as freely as a prostitute may, and enjoys herself like Kali. She has sex accompanied by the chanting of mantras, and meditates upon the union of Mahakala and Kalika. While such an image may initially give an impression of a free woman in the modern sense, this is not the case—her freedom is limited by the roles defined in the *Niruttara Tantra*. She is not a tantric *vesya* if she becomes involved with a man other than her husband; as the text phrases it, if she worships a Shiva other than her own Bhairava, she will live in the fierce hells until the destruction of the universe. If she gets involved with other male practitioners due to passion, desire for money, or other temptations, she will go to hell. She is then called an animalistic prostitute (*pasu-vesya*). Any man involved with her will suffer disease, sorrow, and loss of money. The proper *vesya* must be chaste and pious, doing rituals with her own partner.[8] She cannot be respected and take on a different partner, and thus she cannot instruct other male partners by ritual.

Sexual practice within a single couple is called *lata sadhana*, the spiritual exercise in which the woman is like a vine (*lata*) growing around the man. *Lata sadhana* is individual practice, with a single couple alone practicing mantras, breath control, and other forms of meditation in a ritual context. The *kula cakra* is a group practice, where men and women sit in a circle (*cakra* or chakra) in couples, and perform the ritual of the *pancatattva*, taking the five forbidden things, of which one is intercourse. The tantric texts tend to be rather evasive as to the details of *lata sadhana*; these should come from the guru. However, a good deal of ritual worship is involved, as the *Maya Tantra* states:

4. Bring a woman while she is menstruating, and at midnight worship your *ishtadevata* [personal deity] within her genitals.
5. After that, the practitioner must chant 336 mantras daily [the text does not specify which mantras], for three days. By means of this, he can gain the fruit of one thousand corpse rituals. There is no doubt about it.
6. Here is another type [of ritual], please listen carefully. First, to gain perfection in the four paths, [the practitioner] should chant mantras 108 times. Then he should worship his personal deity in the genitals of a woman who is not his own. Then he should worship Mahamaya 108 times, using menstrual blood.[9]
7. After that, he should offer a burnt offering, and chant mantras 108 times. He should become devoted to the practice, and be continually absorbed in Mahamaya.
8. If he does this daily for sixteen days, he will become rich, powerful, an orator and a poet, and loved by all. There is no doubt about it.[10]

The goal here is the enrichment of the male tantrikas; the woman merely brings along the goddess within her. We see the same problem in the ritual *cakra*, as the *Kamakhya Tantra* states:

35. [The practitioner] will bring an initiated woman, and establish a ritual circle [*kula cakra*].

36. Then the practitioner will joyfully worship the goddess, [especially] her genitals. Then he will sing hymns sweetly and chant mantras continuously, while looking at his partner.

37. He who chants mantras continuously while in this state, will be lord of all supernatural powers in the Kali Yuga.[11]

Here the male tantrika is involved with a woman, with worship and mantras as ritual. The *Kamakhya Tantra* states that the man will gain *siddhis*, or supernatural powers. The effect of this practice on the female tantrika is not mentioned.

The most vivid description of the female role in a more orgiastic style of *cakra* is probably found in the *Kularnava Tantra*. It is an interesting description, as it violates the notions that practitioners should not be desirous, and the text allows them to have other partners. However, the passions are justified because the participants are in an altered state (*ullasa*), and because everything in the *cakra* is transformed (eating becomes fire sacrifice, sight is meditation, sleeping is worship, and union with one's partner is liberation):

67. Intoxicated by passion, the women take shelter with other men, treating them as their own. Each man also takes a new woman [*shakti*] and treats her as his own, when in the state of advanced ecstatic joy.

68. Seized by delusion, the men embrace other men. . . .

71. O Shambhavi! The yogis take the food from each other's plates and dance with their drinking pots on their heads. . . .

73. The women who are not in their normal senses clap and sing songs whose words are unclear, and they stagger while dancing.

74. Yogis who are intoxicated with alcohol fall upon the women, and the intoxicated women fall upon the men, O Kulanayika! They are induced to perform such actions, to fulfill their mutual desires.

75. When this state of ecstasy is not accompanied by corrupt thoughts, the bull among yogis reaches the state of godhood [*devata-bhava*].[12]

The effect upon the cow among yogis is not clear, but one assumes that the women would have similar ecstatic experiences.

Female Gurus

A third female role is that of the guru. In some tantras, we see female gurus idealized. For instance, the *Guptasadhana Tantra* gives a visualization of the female guru: she is located in the Sahasrara lotus above the head, and her eyes look like lotus petals. She has high breasts and a slender waist, and she is shining like a ruby. She wears red clothes and jeweled ornaments. She is seated at the left of her husband, and her hands show mudras giving boons and freedom from fear.[13] She is graceful, delicate, and beautiful. Such an image is quite different from the reality of the physical female tantric gurus, who tend to be older, unmarried, sometimes bald nuns, often toughened from ascetic and outdoor life, looking strong and sometimes grizzled. They generally do not wear jewelry, seeking to avoid the dangers of sexual attractiveness. The last thing they want to be is beautiful and delicate, while sleeping alone on temple floors or wandering on pilgrimage; they often travel alone and need to defend themselves. Their emphasis is on independence and attaining liberation rather than seductiveness.

As we can see, actual female tantrikas do not exactly fit these idealized textual roles. Instead, the female Shakta tantrikas whom I interviewed and who were described by informants during fieldwork in West Bengal tended to fall into five roles:

1. Celibate tantric yoginis, whose status was the highest among the women interviewed, were lifelong celibates. Many were gurus with disciples, and some headed temples, ashrams, or tantric study circles. Some emphasized the importance of devotion toward the goddess or guru; others were believed by their disciples to be partial incarnations of the goddess. Tantra for them was a dedicated practice involving mantras, visualizations, austerities, and ritual actions (kriya). The goal of tantra was to gain liberation and also shakti, both as the goddess and as power. There was little evidence of domesticity, except occasional cooking for disciples and festivals, and service to visitors.

2. Holy women, called grihi sadhikas, had been married but left their husbands and families to follow a religious calling. They had lower status than the lifelong celibates, but some had disciples. Often they would wander, practicing tantric meditation and worship, and live at temples or ashrams. Some would go into states of possession by the goddess (Kali bhava) or other deities, induced by chanting tantric bija mantras or singing hymns to the devi. Tantra for them was devotion and possession, usually in response to a call by the goddess. The goal of tantra was to follow the goddess's will in an ascetic setting. Here, we have traditional domesticity followed by renunciation.

3. Tantric wives performed tantric ritual sex and worship as part of their devotion toward their husbands and gurus. The woman was often initiated by the same guru as her husband and followed his teachings. Tantra was a form of service, involving obedience to husband and guru and following women's marital obligations. The goal of tantra was to fulfill dharma and social obligations. Thus, tantra as practiced within marriage was equivalent to domesticity and followed traditional social norms.

4. Professional consorts were women who performed ritual sex and worship as a way to make a living. The consort and her children were generally supported by the man who was her ritual partner. The woman may have moved from one *sadhu* to another, depending on who would shelter and support her. Tantra here was professional sexual practice, a career choice. The goal of tantra was to help the male tantrika in his practice, make money, and possibly get a permanent home and a male protector. Perhaps such practices might be understood as serial domesticity.

5. Celibate wives and widows were householders who incorporated tantric practice as an aspect of worship. Tantra was a form of devotion, especially in combination with *bhakti* yoga. The goal of tantra was to please the goddess and gain blessings, without sexual practices. Here, renunciation and domesticity were combined in a fashion that was socially respectable and fairly widespread (according to informants).

Let us examine some of these roles in greater detail. As background, I interviewed practicing female tantrikas in West Bengal in 1983–1984 and 1993–1994. Some were ascetics and heads of ashrams; some were householders; some made no secret of their practice; some practiced underground, unknown to family members, coworkers, and neighbors. Most female tantrikas interviewed were not only celibate, but insistently so. Several said that tantric meditation involves purity and concentration and that desire would be a distraction and would cause them to fail.

Celibate Tantric Yoginis and Gurus

I interviewed in depth three women who were female gurus, initiated into Shakta tantric lineages. Two of them practiced tantric rituals themselves, and the third was of the Shakta universalist perspective, and she knew many practicing women tantrikas. All of these women were highly respected, and all of them were celibate. All of the highest-status tantrikas whom I met, male or female, were celibate.

For Gauri Ma, head of an ashram in Bakreshwar, tantric ritual revealed a person's "inner history," giving the power to "see inside," to watch the inner life of the spirit. The goal is to "gain" Shakti (*shakti labh kara*), to have her dwell in the heart. It is Shakti who enlightens you, who brings you to the highest states. Shiva is as useless as a corpse, and that is why he is portrayed as one in the iconography. In her practice of kundalini yoga, the male and female aspects of the person were united, and there was no necessity for any union of physical males and females. In the *pancatattva* ritual, or circle with five forbidden things, the actions are symbolic, with drinking wine representing control of the breath,

FIGURE 9.1. *Sannyasini* Gauri Ma and the author in Bakreshwar, West Bengal. Photo by Jim Denosky.

and ritual sex representing the sort of union seen in yogic meditation. She made a special point of saying that no outward practice of these is necessary for a strong and disciplined tantrika and that tantric rituals are symbolic of inner transformations.[14]

For Jayashri Ma, the female guru of a group of devotees, tantric ritual is a way of getting a fused identity with Shakti, which lasts over a lifetime. Jayashri was initiated by her tantric guru while they sat on matched sets of skulls, and with the mantra came the direct entrance of the goddess Adya Shakti into her heart. The mantras, hand positions, trances, and rituals were ways of preparing her body for Shakti's entrance. Union with Adya Shakti is the highest state possible, for she is identical with Brahman, and mother of the universe. Jayashri came from a tantric family, and her guru was a tantrika who practiced secretly. Jayashri too practices in an underground fashion, for she said that religious practitioners (especially tantrikas) were persecuted by the communist authorities in her area. She has many health problems, but the ascent of the goddess out of her heart and into full consciousness blots these away, and she becomes aware of nothing but the goddess's love and power. She is a celibate tantric guru, who said that she no longer needs to perform rituals because the goddess has already taken up permanent residence in her heart.[15]

For Archanapuri Ma, tantric practice has a strong component of devotion. She is the head of an ashram near Calcutta and a celibate member of a Ramakrishna lineage. Her Shakta guru, Satyananda, began with a Vedanta perspective, but later had a revelation from the goddess Kali Bhavatarini that he must worship her. He performed tantric meditations and offered blood to Kali, and he taught Archanapuri Ma many meditative and ascetic techniques. Her understanding of tantra is heavily infused with devotion, toward both guru and goddess.

In the nineteenth century, the most well-known case of a female tantric guru was probably that of Bhairavi Brahmani or Yogeshvari, a woman tantrika who came to see the Bengali saint Ramakrishna Paramahamsa and stayed with him for about three years. She is described in Ramakrishna's biographies as almost forty years old and attractive, and she validated Ramakrishna's spiritual status. She had him sit on skull seats, chant mantras, eat fish and human flesh from a skull, and perform many practices described in the major tantras. She brought him women with whom Ramakrishna could perform some of the rituals, but the biographies are unclear about his practice with them; Ramakrishna claimed to have fallen into trance and been unaware of performing anything.[16] There is no direct evidence that Yogeshvari at any point lost her celibate status.

Ramakrishna seems to have been quite ambivalent toward these practices, partly accepting her as a guru and partly rejecting tantric practices generally. His followers were also ambiguous about the Bhairavi. Some found her teaching acceptable, as she was high caste, and even sexual practices were allowable if a guru were present (rather like having a chaperone). Others found her a bad influence and were glad when she left.

Tantric Holy Women

In the second role, we have tantric holy women who have been married but left their homes due to a religious call. They have lower status, though their religious dedication and newfound celibacy still gain them respect. The holy woman (grihi sadhika) who has gone out on her own, only returning occasionally to visit her husband and children, does not have an easy life. Often she has been initiated by the family's Shakta household priest (kulaguru) and heard a prophetic call in a dream or vision from a deity, who asked her not to oil her hair, not to eat certain foods, and to go on a pilgrimage. She leaves the household and may survive by begging, telling fortunes, or being possessed and gaining donations from observers. She gains social status when she starts to gain devotees, and sometimes she may have a special set of supernatural powers given by the goddess (especially healing or materializing food). If she undergoes possession, she is usually possessed by the goddess Kali, though she may be possessed by other deities as well.

Such calls often begin while the girl is very young. As an example, the *grihi sadhika* Lakshmi Ma was a devotee of Kali and Tara, both traditionally tantric goddesses in West Bengal, and she used to see Kali and play with her when she was a child. After she married, she continued to see Kali, who would complain if she did not get sufficient offerings. Lakshmi Ma told her family of her visions, and they thought that she was possessed. They bound her with ropes and had her undergo an exorcism. It was unsuccessful, though the exorcist burned her and bound her in iron chains. The family calmed down when her husband had a dream of Kali, telling him to build an altar for her, and they began to worship there. She later lived separately from her husband, performing rituals at Tarapitha and other holy places. She dressed in classic tantric fashion—red clothing, matted hair, heavy *rudraksha* garlands—and she often carried a large trident.[17]

Tantric Wives

For tantric wives who remain in the household, the religious goals tend to be devotion and obedience to husband and guru and desire for union with Shakti. I spoke several years ago with a Sahajiya, or tantric, Vaishnava couple, and the perspectives of the man and the woman in the couple were very different. The man emphasized adventure, pleasure (he claimed that male tantrikas could have sex for four hours), and increased attractiveness (for tantra worked as a sort of birth control and fountain of youth, allowing women not to get pregnant and not to turn into wrinkled old hags by the age of twenty-four years, which he said was what happened without it). Tantra was fun, exciting, and a way to escape the routine. He felt that it made Indian men superior to Western men in endurance.

His wife's perspective was quite different. Tantric practice for her was obedience to guru and god and a way to help her husband and please him. Tantra was not rebellious but rather following *stri-dharma*, for it was the wish of her husband and guru. Tantra was a way to serve them. She was unwilling to give details of her practice unless I was initiated, but she did say that her guru's face was present at all times within her mind during the ritual.

This couple lived in a large joint family which farmed land in rural West Bengal. They would leave the house late at night to practice, after everyone else was asleep, and return in time to get some sleep before the day's chores began. Nobody in the family knew that they were practicing tantrikas. Many householder tantrikas seem to practice this way, where either the family does not know of their practice, or the family is of tantric lineage and they know, but the neighbors do not.[18]

Such practice among couples is often highly secretive, known only to other religious practitioners. Archanapuri Ma knew some women who were in tantric arranged marriages. She described them as married women who were helpers to their husbands. She said that these women were not used and thrown away, as most people believe:

> Tantra is like this: India has always tried to elevate all traits of the human character through religion. The mind is the eternal playground of sensual desire. While Western psychology has understood this carnal tendency of mankind as his original or root [*mula*] inclination, Hindu religion has tried to transform it through the path of spiritual discipline, to divinize all tendencies of the person. This is the basis of tantric *viracara* practice, and it is very difficult, because some rituals involve taking a woman companion [*bhairavi*]. Though these paths appear difficult to us, they are very potent and useful for the deserving aspirants, and have been revealed by liberated people. This practice centers around strength, and requires a powerful mind and great concentration.
>
> We must also pay attention to the female tantrika [*bhairavi*]. Is her part only mechanical, required only by male aspirants to prove their mental and spiritual strength? Is her life useless once the above purpose is served? No, for there are many female tantrikas who can legitimately be called equal travelers of the spiritual path and equal sharers in its benefits. Some have attained to great religious heights, but most prefer to remain inconspicuous, and people do not know about them.
>
> In some cases both husband and wife take part together in the tantric *cakra* ritual and practice together while leading an active householder's life. I have met a few such female tantrikas who are engaged in spiritual practices, despite the responsibility of bringing up children. They only belong to one *cakra*, for a female tantrika who participates in a *cakra* conducted by one male tantrika does not join any other *cakra* conducted by some other male tantrika. In some *cakras*, the mental strength of the tantrika is put to severe tests. A young sixteen-year-old girl is brought to the ritual, who has all of the prescribed auspicious signs, and is pure and holy in both her character and her mind. Her company will lead the tantrika across the difficult path to perfection.[19]

Tantric householder wives are rare, and they tend to identify themselves as basically traditional wives who are following religious teachings. This is because the sexual rituals and their accompanying yogic practices are performed under the instructions of the guru and following her husband's wishes. Some practitioners have said that it is much better to have one's wife as a partner, for otherwise the woman may not be respected.

Professional Consorts

The fourth role includes female tantrikas who are professional ritual assistants, who practice sexual rituals with male Shakta tantrikas. Such a role is a very low-status one in Bengali culture, and nobody that I interviewed was willing or able to tell me anything of such women. They were understood as having a specialty within the profession of prostitution, as some women have skills in dominating men (like Kali). It was rather like an addendum to the courtesan's traditional sixty-four arts, an extra set of skills which professional women could gain. I was told that most of such women were low caste and wanted to gain extra money for the household, or else they were widows (especially child widows) who had no other way to make a living. Some informants actively condemned them, but most pitied them.

This analysis was supported by Bholanath Bhattacharjee's article "Some Aspects of the Esoteric Cults of Consort Worship in Bengal: A Field Survey Report."[20] He interviewed forty-eight women who were professional ritual consorts and gave detailed case histories for four of them. These women were called either *bhairavis* (those involved in Shakta rituals) or *sadhikas* (those involved in Vaishnava rituals). The term *sadhika* is a general term for holy woman or female religious practitioner, while the term *bhairavi* refers specifically to the consort of a *bhairava*, a male Shaivite tantrika. A majority of the women followed this profession as a family occupation; it was almost a caste, as the job was handed down within the family and was hereditary. A minority were converted to the profession by people whom they met. Almost all were initiated and given new names.

Their tantric gurus taught the women breathing techniques and mantras to lessen passion, as well as positions and muscular contractions to control the pace of intercourse. These techniques allow the woman to be qualified to practice with either one man for an extended period, or with a variety of men over time. For those women following their hereditary role, these practices were understood to be both service, helping the male tantrika to gain awareness of Brahman, and following their own caste obligations, which brings spiritual advancement.

Many of these women learned this profession while they were young girls, orphaned or without a father, from much older men. Bhattacharjee's article described four case histories. In the first case, an orphaned girl of seventeen years met an elderly man who taught her these practices; she later practiced with at least fifty other male practitioners in Birbhum. When her main *bhairava* did not practice properly and she became pregnant, he left her. However, he later came back, saying that if his guru liked practicing with her, he would take her back and also pay her rent and support their baby. She stated that she was forced by poverty to agree to this. The guru appreciated her abilities and asked her to become his own consort and leave the other man (he also was willing to support her and her baby). She stayed with him until his death and then lived in a sexual relationship with a *bhairava* who came for shelter to her hut. She trained her daughter as a consort, and the daughter learned the sexual rituals from the *bhairava* with whom they were living.

In the second case described by Bhattacharjee, a widow was forced by hunger to become a prostitute. She later learned tantric sexual skills from a guru. She found living with the guru to be preferable to prostitution, as she did not have to entertain many men, though she still called it hard work. Her guru was almost twice her age. In the third case, the woman was born due to an accident in her mother's ritual practice with a *bhairava*. She felt that she was under obligation to follow in her mother's footsteps and also became a *bhairavi*. She and her own guru initiate couples and teach them techniques of sexual ritual in the same bed (though she seemed more concerned that they practice "even by day, if necessary"). They are taught various rhythms and to think of ocean waves and lions and tigers rather than snakes (which bring loss of control). She said that, in cases of problems in the practice (usually pregnancy), the woman returns to prostitution.

In the fourth case, the consort was the daughter of a cook who was very poor. The cook asked a *bhairava* (who was a relative of the household for which she worked) to find a match for her daughter. He was much older than the girl, and he decided to initiate her as his *bhairavi*. At the time of the article, she had lived with him for nine years. The *bhairava* had also had ritual sex with the girl's mother.

These women have come to accept their roles as consorts as their lot in life. Several were forced by poverty and hunger into these roles, and they needed money to care for their children. Often, they were bound by considerations of dharmic obligation; since their mothers were *sadhikas*, they too must follow that profession. Many of these relationships are semi-incestuous, where the man with whom the mother is sleeping is also sleeping with her daughter. However, because it is placed in a ritual context, the father figure becomes the guru, and the relationship is understood as a sort of religious apprenticeship.

While the consort role is often idealized in the West, representing freedom and liberated sexuality, there are clearly problems for women in Hindu society who are forced into the role and would themselves prefer a more traditional life.

Celibate Wives and Widows

The fifth role is that of the celibate wife, who uses tantric mantras and visualization for worship. The celibate wife remains in the household, has already had children and wants no more, or has been celibate for the entire marriage (as in the famous case of the saint Anandamayi Ma). The wife becomes a devotee and leads a privately ascetic life. She spends most of her time in the worship room before the deity's image, while the husband acquiesces and stays celibate as best he can. Sometimes, the wife may become a worship leader (*pujarini*) for a group of other women, or the leader of a *kirtan* singing group. In such cases, she gains a reputation as a holy woman, while the husband stays in the background. Many husbands are quite amenable to their wives becoming celibate devotees in later years.

We may also see tantric and devotional practices within the home as performed by widows. The householder widow who spends her life in religious ritual and pilgrimage may be respected or disparaged. I have seen Shakta religious widow matriarchs, who are called holy women by members of the extended family, who dominate both their households and the Brahmin priests called in to perform rituals. They hold the keys to the household and the money box, and thus have financial control—despite their renunciation. On the other hand, I have also seen non-Shakta widows ignored, alone and unwanted, where even their gurus look down on them.[21]

In one case in Calcutta, a priest was called in to perform rituals for Durga *puja* by the matriarch of a large joint family. She had been initiated into one of the Ramakrishna lineages, but continued to live in the family home. She was a holy woman who lived a householder life, and she performed daily meditation (involving tantric *bija* mantras but not tantric sexual rituals) and frequent pilgrimage. The priest was ostensibly in charge of the rituals, but the householder matriarch kept correcting him on his Sanskrit pronunciation and his actions, and he acquiesced to her claims of proper ritual behavior. Thus, we have a Brahmin male and a semi-householder female with different types of control over ritual practice. I spoke later with some of her sons and grandsons, who all agreed that she knew more about ritual than most of the priests in the area.

For all of the female tantric gurus interviewed, sexual ritual was understood to be peripheral rather than central. It is a practice done for people who cannot control their instincts, by people (generally male) who do not have the necessary yogic discipline for real practice and need to take a few extra courses to qualify for advanced practice. The issue is not that the sexually active tantrikas are sinful, but rather that they are weak and spending their time at the lower end of practice rather than the higher end. Some female tantrikas implied that men were generally weaker than women in this area and more compulsive about needing sexual interaction. As Gauri Ma stated,

> Most women have no need of sexual ritual [*lata sadhana*]. It is for men, who are bound by lust, and need to overcome it. Then they take a consort. In women, lust is not so strong. Tantric practice is meditation [*kriya*] and worship [*puja*].[22]

None said that *lata sadhana* was evil, or sinful, or scandalous. They did not appear to be hiding their own secret practices. They simply said it was rare and unnecessary. Some female tantrikas were more outspoken, saying that no man was going to take away the power they had gained by hard austerities and long recitation of mantras (several female tantrikas mentioned that sexual ritual involved the loss of their power).

Does tantric ritual empower women in Hindu culture? It depends upon the rituals performed and local understandings of these rituals. Women are empowered by tantric practices that emphasize renunciation and asceticism, especially meditation and the use of tantric mantras. Female tantric gurus have positions of ritual authority usually possessed by males, including running ashrams, taking offerings, and advising householders on life decisions. Celibate tantric holy women often have disciples who support them and whom they bless. Celibate wives and widows may become respected worship leaders in the community.

Female tantrikas who are not celibate are viewed with greater hesitation, and often sexual ritual may act to disempower them. If they are married and faithful to their husbands, tantra becomes a part of their wifely duty, helping the husband in his spiritual development. Tantric ritual is then a part of domestic female obligations. If the female tantrika is acting outside of marriage, though, and performing sexual rituals with more than one man, mainstream society is likely to look down upon her. She is generally pitied as a desperate woman; she is not seen as a wise or compassionate guru. She may be understood to be a prostitute, or a woman deserted by her husband who must feed herself and her children, and she may be called either immoral or unfortunate. In this case, tantric ritual disempowers her. The notion of tantric ritual as "free love," independent of marriage or commitment, is not appropriate to the Bengali Shakta tantric tradition. In West Bengali society, tantric spiritual practices may sacralize a woman's life and actions, or cause her to be rejected by the community, depending on the type of ritual involved.

It is accepted in the tantric texts that women have a special aptitude for both devotion and ritual practice. Both living in the home and leaving home can be sacred acts for women. But women's roles as renunciants are in direct conflict with their obligations as childbearers; it is the classic opposition between *dharma* and *moksha* (ordinary responsibility to the social order and the extraordinary state of liberation), which produces a tension in the lives of all religious people in the Hindu tradition, male or female. While "domestic tantra" exists, it is rare, and women do not generally admit to it (even to family members). For most women, domestic life and renunciant life are opposed, and one cannot simultaneously be the domestic mother of the household and the tantric Mother of the Universe.

NOTES

1. *Kularnava Tantra* 7.47–49.
2. *Kularnava Tantra* 7.49–51.
3. *Kali Tantra* 8.5–10.

4. Banerji 1988, 222–223.
5. Banerji 1988, 183.
6. Finn 1986, 95–96.
7. Banerji 1988, 261.
8. Banerji 1988, 262–263.
9. Literally *navapuspa*, or new flower.
10. *Maya Tantra* 12.1–8.
11. *Kamakhya Tantra* 4.35–37.
12. *Kularnava Tantra* 8.67–75.
13. Banerji 1988, 184.
14. Interview, Gauri Ma, Bakreshwar, 1994.
15. Interview, Jayashri Ma, Birbhum, 1994.
16. Saradananda 1978, 220–227.
17. For further details of her life, see McDaniel 1989, 215–220.
18. Interview, Sahajiya informants, Birbhum, 1983.
19. Interview, Archanapuri Ma, Calcutta, 1994.
20. Bhattacharjee 1977, 385–397.
21. I have only seen this attitude of scorn toward widows among Vaishnava groups, however. The Shakta widows I have personally seen were strong women and respected by both families and teachers.
22. Interview, Gauri Ma, Bakreshwar, 1994.

REFERENCES

Banerji, S. C. 1988. *A Brief History of Tantra Literature.* Calcutta: Naya Prokash.
Bhattacharjee, Bholanath. 1977. "Some Aspects of the Esoteric Cults of Consort Worship in Bengal: A Field Survey Report." *Folklore* 10 (December): 385–397.
Das, Upendrakumar, ed. 1976. *Kularnava Tantra: Mula, Tika, O Banganubadsaha.* Calcutta: Nababharat.
Dasa, Jyotirlal, ed. 1978a. *Kamakhya Tantram.* Calcutta: Nababharat.
———. 1978b. *Maya Tantra (Mula Samskrta O Banganubad Samet).* Calcutta: Nababharat.
Finn, Louise M., trans. 1986. *The Kulacudamani Tantra and the Vamakesvara Tantra, with the Jayaratha Commentary.* Wiesbaden, Germany: Otto Harrassowitz.
McDaniel, June. 1989. *The Madness of the Saints: Ecstatic Religion in Bengal.* Chicago: University of Chicago Press.
Saradananda, Swami. 1978. *Sri Ramarkrishna: The Great Master.* Translated by Swami Jagadananda. Mylapore: Sri Ramakrishna Math.
Smrititirtha, Pandit Srinityananda, ed. 1981. *Kali Tantram: Mula, Tippani O Banganubadsaha.* Calcutta: Nababharat.

10

Performing Arts, Re-forming Rituals: Women and Social Change in South India

Vasudha Narayanan

On Sunday mornings, at a time quite popular for television viewing, Jaya TV, a popular television channel in South India, presents
a show called *Thaka dhimi tha*. The title of the show refers to the
syllables used for rhythmic steps in Bharata Natyam, a form of classical South Indian dance. In the course of this well-watched show,
girls and women of varying ages perform classical Bharata Natyam
dance in an easily recognizable game show format and are judged in various competitive categories. In a typical show (e.g., 27
February 2005), three young girls around eight to ten years of age
were introduced by a teenaged girl, who seemed to be a dancer herself.
They then participated in various competitions and were judged—
based on the innovative and imaginative nature of their choreogra-
phy as well as for showcasing traditional dances—for a grand prize.
The dances were enacted against a background of a large floor-to-
ceiling illustration of a dancing Shiva known as Nataraja, the Lord
of the Dance. The dances included praise and adoration to various
deities, including Ganesha. There were short segments where the
young girls choreographed popular film music in the Bharata
Natyam style in the game show—something of which many purists
would not approve but which evidently make the ratings soar. At
the end of the program, the judge, a noted dancer herself, performed
a short piece to a song composed by Mira, the well-known sixteenth-
century woman poet. This song expressed Mira's love and passion
for lord Krishna, and in the refrain she sang about the chiming of
her anklets to the music and dance. As the dancer emoted the poet's
passion and swirled around the stage, the viewers were drawn into

the drama of the love among Mira the poet, Lakshmi the dancer, and Krishna; the music and the lyrics, hauntingly familiar, recreated that arena of devotion in a television program sponsored by corporate giants.

The program showcases a justifiable pride in classical dancing and Hindu culture. It was conceived by Radhika Shurajit, a dancer and choreographer who is making this classical Bharata Natyam form popular among children and a large television audience, and the show was still running when this book went to press in 2006. And yet it was only in the 1930s that this form of dance was introduced from temple and private settings onto the "secular" stage and into community halls and auditoriums. Through the regularizing of shows like *Thaka dhimi tha*, the dance is now reaching tens of thousands of people, not just in South India, but in many parts of the world through various satellite providers, such as Asianet.

While young boys are taking to this dance occasionally, it is primarily women who are exponents of Bharata Natyam. According to some informal estimates, about 5 percent of the performers are male; the most generous estimates put it at 10 percent.[1] The show, presented as a cultural program, takes for granted the popularization of this form of dance and the accompanying music in the mid-twentieth century. It takes place on a secular stage with multinational corporations sponsoring the program; the decor of the stage, the lyrics, the music, and the devotional themes of the dance intertwine with fusion music and some popular film music to present an unusual combination of religion and art.

Are the program and the dances it showcases to be seen and experienced as culture, religion, art, or secular entertainment? Dancers would probably say it is all of these, and many academics consider the categories to be fluid with porous boundaries. Within the Hindu traditions, religion, art, and culture often merge seamlessly, and certainly programs such as these make us question the artificial lines between disciplines in Western academia. But more important, what we are looking at here is the transition of dance from temples, courts, and private homes to the public sphere and the transition of what women consider to be authority in the re-formation and the reconfiguration of rituals. When, in the early twentieth century, there were massive efforts to reclaim or, as others would say, appropriate classical Bharata Natyam dance from the exclusive province of the temple dancers and some classes of women and make it available for all people, there were deliberate moves to take it away from the temple milieu to the secular stage. When that was accomplished, ironically, the secular stage became transformed into a shrine replete with icons of the dancing Shiva or Krishna, lighted lamps, incense, and flowers. The dance itself became an act of ritual religious offering to the deity.

This chapter looks at ritual as performance and performance as ritual. It explores the performing arts as ritual acts of worship and social resistance in which women, as ritual agents, "reshape values and ideals that help mold social identity" (Bell 1997, 82, 73). It is through being re-formers that women became performers in public forums; and women of various classes and categories ritualized their performances as worship. By revising and recreating texts, these women use the performing arts as agents of social reform.

Although the move from temples and private courts in the houses of patrons to the secular stage is significant in the history of twentieth-century classical dance in India, the association of music and dance with temples (albeit somewhat romanticized) is still very strong in the Hindu consciousness.

In classical dance performances in the United States, one specifically sees a nostalgia for the temple as a backdrop and as the frame for the dances. In 2001, for instance, there was a scintillating dance performance, *Saptapadi* ("seven steps," a term that ordinarily refers to the seven sacramental steps taken by the bride and groom in a wedding ceremony), in which several prominent dancers of the metropolitan Atlanta area participated. The choreographer of this program, Dr. Seshu Sharma, a local physician with considerable involvement in the performing arts, envisioned the dances as a ritual offering in the context of Indian temples and wanted them to be framed with slides of Hindu temples and architecture from India. Each dance was preceded by slides of one relevant temple in India where that particular style of dance flourished or where the deity depicted in the dance was worshipped. Then, as the priests from the local Atlanta temple recited Sanskrit verses to the deity who would be praised in the dance, the dancer entered the stage against the backdrop of a slide of the Indian temple. It is this framing of classical Indian dance today by a romanticized temple culture that is striking. This format was repeated in December 2004 for a similar mega dance program called *Sivoham Sivoham*[2] ("I am Shiva, I am Shiva"). Both dance programs were organized by the Hindu Temple of Atlanta but performed in the sumptuous auditorium of Georgia Tech University. They portrayed the dances as a significant expression of Hindu religiosity and larger culture and specifically portrayed dance and music as ritual expressions of worship. While all of the dancers in *Saptapadi* were women, there were one or two male dancers in *Sivoham Sivoham*.

This chapter explores the expression of women's religiosity through classical music and dance in public forums in South India. Straddling the fuzzy boundaries among religion, culture, and entertainment, we will look at women who serve as exemplars of devotion—devotion for the arts and devotion for the deity—as well as at what they considered to be authority in the course of this reformation of the classical performing arts such that it became accessible to women of many castes and classes. We will also look at those women who now use these art forms as vehicles to raise social consciousness. Parts of this chapter are, in a sense, a flashback which will explain how the dance milieu described in the TV game show *Thaka dhimi tha* and the temple framework for *Saptapadi* and *Sivoham Sivoham* are recalled and reconfigured from the past and reframed for dancers in the present. We will initially discuss the importance of music and dance in the larger South Indian Hindu culture and, against this background, look more closely at three topics: the role of a ninth-century woman poet-saint in inspiring public expressions of women's religiosity in the twentieth century; the efforts of three women in mainstreaming classical music and dance in South Indian culture; and finally the movement by some dancers, like Mallika Sarabhai, in using this dance form to raise people's awareness of social issues, including the status of women.

The inclusion of the fields of music and dance underscores more than creating the opportunity for the entry of women into the realm of the arts; it acknowledges the efforts of women who made it possible for others to *publicly* express their devotion and spiritual longing in ways that were not available to them earlier. But while this freedom to publicly portray devotion through the performing arts is seen as laudable, we also raise a question in the end: did this opening up of the performing arts come at the expense of taking it away from those women, the *devadasis*, the servants of god, who had safeguarded it for centuries? Was it a creation of new ritual space for women or an appropriation of dance forms by high-class women from the courtesans who came to be increasingly marginalized during the colonial era? Before we discuss these issues, let us look first at the position of music and dance in India.

Social Values and Perceptions of Performing Arts

Hindu women—as women in many other cultures—have been both empowered and subjugated by religious traditions over the centuries. Some of the dancers loosely gathered under the umbrella term *devadasi* had agency and control over their property, on the one hand, but were also objects of "enjoyment" (*bhogam*), on the other. The contrast drawn in literature—even in texts such as the *Kama Sutra* and the Tamil work *Silappatikaram*—is between the decorum of wives, who were dependent on their husbands, and the activities of courtesans, who did not marry and were independent agents in many ways. The Brahminical Hindu tradition has been marked by the curtailing of freedom to women in the spaces connected with dharmic roles. And yet, it may also be argued by some that women in Hindu traditions—either because of or in spite of gender, caste, and class restrictions—have continuously found opportunities to create new spaces for artistic expression and paths to salvation. One can also note that the curtailment they faced in many social spheres was paralleled by a lack of similar opportunities for men; in other words, gender was only one factor among many in determining how one could have the life one wanted to live. It is in this context that we can understand the attitudes toward the performance of classical music and dance by women.

A popular Sanskrit saying ascribed to various sources expresses clearly that the term *sangita*, usually translated as "music" in English, really includes vocal and instrumental music as well as dance (*gitam vadyam tatha nrityam trayam sanitam uchyate*). Music and dance are intertwined in the Hindu traditions, and in this chapter, we will deal with both.

The place of music and dance and of the musicians and dancers in precolonial and colonial India is a very complicated topic. There were, of course, many kinds of classical and popular music and dance performed at homes and in temples. The received narrative tradition today is that classical dance was safeguarded by the *devadasis*, or temple dancers, and that the temple dancers who practiced erotic arts as well as the dance form itself were "emancipated" by the British overlords and several social reform movements. The story from the viewpoint of the *devadasis*, ritual specialists at the temples and in some domestic events as well, is different; they claim that they did not need any emancipation and that their arts were appropriated, indeed, hijacked by the social elite.

Music and dance were performed in many forums in precolonial and colonial India by women from many classes. While classical vocal music was probably part of domestic rituals for upper-class women, playing instruments and performing classical dances in public were within the province of *devadasis*. *Devadasi* is a shorthand term for a variety of practitioners, not all of whom were either dancers or courtesans or performed in temples. Some of them were dedicated to the temple, some served at the local ruler's pleasure, some were simply born into matrilineal families associated with these arts. Dancing was associated with courts, temples, and halls of rich patrons; in some areas, there were different classes of dancers for each of these arenas, while in other regions, the same dancers participated in all three. There were also many categories of lifestyles within these streams, and women associated with the temples were ritual specialists with very specific roles to play in daily, periodic, and annual events. They were paid largely through endowments made to the temples. A few women were long-term companions of patrons. In the colonial era, however, they came to be generically portrayed as women of loose morals, or even as prostitutes. The *devadasis* sang songs of love and praise to both the deity and the patron. The music and dance frequently contained double entendres— the words could refer to the king or the deity, and the emotions could be construed as *kama/sringara* (physical, sensual love) or *bhakti* (devotion).

Since many of the colonizing forces in India had dominant anti-dance ideologies, the attitudes toward the dancers and dance in the nineteenth and twentieth centuries have been lamentably negative. The movement to make classical dance available to girls of all castes was not just a struggle against high-caste male resistance or a culture where there were some patriarchal power structures in place, but also against the dominant colonial ideology. In the early part of the twentieth century, the dance known as *dasi attam* (the dance of temple servants or courtesans) and *sadir* (from the Urdu word *sadara*, meaning dance) was renamed Bharata Natyam, the dance according to the sage Bharata. Since the indigenous name for India was the "land of Bharata" (after another legendary Bharata), the renaming itself had nationalistic nuances.

Acting, music, and dance have been considered to be some of the optional ways to salvation within Hinduism. The treatise on theater and dance, the *Natya Sastra*, written by a legendary person called Bharata, is considered to be the fifth Veda or scripture. Dance is said to involve a total control of the body, a control central to the physical discipline of yoga. The *Natya Sastra* is supposed to have originated with a divine being called Brahma and was then passed on to the sage Bharata. Brahma is said to have taken the reading text from the Rig Veda, the earliest and one of the most sacred texts in the history of Hindu literature, music from the Sama Veda, gestures from the Yajur Veda, and *rasa* (lit. essence or juice), that is, the aesthetic element, from the Atharava Veda. Combining the essence of the four Vedas, he compiled a fifth Veda that depicts dance as a way to salvation. In oral tradition, the very name Bharata is said to incorporate the main elements of Bharata Natyam: *Bha-* stands for *bhava*, a state of mind, an attitude; *-ra* for *raga*; and *-ta* for *tala*, or rhythm. In addition to this, music and dance were known as the Gandharva Veda.

One can get liberation either through dancing or by being overwhelmed by the joy which comes by witnessing the dance. This could be any dance; theoretically speaking, all dance is divine. Thus, in classical Bharata Natyam, there are "pure" dances or dances without any particular lyrics and emotions attached to them. Many of the dances, however, are devotional in tone. At times, the dancer expresses devotion through his/her body and soul to get liberation. This is particularly seen in the Bharata Natyam style of South Indian dancing, where the dancer may express her love for the Lord in explicitly erotic terminology. The pining of a human soul for union with the Lord is expressed through passionate longing and a desire to belong to him. The audience is also granted salvation through participation in the divine joy of movement. Either by dancing or by beholding the beauty of the divine dance—whether it is that of Krishna with his cowherd friends, or Shiva, known as Nataraja, or the King of the Dance—one obtains liberation.

Sanskrit texts on dance such as the *Natya Sastra* usually make a distinction between classical and folk dances. These categories have not been immutable; sometimes, the boundaries have been fluid, and both forms have derived inspiration from the other. People from various communities would perform those dances that were part of their traditions both at home and in public—in village streets, on festival days, for example—but classical dancing was regulated. A striking example of public singing and dancing (though originally even these were contained within homes) is the *garbha* dance and worship in the state of Gujarat. This is frequently classified as folk dancing, but as in any other tradition, one cannot draw hard lines between classical and popular dance forms: they are in dialectical relationship with each other. *Garbha* or *garbhi* is "womb," the source of all creative energy; it is the Mother Goddess who is present in the lamp inside the clay pot that is called *garbha*. Women and young girls dance around the *garbha* all night, celebrating the goddess. It seems that when the focus of discussion is *moksha* (liberation), rather than *dharma* (issues of righteousness) in this world, a greater freedom is seen in women's participation in public spaces. Androcentric regulation of women's modesty or actions in public, which were incumbent on some castes and classes, is simply bypassed in cases where the tradition focuses on the salvation potential of all human beings.

The ostensible reason for the "revelation" or composition of the treatise on dance is said to be that of making accessible the difficult statements of the Vedas to *all* human beings. However, it is interesting to note that at least after the fourteenth and fifteenth centuries (or possibly earlier), while we have documentation of male singers (of many castes) and dancers, the only women who sang and danced in public seem to have been courtesans. This was apparently not the case in earlier centuries; even as late as the twelfth century, we see sculptures of women dancers adorning the niches of the Belur temple in Karnataka. Shantala Devi, a Hoysala queen, is said to have been responsible for building this temple. It is also said that one of the dancing figures within the temple is a figure of the queen herself. According to one popular account, her dance was admired by the king and the courtiers, and "the king as desired by the courtiers gave her publicly the titles of 'Natyasarasvati' [the *sarasvati* or goddess of dance] and 'Sakala samaya rakshamani' (Imperial protector of all faiths)" (Nagappachar 1960, 7).[3] The human body is celebrated in these sculptures, and the later restrictions against women from "decent families" dancing in public may have come from a chronologically evolving coalescence of conservative attitudes explicit in many Hindu *dharmic* texts, Islamic mores in India, and the puritanical perspectives of European missionaries.

It is possible that with new attitudes toward the human body (attitudes that reinforce some of the negative statements made in some *Dharma Shastras* about a woman's uncontrollable sexual propensity), perspectives on the overtly sensual presentations involved in the performing arts also changed. Many devotional lyrics, after all, use the rapturous love metaphor in constructing the relationship between the human being and God. The singer or dancer displayed these sensual *bhavas*, or expressions, either with the face or with the entire body in the case of the dancer, and through voice modulation in the case of the singer. While the allegorical meaning of these poems clearly indicated the love to be spiritual, metaphors pertaining to the body were prominently used. Upper-class men would have thought that it was inappropriate for women to display their bodies in public. Women did continue to dance and sing, but it seems to have been within the confines of the home, without a choice of whether they wanted to do this in public. It is possible that women did participate in devotional singing through the streets in some medieval traditions, especially those associated with the movement of Caitanya, but even this is debated and was probably more of an exception.

Thus, while song and dance have been considered to be significant ways to salvation, until the mid-twentieth century, ordinarily only men and female courtesans performed in public. Although music and dance were theoretically considered to be sacred, in time their beauty came to be associated with physical sensuality and the performance of courtesans. It was considered inappropriate for women from decent families and the so-called higher castes to perform in public. We see this illustrated in the life of Sister Subbalakshmi (1886–1969), a child widow (not to be confused with M. S. Subbulakshmi, 1916–2004, the famous Carnatic music singer of South India), who worked hard for the rights of young widows to be educated in schools and universities. Monica Felton, her biographer, records that when young, Subbalakshmi was taught to play the violin. This was an act that brought about the ire of her tradition-bound grandmother. Felton writes:

> It was not, and he knew it, the extravagance of buying such a thing which shocked Grandmother. She had been far from pleased by the decision to give Subbalakshmi an education of a kind that was really only suitable for boys.... These things had been bad enough. The violin was really the last straw. Ladies might sometimes sing, though only in the privacy of their own homes. Even that was very unusual, and no lady would ever, in any circumstances whatever, learn to play a musical instrument. Music was for dancing girls, *devadasis*, as the temple prostitutes were called. Surely Subramania, who came from such a good family, could not really intend to engage a teacher and allow his widowed daughter, of all people, to take lessons? (Felton 1967, 38)

Subbalakshmi's parents taught her to play not only the violin, but also the *veena*, a traditional South Indian instrument. Subbalakshmi eventually became an educator and also provided the infrastructure (a boardinghouse and regular meals cooked by Subbalakshmi's aunt, herself a widow) to facilitate young widows getting a solid public education.[4] It was due in part to the efforts of Subbalakshmi's family and the work of other women like Bangalore Nagaratnammal, Balasaraswati, and Rukmini Devi Arundale (whom we will encounter shortly) that the fields of education and performing arts opened up for Hindu women in the twentieth century.

In southern India, the dynamic creativity in the production and performance of classical song and dance was largely seen in the lives of men belonging to several castes, including Brahmins, and *devadasi* families. The annals of the Tanjore court in the eighteenth and nineteenth centuries are filled with accounts of prominent male singers/musicians and of courtesans (Seetha 1981, 35, 98, 122–126).[5] *Devadasis* performed these arts in temples and were also ritual specialists. There were also other courtesans not necessarily dedicated to temples, patronized by royalty and nobility, who were involved with the performing arts. Courtesans were generally the only women, apart from royalty, to have access to textual scholarship and the arts of singing and dancing for many centuries. They also held the rights to inherit property and to adopt children. But *devadasis* have never served as role models except within their own communities in South Indian society. Although they expressed their *bhakti* through performing arts, the dominant Kalakshetra school of dance and several other dance schools do not look upon them as sources of authority; rather, they appeal directly to texts such as the *Natya Sastra* to derive "authenticity" for their dances.

In the twentieth century, the coming together of nationalistic concerns, an increased consciousness of premodern women poets, a new pride in Indian classical performing arts, and the new public spaces created for expressions of devotion has created a veritable boom in classical music and dance.

One stream that feeds into this appropriation/expression of music and dance is the growing awareness of women poets who lived more than a thousand years ago. While there are records of dozens of such poets all over India—women who composed in local languages such as Tamil—most of them are not known outside a small region. The poets express a passionate desire to unite physically and spiritually with the deity, and this passion is not unlike the songs sung by the *devadasis*.[6] However, the women's groups that sing devotional songs look to the women poets, not the *devadasis*, as role models. In other words, while the passion for the deity is the same in both sets of songs—those composed by the women poets and those sung by the *devadasis*—women in the twentieth century look to the poets as the authority, not the *devadasis*. And although literally hundreds of classical dancers today choreograph and dance Andal's songs, the authority for the performances becomes Andal, on the one hand, and the remote *Natya Sastra*, on the other, and not the *devadasis* from whom the techniques of the dance style are directly derived. The exception, to some extent, is the school founded by Balasaraswati.

Let us now turn to the question of authority and how women have energized classical music and dance and re-formulated them so they can be accessible to women of many castes. We will discuss the impact of the poet Andal as a role model in Tamilnadu and also explore the contributions of three other women, Bangalore Nagaratnammal, Balasaraswati, and Rukmini Devi Arundale, who made a difference in the public performance of music and dance. In the twentieth century, these three women were instrumental in bringing South Indian classical Carnatic music and Bharata Natyam to the public stage and making the performing arts accessible—for performance, audience participation, and viewing by the general public. They thus helped to transform the ritual form of the performing arts. Ironically, Bangalore Nagaratnammal is said to have been the daughter of a courtesan, and Balasaraswati also hailed from a *devadasi* family. Rukmini Devi Arundale, on the other hand, learned dance from a *devadasi* but worked to bring dance out into the public and secular sphere.

The Goda Mandali, or the Circle of Andal

Since the 1970s, many groups of women in the suburbs of Madras, a city in South India, have formed circles (*mandali*) to sing the poems of Andal and other Vaishnavaite Tamil saints. These groups look directly to Andal, an eighth-century poet, as the authority for their *bhakti*. The groups in Chennai have interesting names: Goda Mandali (circle of Andal; Goda is another name for Andal), Sreyas Mandali (circle [leading] to the higher path), Ranganatha Paduka Mandali (circle that venerates the sandals of Ranganatha [Vishnu]), Subhasri Mandali (very auspicious circle), and Bhaktanjali (worshipful circle of adoration). The groups meet once or twice a week to learn devotional songs from a teacher and also perform in music fests (like the Tamil Music Association festival in December) and temples. Sometimes, they raise money for the upkeep of various shrines through their singing. In the last few years, the Goda Mandali located in Thyagarayanagar, Madras, has used the medium of singing to reappropriate and participate in the passion of Andal/Goda.

Goda Mandali, appropriately named after one of the earliest woman poets dedicated to Vishnu, was first formed in 1970 and reorganized in 1982. It has stopped meeting regularly since about the year 2000 after the tragic murder of one of the members, but there are periodic moves to revive it. The women of this group frequently sang for events connected with temples, and occasionally, they sang for a secular audience. The piety of Goda Mandali has also achieved considerable visibility through television and radio, leading to the formation of more circles, through which the passion of Andal lives again. All practice sessions and performances begin with a unique invocation. In the Sri Vaishnava community, recitation of the songs of the Tamil saints generally begins with the line "I take refuge with the sacred feet of Nammalvar [a male poet-saint who lived in the ninth century] and Emperumanar [Ramanuja, a male theologian of the twelfth century C.E.]." Goda Mandali, however, begins with the line "I take refuge with the sacred feet of Nammalvar, Andal, and Ramanuja; I take refuge with the sacred feet of Andal." This special emphasis on Andal is unique to this circle of her companions in Goda Mandali and in some of the other women's groups. Goda Mandali also has a unique *mangalam*, or last song. In almost all classical South Indian (Carnatic) music concerts, the last "auspicious" song focuses (by tradition) on the male god Rama, and either a song of Tyagaraja (eighteenth century) or Ramdas (seventeenth century) is sung. Goda Mandali, however, sings a song praising the goddess Lakshmi in her manifestation in the temple of Srirangam.

There are also dozens of dancers who choreograph and dance Andal's songs. Srinidhi Rangarajan, a physician and noted Bharata Natyam dancer, in Madras, Tamilnadu, rearranged the verses of *Tiruppavai* (a song composed by Andal) to reflect her experience of a spiritually progressive sequence and choreographed it. This performance was held in December 1994 to inaugurate the Festival of

Tiruppavai. Following the performance of Dr. Rangarajan, students and teachers from a large school in Madras went around the streets in a lighted float, singing the verses of Andal. This float was subsequently taken out at dawn for several days in the month of Markali (December 15–January 13, a month that is considered to be sacred to Andal) and traveled through the city of Madras. These new rituals highlighting women's piety and public role in religious expression are becoming increasingly common; their popularity is attested to by the fact that the Festival of the *Tiruppavai*, the dance by Dr. Rangarajan, and the floats were all sponsored by the Indian Bank, a leading commercial institution in India.

And who is this Andal, the role model and authority for these women singers and dancers? She was an eighth-century poet-devotee who sought the deity Vishnu as her beloved.

Andal, an Eighth-Century Devotee, and the Performing Arts

Normative texts and oral tradition in some Hindu communities held that revering one's husband as a god was enough to attain liberation. While there are several narratives to exemplify this ideal, there is no indication that many women took this notion literally. Andal did not want to get married and consider her husband as a god; she wanted God as her husband. Andal is the only woman poet-saint venerated by the Sri Vaishnava community of South India. In two poems, the *Tiruppavai* ("Sacred Lady") and the *Nachiyar Tirumoli* ("The Sacred Words of the Lady"), she expresses her passionate desire to marry lord Vishnu, whom she sees in the forms of Krishna or Rama (incarnations of Vishnu), or as the resident deity in the temple. In the *Tiruppavai*, she imagines herself as a young *gopi*, or cowherd girl, in the village where Krishna grew up. She wakes up her friends very early in the morning in the month of Markali, and they all go to wake up Krishna and give him their petition: their longing to be with him and to serve him for all time. Andal asks her friends to come with her to "bathe"; the Tamil word *niratal* or bathing, was frequently used to indicate a sexual union in Tamil literature. Since Vishnu is compared to a lotus pond frequently, Andal's intentions would be clear to those who recite the poem, and if they are not, the commentators articulate this concept quite well.

Andal's life offers not just a theological model for all human beings, but a model of love that women may use in approaching God. Women see in her a person who attained salvation not by worshipping her husband as a deity (as Manu would have it), but by approaching the deity directly and seeking union with him. What Andal and other women poets did by living the way they did was to negotiate a space within a marriage-dominated society and force at least some sections of the society to make room for them. The typology of women that we see in the law books (*Dharma Sastras*) are young unmarried girls, married women, and widows: single women who either reject marriage or who walk out on their husbands are not even recognized. But by the power of their love and the consolidation of their aspirations, the women poets carve out a different space for themselves.

Andal's songs have been recited daily in domestic and temple liturgies, and her lyrics have been set to *ragas* and performed on sacred and secular stages. Her songs have been part of the repertoire for all classical Bharata Natyam dancers since the 1970s. More important, Andal, Mira, and other women poets have become the focus of inspiration and the authority for *bhakti* for many women's groups in India.

How do these women who dance and sing Andal's songs relate to Andal? In Sri Vaishnava theology, Andal is clearly a paradigmatic devotee and by identifying with or imitating her love, it may be possible to reach Vishnu. Parasara Bhattar, a twelfth-century theologian, is quoted as advising a male disciple that one ought to recite the entire *Tiruppavai* every morning and experience its emotions. If it is not possible to recite at least one verse, he is advised to just think of the way he has experienced the joy of the verses. In other words, the experiencing of the path taken by Andal, however vicariously, is highly recommended for both men and women. Commentaries say that by the practice of some rituals, the cowherd girls got Krishna; by the imitation of those rituals, Andal reached Krishna. By ritually making the words of Andal her words, the devotee is extolled to be like Andal, imitating her passion, emulating and appropriating her devotion (Periyavaccan Pillai 1974, 202–203). In other words, one seeks union with Vishnu through the words of Andal and by sharing her passion and her power.

The women of Goda Mandali see Andal's words and the words of the other saints as portraying their own emotions and spiritual longing and as ritually giving them direct access to the Lord. Chitra Raghunathan, one of the members, says that singing with this group is the most fulfilling aspect of her religious life: in fact, she added, this is her only real religious life; this is her direct prayer, her ritual. In temples, special groups (like the *adhyapakas* and *araiyars*, the traditional male cantors) have the religious and often the legal right to recite and pray; in household rituals, a man may officiate; but through singing and dancing, the women communicate directly with the deity. In this context, two factors are important: the companionship of the group, which is like the collective prayer of Andal and her friends, and second, the opportunity to sing the sacred words in private and in public forums. The growing popularity of these women's groups, which sing the prayers in sacred and secular forums, is leading to an increase in the transformation of ritual patterns in some Hindu communities.

Hundreds of women's groups like Goda Mandali have become popular all over the world largely due to the pioneering efforts of Bangalore Nagaratnammal, who helped to create a public space where women could participate in singing classical music. Classical Carnatic music in South India is almost completely devotional in tone, and the lyrics explicitly express one's *bhakti* to a deity.

Bangalore Nagaratnammal

Bangalore Nagaratnammal (1878–1952) was the daughter of a courtesan-singer in the royal court of Mysore. Coming from a community that was low in social status from certain Brahminical perspectives, it was nevertheless one that accorded young women the privilege of education of every kind. A celebrated singer and musician, Nagaratnammal was responsible for instituting a music fest in honor of the male composer Tyagaraja (1767–1847) in the town of Tiruvaiyaru. This festival was instituted to encourage all singers—male, female, famous, and unknown—to participate equally, with equal time and opportunity for all to celebrate the piety of Tyagaraja's music.[7] This was more than a music festival; the music itself is considered to be a form of worship and is also accompanied by religious rituals, extolling the musical composer and, now, Bangalore Nagaratnammal.

Nagaratnammal's authority for institutionalizing this festival of music was *not* derived from the *devadasi* community; rather, she appealed to the authority of dreams. She was apparently led by dreams to Tiruvaiyaru, a small village in Tamilnadu where the composer Tyagaraja had lived. She cleared the land where he had been buried, tirelessly collected funds to build a temple nearby, and then instituted the music festival. She befriended and encouraged younger women to sing and perform, singing to celebrate the deity and to give full expression to their talents and fervor. Bangalore Nagaratnammal is to be remembered for creating the public space for women and men to participate in a festival where one can sing the devotional lyrics of Tyagaraja and participate both in a choral and individual expression of reverence.

The Tyagaraja Utsava (Festival of Tyagaraja) was and remains a grand vision and celebration, and it has grown to be one of the best-known music festivals in India and for Hindus in the diaspora. Tyagaraja Utsavas are celebrated with great *eclat* not just in Tiruvaiyaru, but now in every major city in the United States and Canada with the most prominent one being in Cleveland, Ohio. The lead singers in many of these festivals in India and abroad are now women musicians. The establishment of this public, devotional forum for the display of talent—of both men and women—is due to the efforts of Bangalore Nagaratnammal. While during the early part of Bangalore Nagaratnammal's life, Carnatic music was not sung in public by high-caste women, they are now conspicuous by their presence.

The opening up of classical dance and music to men and women of the "higher castes" is an important development in the twentieth century. While this is particularly true of Carnatic music, it is also true of the performing arts all over India. It was only in the twentieth century that the pioneering efforts of Balasaraswati and Rukmini Devi Arundale resulted in making Bharata Natyam accessible to women of all castes.

Balasaraswati and Rukmini Devi Arundale

While Vallathol in Kerala and Rabindranath Tagore—two men—worked for the revival of classical dance forms in Kerala and in Bengal, the classical Bharata Natyam dance became popular in Tamilnadu with the efforts of both a man (E. Krishna Iyer) and two women, Balasaraswati (1918–1984) and Rukmini Devi (1904–1986). Balasarawati's impact on the field of dance was tremendous:

> No dancer captured the public imagination as Balasaraswati did in the thirties and forties. Bharatanatyam to the public until then was an esoteric art practised for the pleasure of a few connoisseurs and dilettantes. Outside the pale of the temple and court there were hardly any public performances. Balasaraswati made the public aware of Bharatanatyam, not by deliberate efforts as a reformer, but by the beauty and the eloquence of her dancing. It was left to others to fight prejudices and stupidity, do research, delve into the past, give the dancer's profession respectability and so on.[8]

Narayana Menon's account of Balasaraswati makes an important point—that she made this classical dance form popular, "not by deliberate efforts as a reformer, but by the beauty and the eloquence of her dancing." This is, perhaps, the primary difference between her efforts and those of Rukmini Devi.

Balasaraswati came from a family of courtesans and Rukmini Devi from a Brahmin family. Balasaraswati learned dance from the time she could walk and had her stage debut (*arangetram*) when she was seven years old; Rukmini Devi learned Western dance first, was a friend of Anna Pavlova and learned Bharata Natyam when she was much older from Gowri Ammal, a *devadasi*, and had her stage debut when she was in her mid-thirties. Balasaraswati sought the authority for her style of dance and the traditional sequence of Bharata Natyam recitals from her own family heritage; Rukmini Devi from Sanskrit, pan-Indian sources.

Biographies of Balasaraswati frequently speak of her ancestors and her place in a lineage of people who had dedicated themselves to the arts. She was proud of this heritage and fought to preserve and transmit this authenticity of the received tradition. For her, this tradition was local and the authority came from her foremothers. Rukmini Devi's school of dance, on the other hand, emphasized the pan-Indian heritage of this dance form with a serious study of the *Natya Sastra* composed by Bharata and also the *Abhinaya Darpana* (ca. fourth through sixth centuries), a Sanskrit text attributed to Nandikeswara (O'Shea 1998).

Both Balasaraswati and Rukmini Devi agreed firmly that the Bharata Natyam was a religious art; we find this over and over again in their speeches and talks. Even when a piece was dedicated to a human patron, Balasaraswati explained that it ultimately addressed the supreme being:

> The composer of a Sabdam or a Varnam might have dedicated it
> to a prince or a noble man. But as far as the dancer is concerned,
> the hero can only be the King of Kings, the Lord of the wide world.
> It is impossible for her to dedicate her art, which has sanctified her
> body and has made her heart sacred, to a mere mortal. She can
> experience and communicate the sacred in what appears to be sec-
> ular. After all, our composers have been steeped in the tradition of
> *bhakti*.[9]

While both dancers spoke of dance as a religious exercise, Balasaraswati is credited with the saying that *sringara* is the highest form of expression in Bharata Natyam (O'Shea 1998). *Sringara* is romantic love; some translate it as passion or sexual love. Balasaraswati firmly thought—as we can see from the following passage—that this was not carnal. However, Rukmini Devi seems to have thought that the erotic elements should be removed from Bharata Natyam and that passion should be sublimated and expressed as *bhakti*. Balasaraswati did not think that Bharata Natyam had to be "purified" in any way:

> It is this stream of *sringara* that swells into the mighty river of the
> lover-beloved songs of the Vaishnava and Saiva saints, the *Ashtapadi*
> of Jayadeva and the compositions of Kshetragna. In Bharatanatyam,
> too when it comes to *abhinaya*, *sringara* has been the dominant mood.
>
> NOT CARNAL
> I emphasize all this because of some who seek to "purify" Bhar-
> atanatyam by replacing the traditional lyrics, which express *sringara*
> with devotional songs. I respectfully submit to such protagonists that
> there is nothing in Bharatanatyam which can be purified afresh; it is
> divine as it is and innately so. The *sringara* we experience in Bhara-
> tanatyam is never carnal; never, never. For those who have yielded
> themselves to its discipline line with total dedication, dance, like music
> is the practice of the Presence. It cannot be merely the body's rapture.
>
> Bharatanatyam is an art, which consecrates the body, which is
> considered to be in itself of no value. The yogi, by controlling his
> breath and by modifying his body, acquires the halo of sanctity. Even
> so, the dancer, who dissolves her identity in rhythm and music,
> makes her body an instrument, at least for the duration of the dance,
> for the experience and expression of the spirit.[10]

Even though Balasaraswati emphasized the religious and spiritual nature of dance, her critique of the attempts to purify—that is, get rid of—the *sringara*, or the passion in the dance, made her school distinct from that of Rukmini Devi. It was by the beauty and the aesthetic nature of her dance and by dancing in public that she popularized it. Rukmini Devi, on the other hand, started a school with a regular curriculum. As noted earlier, she appealed to the authority of *Natya Sastra* and other texts to frame the dance form as classical and all-Indian.

Rukmini Devi Arundale, dancer, educator, and nominee to be president of India in 1977, was born in a Brahmin family and is best known for her establishment of a school of classical music and dance. Here, the dancers not only learn from teachers, but see their art as having a continuous connection with the Sanskrit texts on dance composed centuries ago. Rukmini Devi's parents belonged to the progressive theosophist movement and were closely associated with Annie Besant, the Theosophy leader. Rukmini Devi herself broke with orthodox tradition in many ways. When she was sixteen, she married an Englishman. She later learned ballet from Western teachers and Bharata Natyam from Mylapore Gowri, an eminent dancer from a traditional family of courtesans. In 1935, Rukmini Devi gave a public recital of dancing "in the midst of dissent and fury" (Rajagopalan 1990a, 256). The storm of protest was evidently against the idea of a "high-caste" woman giving a public dance performance. Rukmini Devi persisted in her efforts and started the Arena of Art (Kalakshetra), an international academy of the arts in 1936. Classical music and many kinds of South Indian classical dance were taught there for all those who desired to find fulfillment through these artistic forms. It is hard to imagine that Bharata Natyam, a field that is dominated by Brahmin women and girls today, was completely forbidden to them until late into the twentieth century.

Social Change and Dance

The performing arts now serve as vehicles for further dynamic reform in a way that is unparalleled within the Hindu tradition. The fight to render erotic/spiritual longing in artistic ritual form in public forums was a major landmark of the twentieth century. The performing arts are now used with skill by celebrated dancers like Mallika Sarabhai and Chandralekha to express themes of anguish and strength that pertain to women's issues. What is striking is that unlike some of the women mentioned above, who looked at earlier paradigmatic poets, dreams, or Sanskrit texts for inspiration and as a validation of their innovation, people like Dr. Sarabhai do not necessarily retrieve authority figures or texts from the past to mount their challenges.

Mallika Sarabhai's new school of dance, dedicated to her mother, is called Natarani, or Queen of Dance. This is a deliberate change from the name Nataraja, or King of the Dance, a popular name of lord Shiva, also known as the Lord of the Dance. Mallika Sarabhai has utilized the forms of mime and dance to underscore some of the injustices done to women. She initially set the feminist agenda through "Shakti: The Power of Women" and has continued explorations of feminist issues through her recital "Sita's Daughters." "Shakti" is a solo performance in which Dr. Sarabhai portrays women whose power has been negated or neutralized by male society.

"Sita's Daughters" starts with a focus on an episode from the *Ramayana*, an epic which is probably the best-known story in the Hindu tradition. At the end of the story, Prince Rama, who is regarded as an incarnation of lord Vishnu, questions his wife, Sita, about her chastity. In the last segments of the epic, Rama banishes the pregnant Sita. Several years later, when he meets his twin sons and Sita, he says he will accept her if she can give him some "proof" that she is chaste. Sita proves this by an "act of truth." This is an act by which a person swears that, if something is true (for example, her love for a particular person), then a miracle will happen. Sita now swears and says that, if it is true that she has always been faithful to Rama, Mother Earth will open up and swallow her. The earth opens up and accepts Sita. Sita proves to Rama that she is indeed chaste, but Rama does not get his wife back.

Dr. Sarabhai sees these instances of Rama's questioning and seeking of proof of chastity as a paradigmatic instance of injustice to women. This initial episode frames the later sequences of the dance, when she portrays instances in which some hegemonic segments of the religious culture sanction the instances of gender inequity. She also portrays the current struggles of women in the northern Doon Valley who work for ecological preservation and try to prevent trees from being cut down. This movement, called Chipko, is a protest against the developers who seek to level the land in the name of development without heed for the future. Using very few props, Dr. Sarabhai focuses on women who refused to give in to the pressures around them, women who did not accept, but who questioned and chafed. These women are called the "Sitas who refuse ever again to submit to the tests and trials of weak and doubting men."[11] In "Sita's Daughters" and other performances, Dr. Sarabhai uses dance as a ritual vehicle to publicly portray social causes.

Courtesans like Bangalore Nagaratnammal and Brahmin women like Balasaraswati and Rukmini Devi Arundale did not see themselves as radicals or feminists—they were driven by an ardor to share their joy of learning, music, or dance with others and not have it restricted to certain segments of society. One may ask, however, if these efforts through which all women had the right to learn and perform music and classical Bharata Natyam dance in public should be seen from another perspective—that of the *devadasi*. Was this a process of opening up the arts or one by which they were wrested, indeed hijacked by some upper-class women?

The answers are complicated because these efforts came at a time when there were legal and social measures to make the *devadasi* system illegal. One may also note that Balasaraswati, herself from a *devadasi* family, worked hard to change the conservative—and negative—perceptions about Bharata Natyam by performing all over India and then in other countries as well, attracting not just connoisseurs and admirers but also a devoted group of students.

The nationalistic fervor of the 1930s and 1940s formed a backdrop to and helped Rukmini Devi's efforts in framing this dance as a national heritage of India. From her perspective—and the hundreds of students in her school—the transformation of ritual music and dance was an attempt to make opportunities available to women by breaking down social barriers based not only on gender, but also on social caste, economic class, and colonial dominion.

Ironically, in Tamilnadu, in an attempt to improve the status of the *devadasis*, the courtesans who danced in temples, several legal measures were enacted to ban not just the dedication of girls to temples, but any dancing by any woman in temples. Part 3, section 3, of the Devadasi Act of 1947 reads, "Dancing by a woman . . . in a temple or religious institution . . . or procession or at any festival or ceremony . . . is declared unlawful."[12] This law, which is supposed to avoid treating women as commodities just used to entertain, also denies them the freedom of expression to use music and dance as a ritual of worship. Happily, in contemporary India, this law is ignored by everyone, including the government of India. Several dance festivals have been initiated in temples, and women do sing and dance in processions. Sometimes the temples are used as dramatic, aesthetic backdrops, as in the Mahabalipuram dance festival in January and the Khajuraho festival in early spring. Almost every major temple complex—Konarak, Pattadakal, Khajuraho, Modhera—has an annual dance festival, which is seen as a tourist attraction and cultural entertainment. In many other temples however, like Chidambaram, the dance festival (called Natyanjali, or Worship through Dance) coincides with the holy day of Maha Sivaratri, the Great Night of Shiva, and is seen explicitly as a devotional exercise. Accounts like the following are seen on Web sites:

> The Natyanjali festival dedicated to Lord Shiva is celebrated every year during February–March for five days in the temple premises. This is an opportunity for all dancers, from all over India, to perform and to pay their tribute to Lord Nataraja. It begins on the auspicious occasion of Maha Shivaratri. During this time leading dancers from all parts of India congregate and dance in the temple as an offering to Nataraja. Many dancers think it is a blessing to be able to perform their "arangetram" (first stage performance) in the vicinity of the sanctum sanctorum of Lord Nataraja in Chidambaram. The festival lasts for 5 days.

> Natyanjali festival is jointly organised by The Department of
> Tourism, Government of Tamilnadu, The Ministry of Tourism, Gov-
> ernment of India and The Natyanjali Trust, Chidambaram. It is
> designed to promote a universal message of "Unity in Diversity"
> conveyed in the universal language of music and dance.[13]

Several factors, therefore, have come together in the use of performing arts
to showcase new spaces in women's agencies. In this process, there have been
appeals to multiple sources of authority, including personal experiences as articulated in dreams, the life histories of renowned women saints, and the re-
vived clout of Sanskrit texts as powerful storehouses of wisdom and practice.
Two important factors contributing to the success of these measures are the
internal paradigms of granting spaces to women along the path to liberation
and the overall significance of custom and practice in the many Hindu traditions. The latter allows for flexibility, revival and re-formation of paradigms,
appropriations, and the co-opting of concepts and rituals. But in the process of
people from various castes and classes reclaiming this heritage, did the art of
those women, the many kinds of courtesans, the many *devadasi* communities,
who had performed for centuries get taken away from them and commer-
cialized in a different way? The answers, as we saw, are complex.

Time and space have also been significant in these rituals of devotional
offering. These changes can only be seen in the context of the times. The early
twentieth century was a time when the ardor of nationalistic fervor, the desire
for an independent India free of colonial rule, proud in its history and heritage,
and united in culture was widespread. The upper-class women who began
showcasing the temple arts, this proud heritage, not in the temple but on the
secular stage, were a symbol of this new Bharata. This was the dance of India,
the dance according to the legendary Bharata, the Bharata Natyam. The narrative of women's ritual roles began to extend beyond the home altar and temples to newer, hybrid, public spaces. These hybrid spaces were—and remain—
the great community halls and stages where classical music and dances take
place. And now, it has come full circle and come back to the temples. For many
women, these performances have become a professional art; for others, their
performances were and continue to be acts of worship. In temples in India and
the United States, women now perform music and dance as part of their devotional offerings. But whereas women in the mid-twentieth century worked to
bring dance from the temple into the public sphere, now, in shows like *Thaka
dhimi tha*, the public stage and the television platform have become the new
hybrid spaces—extensions of the temple space and domestic altars in secular
forums. This popularization has led to dance and music becoming entertainment for some individuals; for others, it is the language, form, and content of
religious ritual, as well as an agent of social change, leading them to liberation
on earth and then to heaven.

NOTES

1. Personal communication from Professor Davesh Soneji.

2. I was asked by Dr. Sharma to do the narration and show the slides for this program and was involved in the presentation of the dance as part of temple culture.

3. Almost all of the official guidebooks to the area point to the image inside the temple (marked as number 40 now by the government of India authorities and the Archaeological Survey of India) as representing Shantala Devi. There do not seem to be any primary sources that make this identification. The restaurant in the official Indian Tourism Development Corporation hotel at Hassan has named its restaurant Shantala. The general Indian stereotype of wifely virtue is to perceive a woman as the server of food, and it is interesting that of all places, a restaurant is named after this queen, who contributed so much to the fine arts and architecture.

4. I have discussed Sister Subbalakshmi's contributions in my chapter, "Brimming with Bhakti, Embodiments of Sakti: Deities, Devotees, Performers, Reformers and Other Women of Power in the Hindu Tradition," in *Feminism in World Religions*, edited by Arvind Sharma and Katherine Young (Albany: State University of New York Press, 1999).

5. In chapter 3, Seetha discusses the contributions of composers and musicians between the seventeenth and nineteenth centuries in the Tanjore area, and it is interesting to note that all sixty-two musicians/composers on whom she focuses are men. It is evident from other sources also (e.g., Rajagopalan 1990b and 1992b, which lists all the important musicians in South India) that prior to this century almost all musicians who were well known and who gained public approbation were men.

6. It must, however, be pointed out that some of the *devadasi* songs are more explicitly erotic in tone and have overt sexual imagery attached to them. See for instance, Soneji 2004; Ramanujan, Narayana Rao, and Shulman 1994.

7. Adapted from a booklet containing the biography of Bangalore Nagaratnammal, written in Tamil by her disciple Banni Bai.

8. From Narayana Menon, *Balasaraswati*. Inter-National Culture Center, New Delhi. Available at http://www.tamilnation.org/hundredtamils/balasaraswati.htm.

9. Balasaraswati, Presidential Address, Tamil Isai Sangam. Available at http://www.carnatica.net/dance/bharatanatyam1.htm.

10. T. Balasaraswati, Presidential Address, Tamil Isai Sangam. Available at http://www.carnatica.net/dance/bharatanatyam1.htm.

11. This is from a publicity pamphlet for "Sita's Daughters" by Darpana Academy of Dance.

12. This is quoted in "Devadasis, Part IV," *Hinduism Today*. Available at http://www.spiritweb.org/Hinduism Today/94–01-Devadasis_Part_IV.html.

13. Available at http://www.webindia123.com/festival/dance/chidam.htm.

REFERENCES

Allen, Matthew Harp. 1997. "Rewriting the Script for South Indian Dance." *The Drama Review* 41, no. 3: 63–100.

Andal. 1971. "Nacciyar Tirumoli." In *Nalayira tivviyap pirapantam*, ed. P. B. Annangaracariyar, 88–109. Kanchi: V. N. Tevanatan.

Bell, Catherine. 1997. *Ritual: Perspectives and Dimensions*. New York: Oxford University Press.

Coorlawala, Uttara Asha. 2005. "The Birth of *Bharatnatyam* and the Sanskritized Body." In *Rukmini Devi Arundale (1904–1986): A Visionary Architect of Indian Culture and Performing Arts*, ed. Avanthi Meduri, 173–194. New Delhi: Motilal Banarsidass.

Falk, Nancy Auer, and Rita M. Gross. 1989. "Women's Power: Mythical Models and Sacred Sources." In *Unspoken Worlds: Women's Religious Lives*, ed. Nancy Auer Falk and Rita M. Gross, 233–234. 2nd ed. Belmont, CA: Wadsworth.

Felton, Monica. 1967. *A Child Widow's Story*. New York: Harcourt, Brace and World.

Ganguly, Rita, and Vidya Hydari. 1986. "From Mother to Daughter: Women in Classical Music." *Manushi* 6, nos. 3 and 33: 10–14.

Kishwar, Madhu, and Ruth Vanita. 1983a. "A Grand Old Lady of Music: An Interview with Asghari Begum Sagarwali." *Manushi* 3, no. 3: 2–10.

———. 1983b. "'Bhairav se Sohni': Geetika's All-Women Classical Music Festival." *Manushi* 3, no. 3: 8–10.

Meduri, Avanti. 1988. "Bharata Natyam, What Are You?" *Asian Theatre Journal* 5, no. 1: 6.

Mukherjee, Sharbari. "Women and Traditional Indian Music." In a brochure published by Geetika, a music organization for women.

Nagappachar, B. 1960. *The Belur Temple*. Saklaspur, Karnataka: Sri Krishna Power.

Narayanan, Vasudha. 1991. "Hindu Perceptions of Auspiciousness, and Sexuality." In *Women, Religion, and Sexuality: Studies on the Impact of Religious Teachings on Women*, ed. Jeanne Becher, 64–92. Geneva: World Council of Churches Publications.

———. 1999. "Brimming with Bhakti, Embodiments of Shakti." In *Feminism in World Religions*, ed. Arvind Sharma and Katherine K. Young, 25–77. Albany: State University of New York Press.

O'Shea, Janet. 1998. "'Traditional' Indian Dance and the Making of Interpretive Communities." *Asian Theatre Journal* 15, no. 1: 45–63.

Peryavacchan Pillai. 1974. *Turuppavai Muvayirappati Vyakyanam*, ed. P. B. Annangarachariar. Kanchi: Editor.

Rajagopalan, N. 1990a. "Rukmini Devi Arundale." In *A Garland: Biographical Dictionary of Carnatic Composers and Musicians* (vol. 1), 255–257. Bombay: Bharatiya Vidya Bhavan.

Rajagopalan, N. 1990b. *A Garland: Biographical Dictionary of Carnatic Composers and Musicians* (vol. 1). Bombay: Bharatiya Vidya Bhavan.

———. 1992a. "Balasaraswati." In *Another Garland: Biographical Dictionary of Carnatic Composers and Musicians* (vol. 2), 104–105. Bombay: Bharatiya Vidya Bhavan.

———. 1992b. *Another Garland: Biographical Dictionary of Carnatic Composers and Musicians* (vol. 2). Bombay: Bharatiya Vidya Bhavan.

Ramanujan, A. K., Velcheru Narayana Rao, and David Shulman, eds. and trans. 1994. *When God Is a Customer: Telegu Courtesan Songs by Ksetrayya and Others*. Berkeley: University of California Press.

Rangacharya, Adya, trans. 1998. *Natyasastra*. Delhi: Munshiram Manoharlal.

Rao, V. Narayana, and D. Shulman. 1989. "History, Biography and Poetry at the Tanjavur Nayaka Court." In *Identity, Consciousness and the Past: The South Asian Scene*, ed. H. L. Seneviratne. *Social Analysis: Journal of Cultural and Social Practice*, no. 25 (September): 115–130.

Seetha, S. 1981. *Tanjore as a Seat of Music*. Madras: University of Madras.

Soneji, Davesh. 2004. "Living History, Performing Memory: Devadasi Women in Telugu-Speaking South India." *Dance Research Journal* 36, no. 2: 30–49.

Wagoner, Phillip B. 1996. "'Sultan among Hindu Kings': Dress, Titles, and the Islamicization of Hindu Culture at Vijayanagara." *Journal of Asian Studies* 55, no. 4: 851–880.

Index

"playing," 149–50, 155
Pongal festival, 85, 99
possession
    and goddess rituals, 12, 149–57
        in context of "play," 149–52
        description of rituals, 154–56
        and matajis, 152–54, 157–58n1
        and women's space, 156–57, 158n3
    and matammas, 36, 44, 47, 51
    and ratijagas ("wake" rituals), 79–80
    and tantric rituals, 160, 165, 168–69
pottus, 10, 85–87, 90–96, 100–101, 103, 103n2
    and householder ideology, 100–101
    and moral status, 103
    presence/absence of, 91–96
power, 13
    and goddess possession rituals, 149–50,
        152
    and kolams/pottus, 87–88, 91, 95, 103
    and medieval Tamil inscriptions, 124n6
    and performing arts, 193
    and ratijagas ("wake" rituals), 75–79, 81n18
    and talis of women, 39, 41
    and tantric rituals, 165
prabandha literature, 144n9
praise poems, 133
Prakash, Ved, 59
Prakrit Dictionary Project, 28
pregnancy, 42, 171–72, 193
presence/absence
    and kolams/pottus, 87–92
    memories of, 92–96
primogeniture, 77, 81n23
Proctor-Smith, Marjorie, 5
prostitution
    and matammas, 46
    and performing arts, 181, 184
    and tantric rituals, 162, 171–72, 174
puberty
    and matammas, 9, 36, 39–41, 43, 45–46
    and pottus, 91
public spaces
    and goddess possession rituals, 156–57
    and kolams, 96–97
    and performing arts, 182–83, 185,
        188–89, 195
    and ratijagas ("wake" rituals), 65–66, 71–72,
        75, 80
pujarini, 173
puja rituals
    Durga puja, 118–19, 161, 173
    and goddess possession rituals, 12, 149
    Kartik puja, 3–4, 56
    kumari puja, 161
    and matammas, 48, 53n7

and ratijagas ("wake" rituals), 65
and sakhis ("female friends"), 58–60
and Sanskrit language, 24–27
stri/shakti puja, 161
and tantric rituals, 160–61, 173
Pullappai, 112
Punitavati, 11–12, 133–34
puram poetry, 138
Puricanti, 113
purity
    and kolams/pottus, 10, 86–88, 91,
        95–98, 102
    and medieval Tamil inscriptions, 112
    and Sanskrit language, 21–22, 26, 28
puttininti tali ("mother's tali"), 40, 53n7

Radha-Krishna, 56–57, 61
radio, 186
Raghunathan, Chitra, 188
Raheja, Gloria, 7, 61
Rajasthan (North India), 9–10, 65–80
Rajendra I, 124–25n9
Rama, 125–26n16, 186–87, 193
Ramakrishna Paramahamsa, 168
Ramanuja, 186
Ramarakshastotram, 25, 30–31
Ramayana, 193
Ramdas, 186
Ranganatha Paduka Mandali, 186
Rangarajan, Srinidhi, 186–87
Rangaswamy, Dorai, 145nn14,15
rasa-lila ("circle dance"), 56
Rashtriya Sanskrit Sansthan, 20
ratijagas ("wake" rituals), 10, 65–80
    and Chocolat (film), 70–73
    locative dimension of, 65–70
    and spheres of influence, 73–80
Ratnaparakhi, A. R., 23
red dots. See bindis; bottus; pottus
reform movements
    and Karaikkal Ammaiyar, 133
    and matammas, 36–37, 39, 52
    and performing arts, 13, 178–81, 192–95
    and Sanskrit language, 21–22
relational love, 62
religious life in medieval Tamilnadu, 11,
        109–23
    gift giving, 11, 115–23, 125–26nn13-18
    vow taking/self-offering, 11, 110–15,
        123nn1,2, 124nn4-7, 124–25nn9-11
renunciants
    and goddess possession rituals, 12, 152, 154
    and kolams/pottus, 101
    and medieval Tamil inscriptions, 109,
        112–13, 115, 124nn4,7